Precariat: Labour, Work and Politics

In his recent work, Guy Standing has identified a new class which has emerged from neoliberal restructuring with, he argues, the revolutionary potential to change the world: the *precariat*. This, according to Standing, is 'a class-in-the-making, internally divided into angry and bitter factions' consisting of 'a multitude of insecure people, living bits-and-pieces lives, in and out of short-term jobs, without a narrative of occupational development, including millions of frustrated educated youth. . ., millions of women abused in oppressive labour, growing numbers of criminalised tagged for life, millions being categorised as "disabled" and migrants in their hundreds of millions around the world. They are denizens; they have a more restricted range of social, cultural, political and economic rights than citizens around them'.

This present book explores the nature, shape and context of precariat, evaluating the internal consistency and applications of the concept. Demonstrating the sheer breadth and depth of application, the chapters cover a wide-range of topics, from the relationships between precariat and authoritarianism, multitude (another concept to achieve popular consciousness), and place as well as the nature of precarious identities and subjectivities among those working in immaterial labour. The book concludes with a reply by Standing to reviews of *Precariat*.

This book was originally published as a special issue of *Global Discourse*.

Matthew Johnson is a Lecturer and British Academy Postdoctoral Fellow in Politics, Philosophy and Religion at the University of Lancaster. He is interested in the evaluation of culture and the effect of forms of intervention on wellbeing. He has authored *Evaluting Culture* (Palgrave) and has edited *The Legacy of Marxism* (Continuum).

Precariat: Labour, Work and Politics

Edited by
Matthew Johnson

Routledge
Taylor & Francis Group
LONDON AND NEW YORK

First published 2015 by Routledge

2 Park Square, Milton Park, Abingdon, Oxon, OX14 4RN
605 Third Avenue, New York, NY 10017

Routledge is an imprint of the Taylor & Francis Group, an informa business

First issued in paperback 2020

British Library Cataloguing in Publication Data
A catalogue record for this book is available from the British Library

ISBN 13: 978-1-138-80320-6 (hbk)
ISBN 13: 978-0-367-73951-5 (pbk)

Typeset in Times New Roman
by RefineCatch Limited, Bungay, Suffolk

Publisher's Note
The publisher accepts responsibility for any inconsistencies that may have arisen during the conversion of this book from journal articles to book chapters, namely the possible inclusion of journal terminology.

Contents

Citation Information

The chapters in this book were originally published in *Global Discourse*, volume 3, issue 3–4 (September–December 2013). When citing this material, please use the original page numbering for each article, as follows:

Chapter 1
Introduction: The precariat
Matthew Johnson
Global Discourse, volume 3, issue 3–4 (September–December 2013) pp. 385–387

Chapter 2
Authoritarianism and the precariat
Bill Jordan
Global Discourse, volume 3, issue 3–4 (September–December 2013) pp. 388–403

Reply to Bill Jordan's 'Authoritarianism and the precariat'
Daryl Glaser
Global Discourse, volume 3, issue 3–4 (September–December 2013) pp. 404–405

Chapter 3
From the precariat to the multitude
Ben Trott
Global Discourse, volume 3, issue 3–4 (September–December 2013) pp. 406–425

Self-nomination and autonomy: a reply to Ben Trott
Timothy S. Murphy
Global Discourse, volume 3, issue 3–4 (September–December 2013) pp. 426–429

Chapter 4
Breaking the heartland: creating the precariat in the US lower rust belt
Joseph J. Varga
Global Discourse, volume 3, issue 3–4 (September–December 2013) pp. 430–446

Breaking the heartland: creating the precariat in the US lower rust belt: a response to Joseph J. Varga
Angela Wigger
Global Discourse, volume 3, issue 3–4 (September–December 2013) pp. 447–449

Chapter 5

Precarity of place: a complement to the growing precariat literature
Susan Banki
Global Discourse, volume 3, issue 3–4 (September–December 2013) pp. 450–463

Some thoughts on 'precarity of place': a reply to Banki
Wanda Vrasti
Global Discourse, volume 3, issue 3–4 (September–December 2013) pp. 464–466

Chapter 6

Precarious work, entrepreneurial mindset and sense of place: female strategies in insecure labour markets
Hanna-Mari Ikonen
Global Discourse, volume 3, issue 3–4 (September–December 2013) pp. 467–481

Precarious work, entrepreneurial mindset and sense of place: female strategies in insecure labour markets: a response to Hanna-Mari Ikonen
Jeremy Morris
Global Discourse, volume 3, issue 3–4 (September–December 2013) pp. 482–485

Chapter 7

The precariousnesses of young knowledge workers: a subject-oriented approach
Emiliana Armano and Annalisa Murgia
Global Discourse, volume 3, issue 3–4 (September–December 2013) pp. 486–501

The production of precariousness and implications for collective action: a reply to Emiliana Armano and Annalisa Murgia
Nancy Ettlinger
Global Discourse, volume 3, issue 3–4 (September–December 2013) pp. 502–506

Chapter 8

Precarious subjectivities are not for sale: the loss of the measurability of labour for performing arts workers
Mauro Turrini and Federico Chicchi
Global Discourse, volume 3, issue 3–4 (September–December 2013) pp. 507–521

A reply to 'Precarious subjectivities are not for sale: the loss of the measurability of labour for performing arts workers' by Mauro Turrini and Federico Chicchi
Heather McLean
Global Discourse, volume 3, issue 3–4 (September–December 2013) pp. 522–524

Chapter 9

Book Review Symposium: The Down-Deep Delight of Democracy*, By Mark Purcell*
Review
Mark Edward 525
Review
Stuart Elden 527
Review
Ian Buchanan 529

Managing ourselves
Mark Purcell 532
Global Discourse, volume 3, issue 3–4 (September–December 2013) pp. 525–535

Chapter 10

Book Review Symposium: The Precariat: The New Dangerous Class, *By Guy Standing*
Review
Catherine Lawlor 536
Review
Jörg Wiegratz 538
Review
Jo Grady 543
Where's Howard?
Guy Standing 546
Global Discourse, volume 3, issue 3–4 (September–December 2013) pp. 536–553

Chapter 11

Conclusion: The precariat, intergenerational justice and universal basic income
Juliana Bidadanure
Global Discourse, volume 3, issue 3–4 (September–December 2013) pp. 554–560

Please direct any queries you may have about the citations to
clsuk.permissions@cengage.com

INTRODUCTION

The precariat

In his recent work, Guy Standing has identified a new class which has emerged from neo-liberal restructuring with, he argues, the revolutionary potential to change the world: the *precariat*. This is 'a class-in-the-making, internally divided into angry and bitter factions' consisting of 'a multitude of insecure people, living bits-and-pieces lives, in and out of short-term jobs, without a narrative of occupational development, including millions of frustrated educated youth who do not like what they see before them, millions of women abused in oppressive labour, growing numbers of criminalised tagged for life, millions being categorised as "disabled" and migrants in their hundreds of millions around the world. They are denizens; they have a more restricted range of social, cultural, political and economic rights than citizens around them' (Standing 2011b). Like multitude before it, precariat has reached the popular consciousness both because of timely salience and comprehensible articulation. In essence, Precariat taps into increasing discontent and dissatisfaction among a range of groups and stokes in people – particularly educated younger people in Western countries – the hope of connection and collaboration with radically different cohorts from radically different backgrounds – a hope which significantly pre-dates the activities of 1968. Succinctly placing the possibility of praxis within dispiriting global circumstances, Standing has produced a foundation upon which, potentially, a host of academic and political programmes may emerge.

This issue of *Global Discourse* seeks to explore the nature, shape and context of precariat, evaluating the internal consistency and application of the concept, particularly with regard to: changes in the sociology of class; democracy, participation and representation; the relationship between precariat and multitude; the means by which precariat might become a 'class-for-itself'; place, migration and globalization; poverty and precarity; the subjective experience of precarity, and forms of resistance. The articles published reflect the extent, both with regard to paradigmatic engagement and site of study, to which the concept has permeated the consciousness of academics and those subject to precariousness (indeed, the former appear increasingly to be included in the latter).

The issue begins with Bill Jordan's (2013) examination of the political relationship between precariat and authoritarianism, in which he traces, through the course of over one hundred years of policy debates, the development of two approaches – liberal and paternalist – to the treatment of precarious employment in capitalism. Examining the possible role played by basic income provision in these debates, Jordan outlines reasons to be cautious about the potential for radical responses to Europe-wide problems. Daryl Glaser (2013) replies. Ben Trott, with a reply by Tim Murphy (2013), considers the relationship between precariat and multitude, arguing that Standing dislocates his analysis of precarious circumstances from utopian emancipatory praxis, before discussing potential examples of transformative projects which transcend differences and spaces. Next, Joseph Varga (2013) analyses the creation of the precariat within the lower Rust Belt of the US Midwest through the production of anti-union legislation and dissolution of forms of security engendered during the New Deal era. Varga then outlines the effects of this shift from proletariat to precariat in political, social and cultural terms. Angela Wigger (2013) responds, outlining the broader, divisive implications of this process, noting, for example, the contribution of precariousness to, for example, the emergence of the Tea Party.

Next, Susan Banki (2013), using illustrations drawn from the lives of Burmese migrants in Thailand, attempts to introduce a new concept of precarity of place to describe the experiences of non-citizen living, which is distinct from, but to be considered in conjunction with, precarity of labour. In replying, Wanda Vrasti (2013) interrogates the concept further, noting possible characteristics of disadvantage, with regard to race, class and gender, which may make precariousness all the more arduous. Hanna-Mari Ikonen (2013) complements the focus on place through her examination of the relationship between entrepreneurship and employment, exploring strategies for surviving in precarious circumstances and emphasising the importance of place to achieving permanence. Jeremy Morris (2013) replies critically, considering the identities at play in Ikonen's empirical work, suggesting that Ikonen's use of entrepreneurship does 'violence to the notion of craft, of the socially-dwelt-in meanings of work that still exist for such people', while emphasising the need for working class studies to engage fully with the concept of precariat.

Emiliana Armano and Annalisa Murgia (2013) then consider the lives of young, educated knowledge producers, seeking to explicate the ways in which this cohort understands and deals with their precariousness, particularly with regard to self-identification, self-exploitation and experience of misalignment. In her reply, Nancy Ettlinger (2013) considers, among other things, the exploitative and deleterious aspects of crowdsourcing, arguing that collective refusal to engage in such activities may be one means of opposing precariousness, with a greater emphasis on bottom up activities needed. Finally, Mauro Turrini and Federico Chicchi (2013), with a reply by Heather McLean (2013), examine the subjective experience of precarity among performance artists, whose lives they regard as being especially instructive insofar as they 'are in many ways a laboratory of job flexibility, where innovative contractual arrangements and professional trajectories have been developed'. Using rich empirical data from quantitative and qualitative research, they note the ways in which performance artists escape from the confines of wage labour to achieve outbursts of professional autonomy, only then to have that autonomy constrained in new ways by precariousness.

In the final part of the issue, there are symposia on Mark Purcell's *The Down-Deep Delight of Democracy*, with reviews by Mark Edward (2013), Stuart Elden (2013) and Ian Buchanan (2013) and a reply by Purcell (2013), and Guy Standing's *The Precariat*, with reviews by Catherine Lawlor (2013), Jörg Wiegratz (2013) and Jo Grady (2013) and a substantive reply by Standing (2013) himself. The issue concludes with Juliana Bidadanure (2013) speculating on the future development of precariat as a concept.

I wish, at this point, to place on record my gratitude to Guy Standing for his support of the issue, advice on its development and participation in the review symposium. I hope that the issue will stimulate further discussion of the concept.

References

Armano, E. and Murgia, A. 2013. "The Precariousnesses of Young Knowledge Workers: A Subject-oriented Approach." *Global Discourse* 3 (3–4): 486–501.

Banki, S. 2013. "Precarity of Place: A Complement to the Growing Precariat Literature." *Global Discourse* 3 (3–4): 450–463.

Bidadanure, J. 2013. "The Precariat, Intergenerational Justice and Universal Basic Income." *Global Discourse* 3 (3–4): 554–560.

Buchanan, I. 2013. "*The Down-deep Delight of Democracy*, by Mark Purcell. Review." *Global Discourse* 3 (3–4): 529–532.
Edward, M. 2013. "*The Down-deep Delight of Democracy*, by Mark Purcell. Review." *Global Discourse* 3 (3–4): 525–527.
Elden, S. 2013. "*The Down-deep Delight of Democracy*, by Mark Purcell. Review." *Global Discourse* 3 (3–4): 527–529.
Ettlinger, N. 2013. "The Production of Precariousness and Implications for Collective Action: A Reply to Emiliana Armano and Annalisa Murgia." *Global Discourse* 3 (3–4): 502–506.
Ikonen, H-M. 2013. "Precarious Work, Entrepreneurial Mindset and Sense of Place: Female Strategies in Insecure Labour Markets." *Global Discourse* 3 (3–4): 467–481.
Jordan, B. 2013. "Authoritarianism and the Precariat." *Global Discourse* 3 (3–4): 388–403.
Glaser, D. 2013. "Reply to Bill Jordan's 'Authoritarianism and the Precariat.'" *Global Discourse* 3 (3–4): 404–405.
Grady, J. 2013. "*The Precariat: The New Dangerous Class*, by Guy Standing. Review." *Global Discourse* 3 (3–4): 543–546.
Lawlor, C. 2013. "*The Precariat: The New Dangerous Class*, by Guy Standing. Review." *Global Discourse* 3 (3–4): 536–538.
McLean, H. 2013. "A Reply to 'Precarious Subjectivities are Not for Sale: The Loss of the Measurability of Labour for Performing Arts Workers' by Mauro Turrini and Federico Chicchi." *Global Discourse* 3 (3–4): 522–524.
Morris, J. 2013. "Precarious Work, Entrepreneurial Mindset and Sense of Place: Female Strategies in Insecure Labour Markets: A Response to Hanna-Mari Ikonen." *Global Discourse* 3 (3–4): 482–485.
Murphy, T. 2013. "Self-nomination and Autonomy: A Reply to Ben Trott." *Global Discourse* 3 (3–4): 426–429.
Purcell, M. 2013. *The Down-deep Delight of Democracy.* Oxford: Wiley-Blackwell,
Purcell, M. 2013. "*The Down-deep Delight of Democracy*, by Mark Purcell. Managing Ourselves." *Global Discourse* 3 (3–4): 532–535.
Standing, G. 2011a. *The Precariat: The New Dangerous Class*. London and New York: Bloomsbury Academics.
Standing, G. 2011b "The Precariat – The New Dangerous Class." Policy Network, Accessed January 21 2014. http://www.policynetwork.net/pno_detail.aspx?ID=4004&title=+The+Precariat+%e2%80%93+The+new+dangerous+class
Standing, G. 2013. "*The Precariat: The New Dangerous Class*, by Guy Standing. Where's Howard?" *Global Discourse* 3 (3–4): 546–553.
Trott, B. 2013. "From the Precariat to the Multitude." *Global Discourse* 3 (3–4): 406–425.
Turrini, M. and Chicchi, F. 2013. "Precarious Subjectivities are Not for Sale: The Loss of the Measurability of Labour for Performing Arts Workers." *Global Discourse* 3 (3–4): 507–521.
Varga, J.J. 2013. Breaking the Heartland: Creating the Precariat in the US Lower Rust Belt. *Global Discourse* 3 (3–4): 430–446.
Vrasti, W. 2013. "Some Thoughts on 'Precarity of Place': A Reply to Banki." *Global Discourse* 3 (3–4): 464–466.
Wiegratz, J. 2013. "*The Precariat: The New Dangerous Class*, by Guy Standing. Review." *Global Discourse* 3 (3–4): 538–543.
Wigger, A. 2013. "Breaking the Heartland: Creating the Precariat in the US Lower Rust Belt: a Response to Joseph J. Varga." *Global Discourse* 3 (3–4): 447–449.

Matthew Johnson
University of Lancaster

RESEARCH ARTICLE

Authoritarianism and the precariat

Bill Jordan

Social and Public Policy, Plymouth University, Plymouth, UK

This article traces present-day policy debates on precarious employment to the nineteenth century. Liberal and paternalist versions of state authority emerged as responses to early capitalist development, and precariousness was an issue that contributed to the differentiation between them. The author argues that these connections with the bases of state power help explain why radical alternative approaches to today's challenges find it so hard to get a hearing in mainstream political circles.

This article identifies two forms of authoritarianism and analyses how they have handled the phenomenon of precariousness. In the justification of state power under capitalism, the issue of people without regular work played a role in arguments for both these forms, but they engaged with it in very different ways. I examine the implications for state authority of shifts in the dynamic between precarious and secure employment, and contrast the responses of these two types of regime.

Since industrialisation began, peasants, day labourers and women from rural regions have moved to towns, for the sake of higher-paid, higher-productivity work, and this eventually gave rise to better employment contracts and conditions, as well as better social provision. The shift from precariousness to security was never complete, especially for women, but billions of people have ultimately benefited from this process, and are still doing so in the South and East Asia, Latin America and Africa.

In the 1970s, this dynamic changed in the affluent economies. With reserves of rural labour depleted, immigrants were drawn in from developing countries; but numbers of secure, full-time, industrial employments started to shrink, and short-term, part-time or occasional ones, mainly in services, to increase. Governments' responses to this shift reflected the trajectory of their political development during the period of their industrialisation.

I shall argue that the long history of social control through a disciplinary regime for those on the margins of the economy influences these responses. Where political power shifted to capitalists and the urban middle class during the nineteenth century, as in the UK and USA, deterrent and punitive Poor Law administrations focused on the most vulnerable among them. Rootlessness and unruly behaviour justified harsh criminal justice systems. I shall examine the legacy of these forms of discipline for present-day policies.

In countries where the traditional landowning aristocracy and the military retained political power, such as Germany, a more paternalistic type of authority prevailed. The urban middle class and organised labour were included in social insurance schemes, but as an alternative to effective democratic politics. This tradition used the construction of the state's machinery to shape and steer society as a hierarchy of status groups with reciprocal duties (Dyson 1980). It too casts a long shadow over developments in this century, and – through the creation of the Eurozone – this spreads right across the Continent. When demonstrators in Spain and Italy brandish posters to protest the power of the German Chancellor, Angela Merkel, they might more appropriately paint a Bismarck-style walrus moustache on her photograph than a toothbrush Hitler one.

In neither type of regime have those in precarious situations played much direct role in these developments, though they were seen as posing a threat. In liberal polities, they offered supplies of cheap labour power, so long as law and order could be maintained; their dangerousness lay in their perceived potential criminality. In conservative ones, the fear of falling into precariousness was mobilised by rulers to secure the involvement of labour organisations in social insurance systems, and the construction of stratified societies which did not challenge traditional authority. These features of state institutions pre-dated democracy, and have survived all the changes brought about through democratic mobilisations.

With the erosion of secure, male, industrial employment since the 1970s, the logics of institutional adaptations have been in line with these alternative approaches. Governments in the UK and USA embraced 'flexibility' in labour markets. 'Tax Credits' gave income support to households with low earnings, but in ways that enmeshed them in complex administrative processes. Whether they were in work or outside it, these citizens were constantly being monitored by the tax-benefit authorities; they were also targets for sanctions if they failed to take available employment, however insecure.

In Germany, early retirement schemes allowed millions of redundant workers access to disability benefits, especially after the former (East) German Democratic Republic was absorbed into the (West) German Federal Republic. Policy focused on sustaining high-skilled employment in high-tech industries, and export of these products was boosted by the creation of the Eurozone. Only belatedly after 2004 were 'flexibility' and 'activation' adopted as policies. Precariousness was concentrated among immigrant workers, and it was the avoidance of this risk for citizens that legitimated comparatively low levels of economic participation among those of working age.

Historic trajectories have of course been modified by democratic politics and social movements, yet these administrative traditions penetrated new public services. The collective arrangements favoured by social democratic parties required compulsory solidarities to supply income security, but these too were informed by distrust of opportunism among precarious workers. The Scandinavian countries, where these parties were strongest, were among the first to insist that unemployed claimants should take part in state-run programmes of activity until they returned to the labour market. These economies achieved high overall rates of employment, with part-time posts occupied mainly by women (Esping-Andersen 1990, 1999).

My argument is that the increase in precariousness since 2008 challenges both liberal and paternalist versions of state authority, and highlights the differences between them. Philosophically, the liberal approach concentrates on correcting the individual weaknesses signalled by reliance on state support; since Locke (1691), this has supplied the justification for official disciplinary power. In the paternalistic version, the state's authority overrides potentially divisive individual interests, and extends over society as a whole to secure collective harmony through hierarchy (Dyson 1980, 68). Neither has proved effective against the new challenge.

In the UK and the USA, the stagnating or falling earnings of employees have been disguised by a combination of bank credit and 'Tax Credits', made unsustainable by the financial and fiscal crises. As I shall show, unless power-holders abandon the attempt to control and discipline those without employment security, there can be little prospect that any recovery from these crises will benefit the worse-off half of the working-age population, or indeed the majority of its youngest generation.

Meanwhile, it has become obvious that the Eurozone arrangements enabled Germany to sell its products in southern European economies living on various credit-fuelled bubbles. Although Germany's own structures have survived intact, those of the indebted economies face years of extreme stress, with falling levels of employment and earnings, all of which will limit the potential development of northern member states.

So the consequences of Germany's strategy for minimising precariousness among its citizens were in the end, once the credit-driven demand model collapsed, experienced as severe austerity programmes in Italy, Spain, Portugal and Greece. There, not only have precarious employments and unemployment increased, governments have also used the police and courts to enforce their programmes against extensive protest movements.

As Standing (2011) points out, this is new evidence of consciousness and organisation among a precariat, made up of members of an angry generation of well-educated young people with few prospects of attaining secure careers. But their scope for democratic pressure is limited, because – as many of them are aware – it derives in large part from the collapse of the Eurozone's mechanisms. In this sense, they are experiencing the application of German authority by proxy in the responses of their governments to their crises of indebtedness.

The rise of ultra-nationalist and neo-fascist parties all over Europe can be seen as partly related to all these processes – fear of precariousness rather than the precariat, except for that part of it made up of immigrants, blamed for failures of governments to achieve reliable growth in employment and incomes. Here, too, authoritarian policies on immigration control (outside the scope of this article) stem from the ineffectiveness of measures to deal with the new dynamic.

Neither the acceptance of precariousness as a welcome symptom of the operation of a free labour market, nor the exclusion from employment of many of working age, has been able to restore the post-war dynamism. I shall argue that a whole alternative approach is now available, but it is unlikely to be adopted because it would require governments to give up aspects of their historic power over citizens.

Liberalism, precariousness and state authority

The ideal of a society in which all members enjoyed equal autonomy under the law informed the American Constitution (Jefferson 1784), and underpinned the gradual expansion of civil and political rights in the UK from the late seventeenth century (Locke 1690). But the original groundings of this vision (in natural rights and property holdings) had little basis in the realities of economic development under capitalism. Even Adam Smith's (1776) optimistic account of the potential for a growing class of industrial workers to gain 'independence' from traditional power-holders as they moved from country to town was unable to demonstrate how the adequacy or security of their incomes would be sustained.

Capitalism could lead to higher wages and more freedom only if people left the rural sector for the urban one; but this implied that institutions protecting agricultural prices and household living standards must be abolished. So precariousness was a pre-condition for development, and power must pass from the landowning class to those with a stake in the industry. In England and Wales, the reform of the Poor Laws in 1834 was intended to consolidate the gains made by the bourgeoisie in the reform of the parliament in 1832.

Parliamentary support for the reform was assured because of the fear inspired by widespread riots in 1830–1. To make the case against the old Poor Laws, the Commissioners' Report of 1834 presented evidence from villages and small towns to show how corrupt or slack administration and the subsidisation of household incomes had led to idleness, drunkenness, illegitimacy and the further depression of wages. The attempt to protect the rural poor had led to their utter demoralisation, it argued.

> … the severest sufferers are those that have become callous to their own degradation, who value parish support as their privilege, and demand it as their right, and complain only that it is limited in amount, or that some sort of labour or confinement is exacted in return. No man's principles can be corrupted without injury to society in general; but the person most injured is the person whose principles have been corrupted.… New pauperism seems to be an engine for the purpose of disconnecting each member of a family from all others; of reducing all to the state of domesticated animals, fed, lodged and provided for by the parish, without mutual dependence or mutual interest. (Poor Law Report 1834, 167, 177)

Notoriously, harsh conditions for those who applied to the authorities for support was recommended as the main principle of the new system. Individual responsibility was to be enforced, and a free labour market created; but this could only be achieved by an administration which insisted that able-bodied applicants were put to work under conditions which were intentionally more unpleasant than those experienced by the poorest non-applicants.

> The first and most essential of all conditions, a principle which we find universally admitted, … is that his situation on the whole shall not be made really or apparently so eligible as the situation of the independent labourer of the lowest class. (335)

The New Poor Law of 1834 enabled rapid movement of populations to factories, by removing the protections of the old order; state power was directed at the most vulnerable. Precariousness had to be enhanced to bring about the transition to a society based on individual self-responsibility, and to re-moralise the poor. It was only by their own efforts, re-enforced by charity and voluntary association, that working people could achieve reliable material security.

Although the state became increasingly involved in regulation and the provision of urban environmental facilities as the nineteenth century progressed, these two characteristics of liberalism – reluctance to offer income support and the use of state authority to discipline claimants – persisted. Liberal regimes were later to adopt social insurance schemes than their paternalist counterparts, and then only when they became aware that these were giving the latter comparative economic (and ultimately military) advantages (Flora and Alber 1981, 72–73).

In the 1930s and 1940s, policies to expand employment and benefits were justified by insistence that they did not undermine individual responsibility. Keynes argued that the state should intervene to increase aggregate demand in the national economy in times of recession because at such moments the supply of labour power did not create its own demand. Instead of driving down wages, the state could take a role in maximising productive activity while still upholding private property, individual accumulation and competition, as well as individual liberty (Keynes 1936, 376).

This allowed Beveridge (1942, 1944) to assume that 'want' would occur only in certain well-defined circumstances, and to propose a scheme of compulsory insurance, to which employers and the state as well as workers would contribute, against these contingencies. Along with the New Deal in the USA, this represented the first systematic attempt by a liberal regime to minimise precariousness through the use of state power. But it certainly did not reduce the state's role in enforcing employment, whenever this became a viable option for claimants.

Indeed, since the state was acting to make jobs available for all fit to take them, and also providing adequate support by right for short- and long-term interruptions of earnings, this removal of 'natural necessity' as a spur to self-responsibility meant that social security officials had a greater duty to uphold the work ethic by enforcing benefit conditions. The liberal welfare state retained the link between its authority and the discipline of claimants under its more generous regime.

But the assumption that these new institutions and policies had ended the reliance of the capitalist productive system on a labour force exposed to risks of destitution proved to be false. Not only did firms in the USA and UK extend their industrial production activity to the developing world, with its ample supplies of workers in precarious rural situations, they also increasingly recruited for their home-based manufacturing and services under non-standard contracts. The 'rediscovery of poverty' among people of working age in the USA (Harrington 1962) and UK (Townsend and Abel-Smith 1965) signalled a shift back towards precariousness in these countries.

In the face of these challenges, governments in the USA and UK reverted to type; they used selective, means-tested systems to address new forms of poverty, rather than trying to extend the coverage of social insurance ones, or to introduce new universal schemes. During the 20 years since the end of the Second World War, numbers claiming social assistance had grown steadily in both countries, and these consisted mainly of lone parents, for whom there was no social insurance coverage. The expansion of that scheme allowed household means-testing to become consolidated within systems for income support, and made it easier to overcome objections to this method of administration.

In the third section of this article, I shall turn to how measures to address the income needs of precarious employees were implemented in liberal regimes.

Paternalism and the social hierarchy

The form of authoritarianism embodied in the German state was quite different in its origins and out-workings than that of liberal regimes. The German state was built by Bismarck, a Prussian aristocrat, in the second half of the nineteenth century, during the industrialisation of its economy, using foreign wars as well as ruthless domestic *realpolitik*; but it also reflected a long intellectual tradition in which the term *Polizeistaat* (police or policy state) meant a concern with constructing a complex hierarchy of officials to manage society and the economy according to standards of efficiency and security.

As Chancellor, Bismarck mobilised conservative institutions and social forces to outflank both the liberal bourgeoisie and socialist organised labour; he thought that the precariousness that capitalism imposed on peasants and factory workers showed that it supplied no satisfactory basis for a social order. Accordingly, he played socialists off against liberals, and used the fear of disorder among the casualties of economic transformation against both (Taylor 1955; Simon 1968).

As well as introducing laws to suppress the socialist movement in the late 1870s, his plan for social insurance, outlined in 1881, was aimed at creating a direct link between the state and the working class, as an alternative to the civil and political rights favoured by the liberals. This was to be focused on the risks faced by the most vulnerable workers – insurance against industrial injury and illness, not unemployment – and would involve trade unions in negotiation with state officials over the administration of the scheme. Speaking to the Reichstag on his pensions bill in 1889, he said:

> I will consider it a great advantage when we have 700,000 small pensioners drawing their annuities from the state, especially if they belong to those classes who otherwise do not have much to lose by an upheaval and erroneously believe they can actually gain much by it. (Rimlinger 1971, 120)

So the state's authority was used to incorporate those in the most potentially precarious situations into the very machinery of official power, and to give them the kind of reciprocal duties towards civil servants that characterised relationships in Germany's stratified society. In this approach, the national community was threatened as much by bourgeois individualism as by the collective muscle of trade unions, and by the liberal democracy as the militant socialism. Accordingly, paternalistic authoritarianism saw protection against precariousness as a bulwark for the traditional basis of the state – landed and military interests and the monarchy.

In this there were certainly elements of continuity between that period and the Nazi one. Although the 1930s saw a murderous mobilisation of state power against some disabled people as well as Jews, gypsies, gay men and other minorities, racism and eugenics were superimposed on a structure of institutions inherited from the Bismarck era. Economic and political instability during the democratic years of the Weimar republic were used to justify an authoritarian regime which rejected free-market capitalism as much as liberalism as the basis for the social order. But Nazi authorities preserved the social insurance scheme; the only element to be abolished was unemployment insurance, seen as inconsistent with the full mobilisation of the national workforce as the basis for its economic policies.

With the construction of a stable democratic system in West Germany after the Second World War, the scope of these institutions was extended, under the same conservative principles (Esping-Andersen 1990, 1999). Social insurance contributions were earnings-related, as were benefits, so the scheme stratified the population as well as protecting it. Post-war reconstruction led to a period of sustained and rapid economic growth in the 1950s, drawing on a supply of refugees and displaced ethnic German people from Eastern Europe as well as from the agricultural sector.

Post-war German politics was also haunted by the legacy of the hyperinflation of the 1920s, seen as the economic environment which nurtured Nazism. Thus, monetary and fiscal conservatism, as well as Bismarckian paternalism, were the bases for public policy. As we shall see in the fourth section, these principles informed a very different response to the re-emergence of precariousness in labour markets from the 1960s onwards.

The response of liberal regimes to the return of precariousness

In the mid-1960s, the first symptoms appeared of a shift in the dynamic between a growing sector of secure full-time industrial employment for men, paying a 'family wage', and a dwindling residue of rural and other marginal types of labour. The numbers of industrial jobs for men started to decline in the UK, Germany and Belgium, and their overall proportions of employment in the USA. This coincided with the rediscovery of poverty among households with at least one member in employment in the liberal polities.

In the UK, this sparked a political debate about how to relieve poverty in such households, but not about the possible long-term implications of a major change in the labour market. The conservative government of Edward Heath published proposals for Tax Credits (1972) which would have introduced a potentially new principle to tax-benefits administration. One declared aim of the scheme, which would have given individuals weekly payments if they had no other income, and withdrawn this through the tax system at a fixed rate as they increased their earnings, was to reduce administrative costs.

In the event, the government instead adopted means-tested Family Income Supplements for households with children. This very modest measure cost only £8 million in its first year, but it established a precedent for all subsequent policies for dealing with poverty among households with an adult in employment. What eventually came to be called 'Tax Credits' were in fact means-tested benefits of this kind, and these became a very extensive and costly scheme, drawing a large proportion of the working population into complex and continuous assessments by the authorities.

Similarly, in the USA what are called 'Earned Income Tax Credits', introduced by the Nixon administration in 1975 and modified several times in subsequent decades, are also means-tested benefits for low-earning households with dependent children, which have become larger in their scope and costs than the social assistance programme. In the 1990s, the Clinton administration made the latter more conditional and restrictive, and built in education and training for greater 'responsibility' (Waddan 1997; Newman 2002).

By then, these policies were needed to complement the deregulation of labour markets that had characterised the Thatcher-Reagan regimes of the 1980s. Returning to the rationale of nineteenth century liberalism, they embraced the economic forces which were leading industrial firms to lay off semi-skilled and unskilled full-time workers, and service firms to employ more staff on non-standard contracts. The rise in precariousness in the workforce during this period was partly disguised by more married women entering such posts, and hence contributing to household incomes, but also by these schemes for supplementing the low wages paid in many such service employments.

For example, by 2005 Wal-Mart had become the largest company in the world, employing 1.5 million people, mainly women shop assistants, in the USA. Wal-Mart did not allow its members to join trade unions, but it did run classes in how to apply for 'Tax Credits' (BBC World Service 2005), effectively subsidising their profits.

Under the Third Way regimes of the Clinton–Blair era, the increasing precariousness of employment and earnings in expanding service occupations was embraced as an indicator of 'flexibility' in labour markets, which contrasted with the 'rigidity' of their European counterparts. 'Tax Credit' schemes grew to compensate households, but their complexity and administrative slowness gave rise to problems of incentives; claimants were reluctant to leave the security of social assistance support for fear of the mistakes and delays that could occur to payments as their jobs ended or their earnings varied (Jordan et al. 1991).

As a result, the 'activation' elements attached to eligibility for unemployment-related benefits became more prominent features of policies in liberal regimes in this period. While these were justified in terms of preparing claimants for the type of vacancies likely to occur, they were equally used to test motivation and impose discipline. Although in the UK there was nothing as overtly controlling as workfare in the USA, schemes for education and training were clearly serving similar purposes.

In opting for means-tested wage subsidisation and enhanced conditionality of benefits, liberal regimes were therefore consolidating the role of state authority at the same time as increasing precariousness of employment and income. The fact that all this was focused on those members of the population with lowest earning power was in the tradition of their predecessors in the nineteenth century, but without the legitimation in terms of a long-term strategy to transform those on the margins of the economy into higher-earning employees with better prospects.

An influential strand of opinion in the 1980s focused on the 'underclass' that was emerging in cities in the USA, and especially its members' criminality and moral degeneration (Murray 1985). This justified high expenditures on criminal justice systems, and especially on prisons. Not only do regimes with more generous levels of spending on social security and public services have lower rates of imprisonment than these liberal regimes (Hay and Wincott 2012, 127–128); when the costs of crime and prisons are included, these also increase public expenditure by around the amounts that countries like the USA and UK fall short of the social spending of conservative European regimes (Western and Beckett 1999).

Indeed, the whole approach adopted by liberal regimes can be seen as an authoritarian creation of a precariat, whose dismal prospects were masked by the artificial boost to their incomes bestowed as much by the bank credit as by 'Tax Credits'. Ironically, it was the banks' extension of mortgage loans to members of this precariat that led to the financial crisis of 2008, when US lenders became insolvent as a result of these risky transactions.

Governments in these countries both hold these debts as a result of bailing out the banks, and administer the schemes through which members of the precariat are disciplined and controlled under the state authority. The UK government is committed to selling the nationalised banks (less these debts) back to private owners, but not to seeking ways to lift members of the precariat out of their situation through tax-benefit reform. This contrasts with the aspiration of the 1972 investigation into Tax Credits, which argued that they would reduce the role of the state in the lives of citizens:

> Fewer people will be means-tested and others means-tested less often, and for the community there will be a large saving in administrative staff. (Her Majesty's Government 1972, iii)

In the fifth section, I shall consider the origins and implications of liberal regimes' current reluctance to pursue any such goals.

The making of a continental precariat

The processes which led to the emergence of a precariat in southern Europe after 2008 were quite different from those outlined in the previous section. Policies in Germany and the other northern European states were designed to ward off the risks of precariousness in labour markets, and although countries like Greece, Spain and Italy had large informal sectors in which employments and incomes were insecure, they had seemed in the years before the crisis to be gradually reducing these and extending social security coverage.

This reflected the goals of the leaders who sought peace, stability and prosperity for Europe through new institutions for cooperation and exchange after the Second World War. The enlargement of the EU to embrace the newly democratic Mediterranean countries in the 1980s and the former communist ones in the new century signalled success in processes of integrating formerly marginal societies within a model for growth and social cohesion which had been established in the original core member states, especially Germany and France. (The impact of the crisis on the former communist countries of Central Europe is outside the scope of this article.)

In the rhetoric of the European Commission, this was known as the 'European Social Model', as if the primary mode of integration was the inclusion of previously precarious populations in a form of social citizenship. In reality, the principal agenda for the EU was free trade, and this can be seen as a response to the changes in the world economy from the mid-1960s. Hay and Wincott (2012, ch. 3) argue that the rapid increase in rates of movement of capital and products across borders was a process of Europeanisation, not globalisation; since 1980, every one of the EU-15 countries has exported more to other member states than to the rest of the world (81).

As the leading exporter of industrial products on the continent, Germany had played a major role in shaping the EU institutions, so that they allowed its domestic political balance to be preserved, along with its economic interests. Without overt use of nation state or supranational authority, Germany positioned itself so as to be the principal beneficiary of the new arrangements, in ways which became apparent only after the crisis. Above all, it is now Germany which insists on the fiscal discipline that forces debtor countries to cut their wage rates, public services and social programmes, and which is therefore the power behind the police beating back protesters in those countries.

From the middle of the 1960s, German firms responded to globalisation by shifting investment from home production towards southern Europe as well as Asia. The value of foreign investments by German companies increased from US$3 billion in 1967 to US $19.9 billion in 1976 (Hood and Young 1979, 18, table 1.4). As a result of this shift in strategies by northern European companies, growth rates of economies such as Spain and Greece in the 1970s were (at around 5%) much faster than in their home countries. Whereas migrant workers from the Mediterranean states had flocked to Germany during its post-war boom, some now started to return.

At the same time, German governments acted to preserve its institutions of the 'social partnership' between employers, organised labour and the state, and protect citizens' living standards from erosion by market forces. Unlike the competitive political and economic struggles that were taking place in the USA and UK during the Thatcher and Reagan years, they sought to guard solidarity between the partners by giving all a stake in these structures and none incentives to change them in radical ways; by the 1990s this was beginning to be seen as a cause of 'rigidity' (Scharpf 1997). Maintaining the wage levels of a (shrinking) industrial workforce and the replacement rates of unemployment and disability benefits as numbers of claimants rose relentlessly meant that social insurance contributions had to be increased. This in turn made it very expensive to hire new workers (Bleses and Seeleib-Kaiser 2004).

Despite its success in world markets for high-tech products and in constantly improving the skills of its industrial workforce, the German economy therefore faced a continuous struggle with non-wage employment costs; these added an estimated 50% to the expense of hiring an extra worker at the minimum wage, taking account of all taxes and contributions, by the late 1990s (Sharpf 1999; Manow and Seils 2000), with unemployment reaching 5 million in the middle of the following decade (BBC World Service 2005; Möhle 2005).

The rationale for this approach was to preserve the social peace of German society, especially in the aftermath of re-unification after 1989. Both precariousness among the population and political conflict were avoided through the paternalistic power of state-sponsored institutions for cooperation between the classes, hierarchically ordered. But these goals were also pursued through the process of EU economic integration, and especially the establishment of the European Central Bank (ECB), the European Monetary Union (EMU) and the Stability and Growth Pact (SGP) in the 1990s.

> The ECB was closely modelled on the German *Bundesbank*, widely regarded as an exemplar of orthodox monetary policy, while arguably enjoying an even greater measure of formal independence. EMU also made controlling inflation the overwhelming priority for the ECB….[The SGP] was essentially a continuation after monetary union of the public finance elements of the convergence criteria. Pressure for the conclusion of the SPG came primarily from Germany…. (Hay and Wincott 2012, 155–156)

The paradox of this period was that Germany was the most powerful influence on the creation of the Eurozone, but this was the moment at which it was experiencing the greatest challenge to its deeply entrenched principles of monetary and fiscal conservatism. It was the fact that Germany itself failed to meet the convergence criteria for the new monetary union (because the costs of re-unification had led it to exceed prescribed ratio of public debt to GDP) that allowed others with similar problems in their public finances, notably Spain, Portugal and eventually Greece and Italy, to join.

In other words, the institutional rules and structures of the Eurozone reflected the fiscal and monetary standards derived from Germany's 1920s history of hyperinflation and the subsequent disintegration of its democracy; but in practice its member states were able to escape many of these disciplines during the subsequent boom years, and this was in Germany's interests as an investor and exporter. Even so, the German economy remained relatively stagnant, with continuing high rates of unemployment, and this was seen as a symptom of its unwillingness to embrace any form of labour-market flexibility.

Eventually after 2005 a consensus around the introduction of an activation and work programme for unemployed claimants was achieved, implemented through the Harz IV reforms. German unwillingness to allow a precariat to emerge within its labour market had made it the last EU member state to adopt such a set of measures; the very idea of thousands of unemployed citizens on state-directed work schemes had been repugnant to post-war German consciousness.

So, in terms of the liberal regimes' version of authoritarianism, Germany's response to labour market rigidities and high unemployment can be seen to have relied only belatedly and reluctantly on the disciplinary use of state power over benefits claimants. But its broader European strategy, and particularly its role in shaping the institutions of the Eurozone, supplied a framework for exercising a characteristically German form of economic discipline, not only over workers and claimants in southern Europe, but also over their governments.

The ECB represented a supranational form of the kinds of bureaucratic steering arrangements beloved of German elites since the time of Bismarck. It was impervious to democratic influence and its operations were guided by the most severe principles of monetary and fiscal rectitude. Through its authority within the Eurozone, it therefore potentially imposed a German version of central (EU) discipline on governments and their citizens with no means to resist its requirements, and without the benevolent elements in its paternalistic tradition.

By the time the crisis struck in the autumn of 2008, Germany itself had put its public finances back in order; its level of residential mortgage and household debt were also the lowest in the Eurozone (Hay and Wincott 2012, tables 7.1 and 7.2, 209), as was its rate of house price inflation; these actually fell by 10% between 1997 and 2007 (Martin 2010, 593). Along with the Austrian banks, German financial institutions had become the main lenders to housing markets in the Central European post-communist countries as well as in southern Europe. As the leading creditor nation of the Eurozone, Germany had exported the risks of precariousness outside its borders, and was in a position to insist that debtor nations retrench to rebalance their economies.

In the Eurozone's southern states, although the overall shape of welfare institutions was conservative in the Germanic or Austrian tradition, coverage against risks of precariousness was incomplete for people of working age. With the onset of the crisis, their citizens – and especially their young generation – found themselves becoming members of an identifiable new precariat with alarming rapidity.

The impact of the crisis

The collapse of banks, mortgage lenders and insurance companies in the USA and UK in the autumn of 2008 was closely tied to these liberal regimes' approach to sustaining precarious household incomes. As part of their wider strategies for economic growth, both 'Tax Credits' from the state and credit from banks had come to be essential elements in these families' budgets, and the attempt to enlist them in mortgage loans in the USA proved to be the trigger for the crisis.

'Sub-prime' loans to households unable to fulfil the usual income and security requirements had increased from 5% to 20% of new mortgage lending between 1994 and 2006 (Martin 2010, 596). The terms of these loans meant that repayments could be sustained only if interest rates stayed low and house prices continued to rise, as they had been during this period. The risks from mass defaults had been diffused across the affluent world through mortgage-backed securities, but were concentrated in financial centres, especially the City of London. So a sudden rise in interest rates in the USA led quickly to successive waves of bank collapses, first in the US, next the UK and then in Europe.

Although this was clearly a crisis of the affluent countries' financial systems, it should also have been seen as a crisis in their systems for supporting the earnings of households in precarious situations. Instead of bailing out the banks with massive injections of taxpayers' money, governments could have recognised this as a moment to reconsider their roles in labour markets and income security. Indeed, a few commentators did argue that states should redistribute funds towards citizens, not financial institutions, and according to new principles of universality, not selectively to poor people (Jenkins 2008; Monbiot 2009). And this was in fact done, on a very modest scale, in the USA and Australia, at the height of the crisis, when banks stopped lending to their customers.

In the face of slower growth and wider disparities in earnings, liberal values point towards reforms which make incentives for employment more equal, by reducing the poverty and unemployment traps which are a feature of means-tested income support systems, and the coercive elements in welfare-to-work schemes. Proposals for a transition to such an approach had been around for many years (Parker 1989; Offe 1996; Van Parijs 1992), and this was an obvious moment for them to enter the mainstream political debate about the reform of tax-benefits regimes.

I shall argue that the reasons why this was not pursued as an official response to the crisis can be traced to the authoritarian elements in both types of regime. Rather than trying to develop this truly innovative approach to the phenomena of precariousness, governments followed a course in line with their previous policy trajectories, because these allowed them to exercise authority in the ways favoured by their state traditions. As a result, a precariat which is identifiable, both to political observers and to itself, and aware of its interests in opposing state authority, has emerged and become potentially organised and active for the first time in recent history.

Clearly, this is not solely a consequence of developments in labour markets and earnings in the affluent countries; other protest movements, facilitated by internet-based communications between members, have involved a wider swathe of groups within societies. For instance, the movements of the Arab Spring against authoritarian regimes in that region have mobilised a better-educated generation who reject traditional forms of state power; and the protests in Brazil in June, 2013, were mainly about poor quality of public services, not employment and salaries. New opportunities for dissent through better means of communication, and a wider climate of resentment against the limitations of traditional politics, have also played a part in the emergence of precariat-based protest.

The main change brought about by the crisis has been the deterioration of the prospects facing the young generation. In all the affluent countries, both unemployment and the prevalence of short-term and part-time contracts have affected this generation more than their seniors, and there is little evidence since 2008 that government policies are improving longer-term outcomes for the new precariat. However, the nature and distribution of their condition varies with the type of regime identified in this article.

In the USA and UK, well-educated young people, including those with employment-relevant qualifications, are now being forced to remain in posts previously seen as transitional 'entry jobs' for longer, and reaching those more suited to their skills later, than before the crisis. This gives them an extended experience of a precariat existence, during which they are unable to gain the advantages of a career pathway, with access to family formation and owner-occupied housing. It also makes them endure the tutelary authority of the benefits and activation systems for longer.

In the Eurozone, the impact of the crisis was mediated by the ways in which risks had been distributed between economies during the boom years. In the southern European countries, housing bubbles and high public debt exposed populations to increased dangers of precariousness when construction sectors collapsed and state spending was cut. In Germany, although the banking crisis was as serious as that in the liberal regimes, citizens were protected from the worst consequences of this because of the country's sound public finances and low rates of household borrowing. As a result, the German government could insist on strict disciplinary conditions for the loans made by the ECB to its southern counterparts, who in turn imposed austerity upon their new, young precariat – arms' length German authoritarianism.

There were several ironies about these developments. Germany's own banking crisis was largely an indirect consequence of the very conservative nature of its governments' monetary policies. Germany had the lowest rate of house price inflation in the Eurozone (Hay and Wincott 2012, 201, fig. 7.1); German banks bought US mortgage-backed securities partly because they were denied access to that source of profitable returns, and so became heavily exposed to the sub-prime crash. They also fuelled southern European housing bubbles with imprudent loans. Eventually, the state bailed them out to the tune of 480 billion euros.

However, this same German conservatism in public and household borrowing meant that the state could afford to do this without imposing great austerity on its social programmes or changing the direction of its strategy for combatting the threat of precariousness among its citizens. It was those southern European countries which could not finance their own bail-outs which were forced to accept ECB and IMF loans on punitive terms, and in turn to impose austerity on their much less well-protected populations. The German Chancellor played the leading role in setting these conditions.

As a result, regions that had relied most on housing booms experienced the most rapid growth in their youth precariat. Andalucia in southern Spain had general unemployment rates of over 35% of the workforce by the middle of 2013, but youth unemployment of over 65%; construction workers were returning to family farms and young people were unable to find long-term jobs as the proportion of such posts tumbled (BBC Radio 4 2013a).

Southern European welfare states were incomplete versions of the Bismarckian model, and their responses to the labour-market conditions of the period since the 1970s had some elements of the liberal approach. Their governments are now committed to the use of police and other forms of official control to enforce austerity measures on their young precariats. Angry protesters bitterly resent Germany's role in this, but have no alternative approach within which to frame their demands.

Neither type of regime offered these protesters a vision of how their economies could adapt to slower growth in ways consistent with equal citizenship and social justice, allowing paid and unpaid work to be shared without infringing individual freedom; yet such a possibility existed. The basic income principle could be introduced into the tax-benefits systems of both types of regimes in ways that would gradually extend the capacities of citizens to make their own choices about employment, education, training and family formation, even in the face of increasing labour-market fragmentation (Torry 2013). But this new direction in policy would require states to let go of some of their power over their subjects, flying in the face of both these traditions of state authority.

By providing all citizens with unconditional sums without tests of employment orientation, means or social insurance contributions, the basic income approach would increase their autonomy across a range of decisions about work (paid and unpaid), relationships, parenting and child-rearing, enabling them to adapt the way they shared their lives. It would also allow states to focus on the services appropriate for the economic and social environment that is emerging in these countries, rather than policing the precariat. But these advantages remain unrecognised while states in both traditions see their power over citizens as indispensable for a viable social order.

Conclusions

The concept of 'authoritarianism' is not often deployed in relation to welfare capitalist regimes in the affluent countries since the Second World War. This is partly because the term was associated with fascist and Stalinist governments, especially during the Cold War period; but it has also been because, both when state power was focused on benefits claimants and where it was more used to structure economic and social relations, it was disguised within income maintenance provision.

However, since the crisis these features have become more overt; a precariat has emerged, and its existence challenges both forms of state authority even where it has not mobilised in protest. Furthermore, by rescuing their financial sectors from its excesses of the boom years, regimes of both kinds have signalled their continuing commitment to their failed long-term strategies in relation to labour markets and income support, and illustrated the persistent influence of traditions in public policy and administration.

I have argued that the underlying issues for all the affluent states have concerned the reversal of the long-term dynamic of industrialisation; instead of rising salaries and more secure terms of employment, both global and regional (European) capitalist development have been generating falling earnings and increased precariousness for an expanding section of citizens in the affluent countries. Banks have taken the opportunity to enlarge their lending to this sector, as part of the creation of housing bubbles in the USA, UK and southern Europe, and their bail-out after the crisis involves states and central banks directly in these toxic 'assets'.

The only positive feature of this story is that it clarifies the interconnections between the credit extended to the precariat through state benefits and that supplied by the financial sector; each are linked elements in the strategies of both traditions, and both of these now explicitly involve state authority. It is this that makes Standing's (2011) evocation of the precariat as a new class appropriate, because it can identify itself against states' power, even if it has as yet no alternative policies to propose.

The UK supplies a case study in how all this has unfolded. Under New Labour governments, the Third Way orthodoxy presented the broadening of 'Tax Credits' coverage and the expansion of the various activation schemes for claimant groups as 'modernisation' of the Beveridge welfare state in the name of 'tough love' (Jordan with Jordan 2000), and the financial crisis as a kind of global virus, quite unconnected with these issues. Since 2010, the coalition government has introduced 'Universal Credits' as a solution to the problems of incentives for those with lowest earning-power in the most fragmented and precarious forms of employment (Department of Work and Pensions 2010). But whereas the blueprint for this reform (Centre for Social Justice 2009) made almost no mention of conditionality, activation or enforcement, all these elements have been enhanced under the coalition's Work Programme, in tacit admission that the slightly improved incentives of the new means-tested scheme must still be underpinned by official coercion.

This has included a programme for placing young jobseekers in supermarkets and budget stores for unpaid 'work experience' under the threat of disqualification from benefits if they refused (Guardian 2011); and a far stricter regime for testing the work capabilities of claimants with disabilities and long-term illnesses, aimed at transferring them to the jobseekers roll at the introduction of the Employment and Support Allowances, resulting in an increase in appeals of over 300% in 2 years (Channel 4 2011). The Work Programme's success in placing claimants in 'sustainable' employment during its first 2 years was 5% (BBC Radio 4, 2013b).

In the Eurozone, the more pervasive role of state authority in the social order makes the tenuous balances within the whole system more fragile. The debts of bankrupt governments to the ECB and the contributions of solvent ones to its funds are a perpetual reminder of the differential impacts of the crisis on peripheral and central countries, with threats of default and expulsion of the least solvent member states a long-term possibility.

Above all, the fact that a whole generation in the whole region of the Eurozone is now identifiably at risk of precariousness of employment and income focuses attention on the legitimacy of both national and supranational institutions. The authority to enforce cuts in wage and benefits rates as well as public service employment and provision is seen as deeply compromised by corrupt links with financial and construction interests at the national level, and by northern European (and especially German) ones in the actions and policies of the ECB. In combination, they have produced arbitrary exercises in power, such as the closing down of the Greek public television broadcaster ELT on 12 June 2013.

So popular demonstrations, especially in Greece and Spain, constantly supply reminders of citizens' resentment of their rulers' power over them, and of the way in which this is enforced by police and other state agents of control. The fact that this authority is exercised on behalf of distant bodies and anonymous bureaucracies not directly accountable to them increases this resentment. Instead of incorporating them into a system of rule through rational design and managed accommodation of interests, it alienates and angers them.

Both forms of authoritarianism are therefore now confronted with problems that are structural, and neither seems likely to be able to overcome them in the near future through economic growth. Yet, both would also be very reluctant to adopt the basic income route out of their dilemmas in the foreseeable future, unless its demonstrable success in some of the mineral-rich developing countries which are adopting it (Torry 2013, ch. 5) make it difficult to resist this.

References

BBC Radio 4. 2013a. *Today*, June 18.

BBC Radio 4. 2013b. *Today*, June 27.

BBC Radio World Service. 2005. *World Briefing*, March 19.

Beveridge, W. 1942. *Social Insurance and Allied Services*. Cm 6404. London: HMSO.

Beveridge, W. 1944. *Full Employment in a Free Society*. London: Allen and Unwin.

Bleses, P., and M. Seeleib-Kaiser. 2004. *The Dual Transformation of the German Welfare State*. Basingstoke: Palgrave.

Centre for Social Justice. 2009. *Dynamic Benefits: Towards Welfare That Works*. London: Centre for Social Justice.

Channel 4 TV. 2011. *News*, November 21.

Department for Work and Pensions. 2010. *Universal Credit: Welfare That Works*. Cm 7957. London: Department for Work and Pensions.

Dyson, K. 1980. *The State Tradition in Western Europe*. Oxford: Martin Robertson.

Esping-Andersen, G. 1990. *The Three Worlds of Welfare Capitalism*. Cambridge: Polity.

Esping-Andersen, G. 1999. *Social Foundations of Post-Industrial Economies*. Oxford: Oxford University Press.

Flora, P., and J. Alber. 1981. "Modernisation, Democratisation and the Development of Welfare States in Europe." In *The Development of Welfare States in Europe and America*, edited by P. Flora and A. Heidenheimer. New York: Transaction Books.

Guardian. 2011, November 17, p. 49.

Harrington, M. 1962. *The Other America: Poverty in the United States*. New York: Macmillan.

Hay, C., and D. Wincott. 2012. *The Political Economy of European Welfare Capitalism*. Basingstoke: Palgrave Macmillan.

Her Majesty's Government. 1972. *Proposals for a Tax Credit System*. Cmnd 5116. London: Stationery Office.

Hood, N., and S. Young. 1979. *The Economics of Multinational Enterprise*. London: Longman.

Jefferson, T. 1784. "Notes on Virginia." In *The Writings of Thomas Jefferson,* edited by A. Lipscombe. Washington, DC: Jefferson memorial Association.

Jenkins, S. 2008. "Better to Hand Us All a Grand than Hurl Billions at the Banks." *The Guardian*, December 10, p. 33.

Jordan, B., S. James, H. Kay, and M. Redley. 1991. *Trapped in Poverty? Labour-Market Decisions in Low-Income Households*. London: Routledge.

Jordan, B., and C. Jordan. 2000. *Social Work and the Third Way: Tough Love as Social Policy*. London: Sage.

Keynes, J. M. 1936. *The General Theory of Employment, Interest and Money*. London: Macmillan.

Locke, J. 1690. *Two Treatises of Government*, edited by P. Laslett. Cambridge: Cambridge University Press.

Locke, J. 1691. "Some Considerations of the Consequences of the Lowering of Interest, and Raising the Value of Money." In *The Works of John Locke in Four Volumes, (1777)*, vol. 2, edited by W. Strachan, *et al.* Edinburgh: Bell.

Manow, P., and E. Seils. 2000. "Adjusting Badly: The German Welfare State, Structural Change and the Open Economy." In *From Vulnerability to Competitiveness: Welfare and Work in the Open Economy*, edited by F. W. Sharpf and V. A. Schmidt. Oxford: Oxford University Press.

Martin, R. 2010. "The Local Geographies of the Financial Crisis, From the Housing Bubble to Economic Recession and Beyond." *Journal of Economic Geography* 11 (4): 587–618.

Monbiot, G. 2009. "If the State Won't Save Us, We Need a licence to Print our Own Money." *The Guardian*, January 20, p. 25.

Murray, C. 1985. *Losing Ground: American Social Policy, 1950–1980*. New York: Basic Books.

Möhle, M. 2005. "Shifting Frameworks of Welfare, Shifting Needs of Welfare Recipients." Paper given at a seminar on Social Exclusion, University of Plymouth, Plymouth, March 11.

Newman, A. 2002. "When Opportunity Knocks: Economic Liberalisation and Stealth Welfare in the United States." *Journal of Social Policy* 32 (2): 179–98.

Offe, C. 1996. *Modernity and the State*. Cambridge: Polity.

Parker, H. 1989. *Instead of the Dole; An Enquiry into the Integration of the Tax and Benefit System*. London: Routledge and Kegan Paul.

Poor Law Report. 1834. *Administration and Operation of the Laws: Report of the Commissioners*, edited by S. G. Checkland and E. O. A. Checkland. London: Penguin.

Rimlinger, G. V. 1971. *Welfare Policy and Industrialisation in Europe, America and Russia*. London: Wiley.

Scharpf, F. W. 1997. *Employment and the Welfare State: A Continental Dilemma*, Working Paper 9/97. Cologne: Max-Planck Institute for Study of Societies.

Scharpf, F. W. 1999. *The Viability of Advanced Welfare States in the Global Economy: Vulnerabilities and Options*, Working Paper 9/99. Cologne: Max-Planck Institute for the Study of Societies.

Simon, W. L. 1968. *Germany in the Age of Bismarck*. London: Allen and Unwin.

Smith, A. 1776. *An Inquiry Concerning the Nature and Causes of the Wealth of Nations*, edited by E. H. Campbell and A. S. Skinner. Oxford: Clarendon Press.

Standing, G. 2011. *The Precariat: The New Dangerous Class*. London: Bloomsbury.

Taylor, A. J. P. 1955. *Bismarck: The Man and the Statesman*. London: Hamilton.

Torry, M. 2013. *Money for Everyone: Why We Need a Citizen's Income*. Bristol: Polity.

Townsend, P., and B. Abel-Smith. 1965. *The Poor and the Poorest*. London: Bell.

Van Pariis, P., ed. 1992. *Arguing for Basic Income: Ethical Foundations for a Radical Reform*. London: Verso.

Waddan, A. 1997. *The Politics of Social Welfare: The Collapse of the Centre and the Rise of the Right*. Cheltenham: Edward Elgar.

Western, B., and K. Beckett. 1999. "How Unregulated Is the U.S. Labour Market? The Penal System as a Labour Market Institution." *American Journal of Sociology* 104 (4): 1030–1060.

REPLY

Reply to Bill Jordan's 'Authoritarianism and the precariat'

Daryl Glaser

Department of Political Studies, School of Social Sciences, University of the Witwatersrand, Republic of South Africa

This is a reply to:

Jordan, Bill. 2013. "Authoritarianism and the precariat." *Global Discourse*. 3 (3–4): 388–403. http://dx.doi.org/10.1080/23269995.2013.857529

Jordan's paper represents a valuable effort to read the idea of the precariat, and the fear of it, back into the history of Western Europe's and the US's divergent regimes of social control and incorporation. It is illuminating more generally on the evolution of the liberal and paternalist regime alternatives, showing how elements of both of these persist through a long series of epochal policy shifts (for example, the adoption of welfarism by liberal regimes and of fiscal conservatism by paternalist ones). It also shows how both regimes generate various forms of authoritarian control over the socially weaker groups, whether via the state surveillance and coercion associated with means testing and workfare systems favoured in liberal regimes or the hierarchical and authoritarian incorporation that marked the paternalist regimes until after World War Two. Moreover, these characteristics seem, on Jordan's account, largely independent of what many would judge to be crucial developments of the last 150 years, including the advent of strong labour movements and representative political systems based on competing mass-based political parties. States appear as largely autonomous, self-driven, continuous orders, at once responsive to changing conditions and impervious in their adherence to particular modes of response.

While I find this paper insightful and persuasive up to a point, and am attracted to the argument for a universal basic income, the above characterisation also hints at some of my concerns. First, the idea of the two traditions is made to do too much explanatory work. The German tradition, especially as it expresses itself in EU leadership and austerity prescription, seems to me as much influenced by a second and independent (post-Bismarckian) moment in German history as by its earlier traditions, namely the hyperinflation of the 1920s. True, fiscal orthodoxy matches quite nicely with the control obsession of the Bismarck regime, but its effects are, in some ways, distinguishable (for example, they point away from generous insurance schemes, at least absent matching tax increases) and may have outlasted the paternalism. Moreover, Scandinavian social democracy and southern Europe prove to be quite tricky to incorporate into the typology and East-Central Europe is omitted from the picture altogether. It might have been useful to hear a comment on where Netherlands fits in, given its partnership with Germany in pushing fiscal orthodoxy. The paternalist tradition here really reduces to a German one, so much of the force of the argument rests on Germany's considerable weight. And in the end, the liberal and paternalist countries seem to end up in a pretty similar (neoliberal) place. The author implies that the countries originating in different traditions have converged because both traditions have failed, but he is not clear as to whether these resiliently distinctive traditions have now collapsed, ceasing to offer markers of distinction between capitalist lands and types. The notion that the German model is alive and well in southern Europe is less than convincing.

Indeed, and second, the argument gets complicated by the non-confinement of economies to national territorial boundaries. Germany's fiscal conservatism may extend at arm's-length to southern Europe, at least once the post-2008 crisis sets in, but is paternalism does not. True, Jordan does not suggest otherwise, but the upshot is that southern Europeans are now up against specifically German fiscal conservatism, not up against the longer-standing paternalistic tradition. So, maybe, southern Europeans should not be painting Bismarck's walrus moustache over Merkel after all. Moreover, capitalists originating in both liberal and paternalist countries freely exploit under-protected workers abroad, both as labourers and as lenders, and with state support; the range of jurisdiction of the traditions thus becomes more difficult to demarcate. Territory is also breached by human immigration. There is an interesting but undeveloped implication in the paper that paternalism may be for citizens, even only for northern European white ones, whereas both immigrants and non-nationals fall outside the protective paternal net. Something of this dynamic may characterise western democratic capitalism generally. The dynamic may also operate at the expense of long-standing racial minority citizens, such as African Americans, whose survival needs have partly fallen under the jurisdiction of the United States' penal-Keynesian military regime rather than under a protective regime, liberal or otherwise. The political clout of enfranchised domestic white working classes, as distinct from state traditions, may be a causal factor in this inclusion–exclusion dynamic. (Obama's election may signal a decline in its clout.)

Which brings me to my last quibble – the account of the state. Sometimes, Jordan's state appears autonomous, invested in its own 'historic power over its citizens'. At other times, reference is made to external economic ruling classes and their sway – capitalists and urban middle classes in the liberal regimes, the traditional landowning aristocracy in the paternalist ones. But why should the motivations of state officeholders be reduced to a power-maintenance imperative? How is the power of external dominant classes brought to bear? And what of non-dominant classes? The working class and labour movement are sidelined from this discussion, both by the focus on the precariat and by the implication that the state is impervious either to external class power or to external class power not originating in dominant classes. Dominant philosophical traditions are themselves treated in a less than convincing way. Liberalism, in particular, needs further specification. Jordan acknowledges that Anglo-American liberalism acquired a socially protective dimension from the 1930s, but currents of social liberalism can already be detected in Britain by the later nineteenth century (with T. H. Green, later the 1909 People's Budget); some detect it much earlier, even in Thomas Paine. If the author is insightful on the way liberal social protection is infused with certain earlier punitive dynamics, he is nevertheless inconsistent (though, in my view, not wrong) in later appealing to liberalism's egalitarian and libertarian 'values' in making his case for a basic income grant. In any case, how do liberal ideas interact with state and class interests – is the liberal outlook a veneer for interests or a driver in its own right? In short, the actual operation of the state, including the interplay of interests and ideas within and around it, are left under-explored.

RESEARCH ARTICLE

From the precariat to the multitude

Ben Trott

Department of Political Science, JFI Institute for North American Studies, Freie Universität Berlin, Berlin, Germany

This paper situates Guy Standing's recent work on 'the precariat' within a broader body of literature exploring processes of 'precarisation', at work and across the social field. It sets out the differential distribution of 'precarity' (including on the basis of gender, geography, status and sector) resulting from transformations in labour and the political economy, the rollback of social democracy and of 'industrial citizenship' (where these existed), as well as from processes of globalisation. The paper argues that, like many other works, Standing's book, *The Precariat: The New Dangerous Class*, de-couples its discussion of precarious, neoliberal labour and life from the explicitly utopian agenda of radical reform it ultimately proposes. Drawing on Kathi Weeks' engagement with Ernst Bloch's work, the paper suggest Standing's utopianism remains *abstract*, detached from an analysis of the social forces, movements and struggles that might bring it into being. It makes use of Antonio Negri's distinctive, heterodox interpretation of V.I. Lenin to provide a framework for theorising how *concrete utopian* projects of radical political transformation – which is to say, 'realist' or materialist ones – are extrapolated out of spontaneous struggles; the predominant 'will', ethics and structures of which are always largely determined by the social, political and economic context from which they emerge. It is shown how, on the basis of this approach, Negri (in his collaboration with Michael Hardt) has constructed the notion of 'multitude' as a potential model for political organisation today – apposite to the precarious reality described by Standing and others. They draw on Baruch Spinoza's political philosophy – often counterposing it to that of Thomas Hobbes – to affirm the capacity for common political action and decision despite heterogeneity, and to ground political organisation in social conflict rather than contract. Finally, drawing on Alain Badiou's distinction between 'immediate' and 'historical uprisings', the paper explores the degree to which a number of contemporary movements and struggles might have tentatively achieved what he calls 'qualitative extension' – establishing connections and a ground for common action across social spaces and strata – potentially setting in motion enduring projects of political organisation and constitution that resemble the multitude model.

> Politics is always about nomination. It is about naming a political subjectivity and organizing politically around that name.
>
> –Simon Critchley (2007, 103)

In the Anglophone world, the term 'precariat' first came into widespread use among activists at once interested in organising around 'precarious' working conditions – and the way their emergence was intertwined with broader social, political, economic and cultural dynamics – while simultaneously convinced traditional forms of workers' organisation were insufficient for building effective forms of resistance and counter-power. What eventually developed into a network stretching across Europe, and then as far afield as Tokyo, began with a 5000-strong parade in Milan on 1 May 2001. It was organised by a network of labour collectives, students, migrant groups, rank-and-file unions and others from across the country, as well as from France and Catalonia. They mobilised 'young temps, partimers [sic.], freelancers and contract workers, researchers and teachers, service and knowledge workers' (Foti 2004, 21). By 2003, this now annual event had grown to include 50,000 participants, and a year later, 100,000 demonstrators took to the streets of Milan and Barcelona demanding 'social rights' and expressing solidarity with local workers that were 'striking and picketing' for 'decent pay and labor dignity' (Foti 2004, 21). Come 2005, EuroMayDay had arrived in London (along with almost 20 other cities) and Alex Foti, a Milan-based activist involved with the EuroMayDay network, argued the idea was 'to build social self-representation through metropolitan activism by federating autonomist collectives and local unions around the social organization of the precariat' (Foti 2004, 27).[1]

The English-language use of 'precariat' now exceeds that of these activist networks. Several high-profile research projects and social scientific publications have recently made use of the category, garnering considerable attention from major media outlets (e.g. BBC 2013; Savage et al. 2013). While the (Euro)MayDay activists had tended to use 'precarity' to describe 'a generalized condition' – albeit one still 'searching for a radical transeuropean subject' (Foti 2004, 22) – however, its current usage in the social sciences usually associates the category with a distinct social group or class (albeit, in some cases, a rapidly growing one). This emergent precariat has tended to be portrayed as the lowest social or economic strata of society, or as the group that is most insecure and deprived of rights.

1. The precariat

Guy Standing's widely reviewed book, *The Precariat: The New Dangerous Class* (2011), has been among those key works that have drawn popular attention to the term. It charts the rise of, 'a new group in the world, a [global] class-in-the-making' (Standing 2011, vii), which has emerged largely as a result of the flexibilisation and increasing insecurity of the labour market throughout '[t]he globalisation era (1975–2008)', defined in broadly Polanyian terms as, 'a period when the economy was 'disembedded' from society as financiers and neo-liberal economists sought to create a global market economy based on competitiveness and individualism' (Standing 2011, 26).

Standing (2011, 8) describes a 'growing "precariat", flanked by an army of unemployed and a detached group of socially ill misfits living off the dregs of society'. They occupy a social position below not only the 'elite', but also: a relatively privileged '"salariat", still in stable full-time employment, some hoping to move into the elite'; a small group of often high-earning 'professional-' and 'technical workers', referred to as 'proficians'; as well as the 'shrinking "core" of manual employees, the essence of the old "working class"' (Standing 2011, 7–8).

As can only be expected, the data Standing (2011) draw on and the narrative he constructs resonates with and builds on (albeit sometimes questioning) numerous other accounts of the changing world of work, and how this has been caught up with processes of globalisation and the changing role of the state. These are the shifts typically framed in terms of a move from Fordism to post-Fordism, Keynesianism to neoliberalism, the industrial to the information age, and from modernity to post-modernity. My preoccupation in the first Part of this paper is *not* with a precise reconstruction of Standing's (2011) account of the precariat itself, his book's many strengths and occasional shortcomings. For this, the numerous reviews already published (along with Standing's [2011] book itself) will be of far more use. Rather, Part One is an effort to situate some of his observations on the nature of contemporary precarity within a broader literature, providing an outline of the ways that *almost all* social strata are affected by what will be called 'precarisation', as well as closely related phenomena.[2]

In Part Two, however, I point towards an important shortcoming in Standing's book. Specifically, I note a relative blind-spot – one that is by no means unique to the approach of this book or this author – where there is a considerable de-coupling of the discussion of the nature of labour and life today, and the avowedly 'utopian agenda and strategy' the book advances for the forging of 'a new "politics of paradise"' (Standing 2011, vii). Part Three then suggests the concept of 'multitude' – as this derives from the political philosophy of Baruch Spinoza in particular and has been taken up in the more recent work of Michael Hardt, Antonio Negri, Paolo Virno and others – as a tool that might provide a way of theorising *how* form could be given to such an emancipatory politics; and how a *concrete utopianism*, extrapolated from existing struggles, could emerge.

1.1. Precarisation and informalisation

The precariat, then, result from a process of 'precarisation' (Standing 2011, 16). 'To be precaritised', Standing (2011, 16) suggests, 'is to be subject to the pressures and experiences… of living in the present, without a secure identity or sense of development achieved through work and lifestyle'. Judith Butler (2011, 13) has distinguished between a similar process of *precarisation*, 'built into the institutions of temporary labor, of decimated social services, and of the general attrition of social democracy', and *precarity* 'as a structure of affect' which represents 'a heightened sense of expendability or disposability that is differentially distributed throughout society', as well as the *precariousness* 'which characterizes every embodied and finite human being, and non-human beings as well.'[3] I broadly follow these distinctions throughout this paper.

The discussion of *precarious work* (or rather, of work's 'precarisation') in Standing's (2011) book includes, yet extends well beyond, the casualisation of the labour market that has accompanied the erosion of the welfare state in recent decades (where this ever existed) – both of which have been carefully documented by scholars like Anne Gray (2004), and indeed, throughout much of his career, by Standing (e.g. 1997, 2008, 2011, 10–11 and 31–49) himself. It goes on to demonstrate that these processes have now been extended and intensified so that 'informalised' forms of work – like those that Mike Davis, in his book *Planet of the Slums* (2006, 178), shows have become, from the 1980s onwards, 'the new primary mode of livelihood in a majority of Third World cities' – can be found almost everywhere.[4] Certainly they can be identified in what Saskia Sassen (2001, 294–305) calls the 'global cities'; metropolises like London, New York and Tokyo that perform key, strategic functions within the global economy. Immanuel Ness (2005, 22), who echoes aspects of Davis' argument, insists that '[a]lthough informalization is typically associated with underground economies in the developing world, there is a growing recognition of the link between the regulated and the unregulated sectors in advanced industrial regions' like New York City, the focus of his work. Furthermore, this 'is not limited to immigrant workers but also has grown to include a larger share of native-born workers employed in domestic services, personal services, and garment production'

(Ness 2005, 23). Such labour, in other words, can no longer be described in any sense as 'peripheral', but rather as *central* to production today.

1.2. Denizens and the new hierarchies of citizenship

The spread of informalisation is one factor that has contributed to the proliferation of so-called 'denizenship', where some are granted a more restricted range of rights than full citizens (Standing 2011, 14). Standing (2011, 11–12) partly explains this phenomenon through the demise of 'industrial citizenship', which he describes as the 'forms of labour-related security… that social democrats, labour parties and trade unions pursued… after the Second World War'. This included the rights to earn an income, maintain employment and skills within a given niche, develop new skills, earn a sufficient income, work in a safe and healthy environment, and the right to trade union representation and to strike – all of which are being eroded (Standing 2011, 10). This is particularly acute, and the status of 'denizen' often at its clearest, not only for those working within the aforementioned informalised sectors, but also among migrants (domestic as well as international), and those subjected to 'criminalisation' (Standing 2011, 14).[5] Here, Standing's (2011, 14) argument resonates in many ways with a huge body of scholarship on the reconfiguration of hierarchies of citizenship in the globalisation era: from Étienne Balibar's (2004, 44) discussion of the ways the 1992 Maastricht Treaty meant first, second and even third generation migrants were excluded from European citizenship, becoming 'a mass of second-class citizens… even when they enjoy long-term or permanent rights of residency'; through to Pun Ngai's (2005, 41) discussion of the various categories into which legal temporary workers are placed in Shenzen – a city in the Chinese province of Guangdong where many domestic migrants work in high-tech factories located within its Special Economic Zone – determining their entitlement to state welfare and residency rights.

Alongside hierarchies – including but not limited to those of citizenship/denizenship – established, exacerbated, or reconfigured through the erosion of 'industrial citizenship' (which, to be sure, was certainly never universal), gender also continues to serve as a basis upon which precarity is differentially distributed. In 2008, all OECD member countries were still characterised by a gender pay-gap, in terms of the median earnings of full-time workers, and in the majority of these countries, women's percentage share of part-time work rose throughout the first decade of the Twenty-First Century (OECD 2010a, 2010b). Women make up an estimated 90% of the 27 million workers in the world's 'free trade zones', that are often highly precaritised (Davis 2006, 158), and Standing (1999, 599) found that, certainly in the European Union, women tend to have less access to welfare benefits than men when unemployed.

1.3. Graduates in debt, and with no future

There have been many consequences to the changes in the labour-market that have taken place over the last few decades, one of which, Standing points out, is that even though the proportion of the population who access further education is greater than in previous generations, the expectations of graduates (in terms of the quality and security of jobs) are failing to be met. '40 per cent of Spanish university students', he explains, 'a year after graduating find themselves in low-skilled jobs that do not require their qualifications', producing what he calls 'a pandemic of status frustration' (Standing 2011, 67). Paul Mason (2012, 70), in his study of the causes and actors behind the recent wave of protests, from the Arab Spring to Occupy Wall Street, describes this as a generation of 'graduates with no future', facing stiff competition for few jobs, little disposable income, and high interest rates on mortgages (Mason 2012, 71). 'Insult is added to injury', however, when these future-less graduates are 'told they should be committed, happy and loyal in jobs that are beneath their qualifications and must repay debts incurred on a promise that their certificates would gain them high income jobs' (Standing 2011, 68). Maurizio Lazzarato (2012, 7) takes up this issue in his recent book, *The Making of Indebted Man*, showing, '[t]he debtor-creditor relationship… intensifies mechanisms of exploitation and domination at every level of society', and not only among students, effectively producing disciplined subjects *compelled* to labour. 'The debtor is "free,"' he explains, 'but his actions, his behavior, are confined to the limits defined by the debt he has entered into… You are free insofar as you assume the *way of life*… compatible with reimbursement' (Lazzarato 2012, 31).

Such is the pressure to find rewarding work, work that helps escape student or consumer debt, or simply work to meet basic needs, that a growing number particularly of young people find themselves in unpaid internships. In *Intern Nation: How to Earn Nothing and Learn Little in the Brave New Economy*, Ross Perlin (2011, 36 and 185–187) describes how these are no longer confined to relatively high-end sectors in the US, EU and Commonwealth countries, but are also increasingly found in retail and elsewhere, as well as in metropolises across Latin America, the Middle East, and Asia. This partly corresponds (and certainly coincides) with a rise in the demand for 'free labour' – even from those in formal, paid employment who are often expected to work long, irregular hours, and increasingly away from traditional places of work. Such labour is 'free', Standing (2011, 130) insists, 'in that it is unpaid; it is unfree in that it is not done autonomously'. One of the areas this (un)freedom of contemporary labour is at its clearest is in the digital and online work of 'netslaves', to borrow a term from Tiziana Terranova (2004, 73). But their particular work-world reveals much about the world of work in general: they are 'not simply a typical form of labour on the Internet; they also embody a complex relation to labour, which is widespread in late capitalist societies' (Terranova 2004, 73). 'Free labour on the Net,' she points out, is '[s]imultaneously voluntarily given and unwaged, enjoyed and exploited' (Terranova 2004, 74).[6] Offline, 'free labour' – if we follow the distinction Standing (2011, 13) borrows from ancient Greece – could perhaps be understood not as 'labour' at all but rather as 'work', and more specifically, as the growing compulsion *to-work-in-order-to-labour*. The Greek definition, Standing (2011, 13) insists, casts *work* as unpaid, traditionally carried out by citizens as an end in itself, whereas *labour* is exploited, conducted for the benefit of others, and performed by non-citizens – the *banausoi*, *metics* and slaves. Today, we might still want to conceive of labour, as in ancient Greece, as the primary productive activity – productive today, that is, for capital; if we follow Adam Smith and Marx's remarkably similar definitions – even if this is often now performed by (full) citizens (Standing's discussion of precarious denizens notwithstanding). Work, however, is certainly no longer performed simply 'for its own sake, to strengthen personal relationships, to be combined with public participation in the life of the community', as Standing (2011, 13) argues was the case in ancient Greece. Instead, such relationship-strengthening, as well as being seen to participate in *and contribute to* 'the community', to society and to culture, have become a common means of accessing labour – of 'pimping' your CV, for instance – which in turn clearly remains the main way of meeting basic (and all other) needs (Standing 2011, 13).

This, then, broadly describes the organisation of work, of labour, and of social life – as well as their blurring – today. Labour is casualised and increasingly informal, with state welfare provisions greatly curtailed. Citizenship is undergoing new stratifications and 'denizenship' proliferating. Through indebtedness, there is a growing compulsion towards finding any kind of waged-labour; as well as towards working-in-order-to-labour, and indeed labouring for free. The precariat as 'a class in the making' emerges as a consequence of a precarisation that is accelerating, even as its effects continue to be differentially distributed – on the basis of gender and geography, status and sector. It is a body of productive and exploited subjects, far more heterogeneous in its make-up than its predecessor, 'the proletariat'.

2. Utopianism, abstract and concrete

Standing's book is a politically invested one. It proposes forging 'a new "politics of paradise",' described as 'a mildly utopian agenda and strategy to be taken up by politicians and what is euphemistically called 'civil society'' in order to avoid 'a politics of inferno' (Standing 2011, vii). The precariat, he insists, potentially represents 'an emerging dangerous class', detached 'from the mainstream of economic affluence and progress', something which is 'conducive for intolerance' (Standing 2011, 25). This is especially when combined with demonisation, the influence of right-wing populism, and neo-fascist electoral victories in Europe, from Sweden to Hungary (Standing 2011, 145–153). Standing (2011, vii) recognises steering away from inferno and towards 'paradise' will require the precariat to move from its status as 'a *class-in-the-making*' to 'a *class-for-itself*', in the sense Marx famously used this latter, Hegelian-inflected, term in *The Poverty of Philosophy* (1995 [1847], esp. 181–191). While the proletariat might already have existed 'as a mass of people' in 'a common situation with common [objective] interests' – all of them subjected to '[t]he domination of capital' – they only became a class for-themselves through collective struggle, initially around wages and the formation of early trade unions (Marx 1995 [1847], 188–189).

Echoing the sentiments of many EuroMayDay activists, Standing (2011, 168) quite convincingly argues new forms of 'collaborative bargaining' are now needed 'to consider the full range of work and labour activities that the precariat has to undertake and its social aspirations'.[7] These forms would be parallel – if not necessarily an alternative – to trade unions, and he lays out some of the challenges and opportunities that would confront such a project. His primary preoccupation in the final chapter of the book, where he discusses these issues, however, is in laying out a 'political programme' that can move 'from theatre and visual ideas of emancipation' invoked by EuroMayDay and similar movements, 'to a set of demands that will engage the state rather than merely puzzle or irritate it' (Standing 2011, 3).[8] He does so through a series of radical policy proposals that would doubtless drastically improve the lives of the precariat and precaritised.

Essentially, Standing (2011, 155–167) suggests a remaking of society, so that all forms of work are respected (not just waged-labour), a degree of idleness is valued (not just individually, but socially), citizenship rights are extended (to migrants and the 'criminalised', among others), education is an end in itself (and its commodification is combatted), and – crucially – a guaranteed and universal basic income is implemented, at least suggesting a separation of the capacity to meet basic needs from the obligation to sell one's labour. For Standing (2011, 181), this final demand is a particularly important programmatic point, not only enabling people to reassert a greater degree of control over their time, but also, among other things, potentially becoming 'an instrument for encouraging deliberative democracy'.[9]

Individual demands and broader agendas such as these have often, first, aimed at establishing a common ground among diverse social subjects, struggles and desires, and, second, been thought to potentially contain the kernel of more far-reaching transformations. The very 'art of politics', as Slavoj Žižek (2013, 11) has argued, often 'lies in making particular demands which, while thoroughly realistic, strike at the core of hegemonic ideology and imply much more radical change. Such demands, while feasible and legitimate, are de facto impossible' – at least within the social, political and economic framework whose limits this ideology delineates.

David Harvey's (2012, 25) recent discussion of the 'Right to the City' as a political demand would appear to fulfil both these functions. On the one hand, it remains 'an empty signifier', with '[t]he definition of the right... itself an object of struggle, and that struggle' he says 'has to proceed concomitantly with the struggle to materialize it' (Harvey 2012, xv). It provides, in other words, a pole around which political struggle and organisation could occur. Simultaneously, it identifies a structural feature of contemporary capitalism – what Harvey (2012, 25) describes as the need for urbanisation to absorb surplus product – as a potentially strategic terrain of struggle.[10] Moreover, while the demand for greater control over the cities in which we live appears thoroughly legitimate, it also hints not only at a desire to socialise control over surplus but also, perhaps, the conditions of its production (Harvey 2012, 25). The demand for a basic income guarantee has also long been understood as similarly strategic. Partly because it is often proposed as a non-means tested payment, without the requirement to (extra) work (e.g. Raventós 2007, 9; Standing 2011, 171), it could conceivably receive very broad support. Yet its real power is usually understood as lying in the radical shifts it would produce throughout society. Stanley Aranowitz and others, in the 'Post-Work Manifesto', suggested it could transform the welfare, health, and education systems, ideological distinctions between 'workers and "idlers"', and society's perspective on the division of labour – shifting emphasis 'from work toward solving problems, exploring possibilities, and finding new ethical and social meanings' (Aranowitz et al. 1998, 68).[11]

Standing's (2011, 155) 'mildly utopian' agenda is at its best, then, when it shares – as it often does – this tactical and strategic approach. *Tactical* in the sense of formulating concrete proposals aimed at improving the lives of the precariat and the precaritised; and at being understood as such. *Strategic* in recognising (if implicitly) these 'realistic' and 'legitimate' proposals are often, following Žižek's (2013, 11) description, 'de facto impossible', calling into question many of society's ideological presuppositions and the limits imposed by its *Realpolitik*. Utopianism – even of this supposedly 'mild' variety, formulated as it largely is in the language of public policy – thus threatens to place key political questions on the table, even in our a supposedly 'post-political' age.

However, there is of course another, less politically threatening, sense in which utopianism has often been understood, rendering it the object of critique. Indeed, this understanding is the one, as Fredric Jameson (2007, xi) observes, that dominated in most 'older Marxist traditions' which, drawing on Marx and Engels' own polemics, saw utopianism as essentially 'lacking any conception of agency or political strategy', often going so far as to cast it as, 'an idealism deeply and structurally averse to the political as such'.[12]

Kathi Weeks (2011, 175–225) – who shares Jameson's (2007) refusal, from a Marxian perspective, to reduce utopianism to this caricature – sets out what she sees as the necessary relationship between utopia and the political programme; or rather, between utopia, the manifesto and the articulation of demands.[13] Drawing on Ernst Bloch's *Principle of Hope*, she insists that, '[i]n order to be both a useful intellectual exercise and a politically effective force,' utopianism – or, 'utopian hope' – needs to 'be based in analyses of the present conjuncture and in relation to existing tendencies and credible possibilities' (Weeks 2011, 195). She points out that Bloch's distinction between 'abstract-' and 'concrete utopias' was partly intended to address the traditional Marxist critique – essentially, a 'realist' or materialist one – with the former corresponding to the ideal type of utopianism so widely objected to (Weeks 2011, 195). *Abstract utopias*, she explains, 'are conjured up without sufficient regard to present trends and conditions that could render them possible, as opposed to impossible, futures' (Weeks 2011, 195). In contrast, *concrete utopias* are 'developed in relation to what Bloch calls the "Real-Possible". A concrete utopia, as "a dream which lies in the historical trend itself… is," as Bloch explains it, "concerned to deliver the forms and contents which have already developed in the womb of the present society"' (Weeks 2011, 195).

Despite its considerable and aforementioned strengths, both tactical and strategic, Standing's (2011) utopian agenda essentially remains a relatively abstract one, to the extent that it contains little in the way of an account as to *how* it could be rendered possible, or whence it derives.[14] Its strategic strengths are ultimately limited to the transformations that would likely be set in motion by such an agenda being won, yet the tactics and strategy for doing so remain under-developed. Indeed, for something along the lines of this agenda to become a *concrete* utopian project, it would require grounding in – or better, *extrapolation out of* – an analysis of existing social forces, coalitions, movements and struggles. So while Standing is correct to insist a 'politics of paradise', and avoiding the very real threat of 'inferno', will require political *construction*, this cannot of course be reduced, as I am sure he would agree, to *prescription*.

In Part Three below, I suggest the notion of 'multitude', as this has recently been theorised, as a tool for thinking precisely *how* such a project of construction could take place, and the manner in which this would be determined (among other things) by the conditions of precariousness, denizenship, indebtedness and their differential distribution – as well as by the blurring of distinctions between work, labour, and life – set out by Standing (2011), and throughout Part One.

3. The multitude

In discussing the increasing flexibilisation of waged-work, the fluidity of the current division of labour, and the tendency for the workplace to extend into the rest of the world, Standing (2011, 38) refers to a so-called 'Italian school' of theorists who, by drawing on the work of Michel Foucault as well as Marx, have sought to understand this process in terms of an emergent 'social factory' (although he says he is unconvinced by this image himself).[15]

The heterogeneous school of thought to which he is referring is often named either *Operaismo* (which literally translates it as 'workerism') or 'autonomist Marxism'. Theoretical work within this tradition – by key theorists such as Antonio Negri and Paolo Virno as well as, more recently, Michael Hardt – has often been characterised not only by the aforementioned engagement with French post-structuralist thought but also by the work of Baruch Spinoza, and particularly his notion of multitude (e.g. Hardt and Negri 2001, 2004, 2009; Virno 2004). Before examining the potential function of this concept – in terms of extrapolating models of political organisation apposite to our age of precarisation, as well as for thinking political struggles that might give form to a politics of paradise today – however, it will prove productive to take a brief detour through Negri's distinct approach to theorising such questions, which has also informed his collaborations with Hardt.

3.1. Lenin beyond Lenin

In a contribution to an edited volume on *The Philosophy of Antonio Negri*, Hardt (2005) points, among other things, to two of Negri's important and overlapping contributions to thinking workers' resistance that are of relevance here. The first is the extent to which he questions the voluntarism – or 'idealist speculation' – often presupposed by discussions of organisational form, or efficacious modes of struggle, as if this were a matter of 'free will', able to be decided upon entirely by political militants or activists (Hardt 2005, 18). Rather, Negri demonstrates how such 'will' is in fact objectively determined. The second and simultaneous contribution is a 'Marxist reading of Lenin' – by which it is essentially meant an 'historical materialist' reading – which in turn provides a productive way of re-approaching classical Marxist discussions as to the relation between spontaneity and organisation (Hardt 2005, 15).[16]

Negri departs from the most traditional interpretations of Lenin, where the objective *critique of political economy* provided the basis for his theory of workers' (or of *political*) organisation, basing itself on an identification of capital's 'weak links' (Hardt 2005, 14). This approach can certainly be found in Lenin's work, and in 'Contradiction and Overdetermination', Louis Althusser (2005, 97–98) provides a succinct summary of this, arguing the Bolshevik leader understood Russia as the weakest link 'in the imperialist chain' because it 'had accumulated the largest sum of historical contradictions then possible; for it was at the same time *the most backward and the most advanced nation*, a gigantic contradiction which its divided ruling classes could neither avoid nor solve'. Russia was said to be 'overdue with its bourgeois revolution on the eve of its proletarian revolution; pregnant with two revolutions, it could not withhold the second even by delaying the first' (Althusser 2005, 97–98).

The Leninism that Hardt (2005, 14–15) finds in Negri's work, however, founds a project of organisation first and foremost on a *theory of subjectivity*. Famously, in *What is to be Done?*, Lenin (1989 [1902], 107) had stressed the need 'to combat spontaneity, to divert the working class movement' away from its 'trade-unionist striving' for better conditions of exploitation and 'to bring it under the wing' of a project of revolutionary organisation. As Althusser (2001, 31) stresses, however, Lenin's 'critique of "spontaneism"' is not aimed *per se* at 'the spontaneity, resourcefulness, inventiveness and genius of the masses of the people but against a political ideology' – namely that of the 'bourgeoisie' – 'which, screened by an exaltation of the spontaneity of the masses, exploits it in order to divert it into an incorrect politics.' Negri goes further, however.[17] As Hardt (2005, 15) points out, he finds in Lenin's early writings, like *The Development of Capitalism in Russia*, 'the concept of a "determinate social formation"' which became 'a framework for investigating the composition of the working class and for discerning the character of the revolutionary subject.' Negri's reading of Lenin's early writings, in the 1890s, he insists, is filled with observations of 'combativeness' among 'the select group of highly skilled Russian workers' and these struggles – no matter how 'immature' – were said to 'form an organizational stand-point,… a political intuition'; in other words, 'they always allude[d] to political goals' (Hardt 2005, 16). Rather than needing to be 'combatted', the Lenin that Negri discovered saw spontaneity as 'the emergence of working-class subjectivity' and insisted 'the affirmation of this spontaneity of the masses *is the first moment of Leninist organization*' (Hardt 2005, 16, my emphasis).

While the spontaneous, concrete struggles of workers were primary, 'a leap from the particular to the general' needed to entail a project of organisation – albeit one that was *co-extensive* with the spontaneity that set it in motion (Hardt 2005, 16–17). 'If the first moment, the economic struggles of the workers and the spontaneity of the masses, constitutes the intuition of revolutionary organization,' Hardt (2005, 16) explains, 'the second moment, that of political leadership and autonomous organization, is its confirmation; or better, if the first moment is the affirmation of working-class subjectivity, the second moment is the affirmation of that affirmation'. As Negri insists, '[o]rganization is spontaneity that reflects on itself' (cited in Hardt 2005, 17).

While political organisation, then, is determined by spontaneous struggle, spontaneity itself is also determinate, in the sense that the 'will' formed among struggling workers – spontaneous and autonomous in the sense that it 'receives no external organization' – is 'formed in the material work relations in the production process' (Hardt 2005, 18). The efficacy of the Leninist or Bolshevik model of (hierarchical, centralised) organisation, resulted in large part from its reflection of the vertical structure of spontaneous struggles which predated it (discussed below), which themselves corresponded to the structure of relations of production at the time (Hardt 2005, 19). It followed that transformations in the realm of production would produce new forms of workers' subjectivity and resistance, which would in turn transform the nature of the most efficacious modes of organisation.

3.2. From the professional to the socialised worker

A study of Negri's work, as Hardt (2005) effectively demonstrates, reveals the degree to which this reading of Lenin, and the deduction from this of a very distinct approach – which *necessarily* moves beyond Lenin – has characterised his interpretation of the transformations in capital accumulation, the organisation of the labour process, and workers' struggle and organisation since the Russian Revolution. He identified, for instance, the way that Fordism–Taylorism sought 'to isolate the Bolshevik vanguards' – the 'relatively highly "professionalised" sector (typical of engineering)' that were common in Russia and beyond at the time, and upon whose skill and knowledge capital was highly dependent (Negri 1988a, 11). They were expelled 'from their hegemonic producer role, by means of a massification of the productive process and deskilling of the labour force' (Negri 1988a, 11). '[T]he capitalist response to the October Revolution of 1917, to the movement of workers' councils,' he explains elsewhere, 'not only removed the historical possibility of this organisational model' but the process of capitalist restructuring this entailed 'also set in motion an operation of dynamic containment of the struggles of the new massified working class, the 'mass worker' that was coming to the forefront' (Negri 1988c, 109).

While Taylor's scientific management set the pace of work along Ford's assembly line, Ford himself sought (with some success) to shape the family, gender relations and the consumption habits of his workers through social engineering designed to benefit profitability and produce a disciplined work-force. The Keynesian 'planner state', as Negri (1988a, 13) described it, meanwhile attempted to stave off the threat of working class revolution – looming large in the decade that followed 1917 – 'by recognising and accepting the new relation of class forces, while making the working class function within an overall mechanism that would "sublimate" its continuous struggle for power into a dynamic element within the system' (Negri 1988a, 13). Struggles over the wage, then, became crucial to all parties. The role of what Negri (1988b, 83) called the 'mass vanguard' in this period – where the 'mass worker' had become the paradigmatic subjectivity, displacing that of the 'professional worker' – recognised the function played by demands for higher wages, forcing an increase in efficiency and enabling higher rates of productivity to be demanded in return. The power of the mass vanguard, however –

which remained very much limited to struggles on the factory floor – was in demanding *less work for more money.*[18]

Despite his continued use of the term 'vanguard', which Hardt (2005, 23) has noted is paradoxical, Negri here was actually arguing *against* the continued efficacy of the (classical) Leninist model. 'The October Revolution was the work of the genius of the Bolsheviks; but today revolution cannot depend on the brilliant insight of vanguards – it stems directly from the daily experience of the masses' (Negri 1988b, 79). Again the dominant (flat, massified) form of workers' organisation corresponded to the organisation of labour and production.

Out of the struggles of these workers emerged in turn yet another new social subject, the 'socialised worker', later re-theorised by Hardt, Negri, and Virno as the 'multitude'. This subject was said to have come about 'in the period following 1968', and '[t]his new composition arose as a result of the decentralization of production that constituted capital's response to the international wave of struggles by the mass worker during the late sixties… If technical skill and knowledge defined the productive composition of the professional worker and collective discipline defined the composition of the mass worker, then communication and sociability defined the new composition and work discipline of the socialized worker' (Murphey 2005, xxxv). Again transformations in the realm of production generated new forms of struggle, which in turn call for new forms of organisation. It is this that multitude was intended to theorise.

3.3. The multitude in classical political theory

The 'anti-utopian aspect of Spinoza's thought' is well-known, as Filippo del Lucchese (2009, 3) points out – 'as is Machiavelli's influence' upon the early-modern philosopher in this regard. Yet both, he demonstrates in his brilliant study of the two, are simultaneously opposed to 'the ideology of the conservation of power' normally associated with 'realist' political theory (del Lucchese 2009, 4). What I would like to suggest is that, as such, Spinoza (and his theorisation of the multitude, particularly in the way it has been taken up within *Operaismo*) provides a framework for thinking (following Weeks' [2011, 195] definition of the term) a very *concrete utopian* project of political organisation and transformation, which is to say: one that is also realist or materialist. It is one that might prove useful in terms of thinking how, not only the 'precariat' – as a discreet sociologically defined group, identified by Standing (2011) and others – but also the broader spectrum of heterogeneous 'precaratised' social subjects (set out in Part One), may become for-itself, initiating 'a politics of paradise'.

Del Lucchese's (2009, 117) study shows that, although the concept of multitude predates Spinoza's usage, his theorisation lends it a new and revolutionary meaning. The distinction with Thomas Hobbes' understanding is instructive. In both, it refers to a body of the population that exists as a multiplicity rather than a unity, unruled by a sovereign.[19] 'The multitude is a multiplicity,' Hardt and Negri (2001, 103) explain in *Empire*, 'a plane of singularities, an open set of relations, which is not homogenous or identical with itself and bears an indistinct, inclusive relation to those outside of it'. This is part of what distinguishes it from traditional understandings of a 'people', which is said to tend 'towards identity and homogeneity internally while posing its difference from and excluding what remains outside of it' (Hardt and Negri 2001, 103).[20] For Hobbes, one of the key functions of the sovereign is to make One – a people, a unity – out of the very multiplicity of the multitude. 'A Multitude of men, are made *One* Person,' he explains, 'when they are by one man, or one Person, Represented; so that it be done with the consent of every one of that Multitude in particular. For it is the *Unity* of the Representer, not the *Unity* of the Represented, that maketh the Person *One*... And because the Multitude naturally is not *One*, but *Many*; they cannot be understood for one' (Hobbes 1985 [1651], 220).[21] In contrast, del Lucchese (2009, 119) cites Hobbes as arguing, '[t]he People' however 'is somewhat that is one, having one will, and to whom one action may be attributed; none of these can properly be said of a Multitude'.

The multitude, for Hobbes, then, as Balibar (1994, 16) has shown, is the 'always already decomposed' people, 'reduced in advance (preventatively) to the sum of its constituent atoms (people in the state of nature), and capable of entering one by one, through the contract, into the new institutional relationship of civil society'. With Spinoza, however, this is by no means the case. Indeed, the novelty of Spinoza's multitude lies precisely in how – in his *Political Treatise* (2000 [1677])[22] – it allows him to reject what del Lucchese (2009, 117) calls 'the contractualist fiction', bringing 'the idea of an irreducible multiplicity in politics to the fore'. As another Spinoza scholar, Warren Montag (1999, 70), has shown, '[i]n his sole direct comment on Hobbes, Spinoza argues: 'With regard to political theory, the difference between Hobbes and myself... consists in this, that I always preserve natural right in its entirety, and I hold that the sovereign power in a State has right over a subject only in proportion to the excess of its power over that of the subject'. Indeed, 'the political plane' of Spinoza's thought is founded 'on the immanent power of... the multitude rather than on the idea of a transcendent reason of state' (del Lucchese 2009, 4). '[T]he multitude', for Spinoza, in other words, as Virno (2004, 21) points out, is always 'a *plurality that persists as such'*. However, despite, in both the Hobbesian and the Spinozian conception, the multitude being opposed to the sovereign as 'a monopoly of decision-making', Spinoza's notion 'is based... on the premise that *not only the one but also the many* can make political decisions' (Hardt and Virno 2009, 2369, my emphasis). '[A]lthough it remains multiple and internally different,' the multitude 'is able to act in common and thus rule itself' – at least *potentially* (Hardt and Negri 2004, 100). It is partly on the basis of this decision-making capacity of the Spinozian multitude that the concept is distinguished from that of the masses, the crowd, and the mob (Hardt and Virno 2009, 2369).

3.4. The hegemony of immaterial labour

The recent theorisation of the multitude as a potential political project resembles a *concrete utopian* one in the sense that it gives 'a name to what is already going on' and attempts to grasp 'the existing social and political tendency' (Hardt and Negri 2004, 220). The figures that coalesce within the multitude, Hardt and Negri (2004, 158–159) insist, – 'industrial workers, immaterial workers, agricultural workers, the unemployed, migrants, and so forth' – signify 'distinct forms of life in concrete places', yet these 'singular figures of postmodern labor do not remain fragmented and dispersed but tend through communication and collaboration to converge toward a common social being'. Part of what makes this social being common is determined through the hegemony of what Hardt and Negri (2004, 99–157) call immaterial labour, so that its characteristics can be found in all other types of work, from heavy industry to agriculture. Immaterial labour is defined as 'labor that produces immaterial products, such as information, knowledge, ideas, images, relationships, and affects' (Hardt and Negri 2004, 65), and the relations of production and the organisation of this kind of labour – communicativity, horizontal networks, precarity, mobility, the production and management of emotions and human relationships, flexibility – are said to increasingly be found across society, irrespective of sector and geography.

The echoes here with forms of work discussed by Standing (2011) and others, addressed in Part One, should be clear. 'One possibility' for the 'common social being' that makes up the multitude – composed of discreet forms of labour and life that remain singular (immaterial, service, industrial and agricultural labour can still be distinguished from one another) – is that it remains 'enlisted in the global armies at the service of capital… formed into the productive organs of the global social body of capital' (Hardt and Negri 2004, 159). But there is an alternative….

3.5. Multitude as a political project

While Hardt and Negri indeed refer, from time to time, to the multitude in the sense described above – to name the 'becoming-common' of multiple, singular forms of labour under the hegemony of its immaterial mode – they primarily reserve the term to name a potential political project.

The protests against the 1999 World Trade Organisation Ministerial in Seattle are described as marking 'the arrival of the multitude' (Negri 2008, 63), 'the first global protest… the first real *convergence* of the innumerable grievances against the injustices and inequalities of the global system' (Hardt and Negri 2004, 286). The protests were said to offer a model whereby while 'a cacophony of different voices… spoke in common… they remained different and independent but linked together', forming a network which defined 'both their singularity and their commonality' (Hardt and Negri 2004, 288).

Multitude has also been used, as Hardt and Virno (2009, 2371) have noted, by several Bolivian scholars to describe the so-called water and gas wars of 2001 and 2003 respectively, where agricultural, industrial and service workers, indigenous Aymara and Quechua, as well as non-indigenous groups, engaged in common struggles around both economic and racial issues. Each of these examples – Seattle and Bolivia – represented, first and foremost, the emergence of spontaneous struggles. In the former, the primary dynamic component of the protests entailed the involvement of self-organised groups (often made up of young people with little prior experience of political activism) and it certainly exceeded, in terms of the desires it expressed, the goals of even the most radical of organisers. In the case of the latter, mass protests were triggered by the privatisation of utilities and price-hikes, but mobilised those concerned with intersecting 'racial, cultural, or civilizational' problems (Hardt and Negri 2009, 108; see also Olivera 2004). If these represented the spontaneous emergence of the multitude in embryonic form – as a coherent political actor, capable of making decisions *despite* its internal heterogeneity – they were prefigured. It was 'recent social and economic transformations' that contributed 'to the possibility of a politics of the multitude' (Hardt and Virno 2009, 2370). Again, the subjective will these spontaneous struggles expressed could be understood as determined objectively.

A project of political organisation, following Negri's Leninist approach laid out by Hardt (2005, 17), would involve a reflection of this spontaneity back upon itself. To the same extent that subjective struggles are shaped by transformations in the realm of production and throughout the political economy, these forms of resistance determine the most efficacious modes of political organisation. 'The force that the revolutionary organizes and imposes does not appear at the beginning but only at the end of the process: revolutionary realism produces and reproduces the becoming and proliferation of desire' (Hardt and Negri 2004, 356).

4. Conclusion

Radical political transformation, or the giving of form to 'a politics of paradise', then, must take as its point of departure a utopianism (however 'mild') that is thoroughly concrete – one that can only but emerge, develop meaning and force, after the eruption of movements and struggles, from within, and acting back upon them. The usefulness of any programme, such as that laid out by Standing (2011, 155–183), or of any set of demands, will be determined by the extent to which they can contribute to such a process. One of the major challenges that would likely be presented to any project of organisation today – on the basis of the (spontaneous) struggles that have emerged over the last few years – would lie in preserving the heterogeneity of their composition, and ensuring any 'vanguard' function (the bringing together and construction of a coherent social force able to act and to decide) was a decentred or dispersed one. Rodrigo Nunes (2012) has argued that the movements that erupted in 2011 – starting from the overthrowing of Zine El Abidine Ben Ali in Tunisia and Hosni Mubarak in Egypt, via the occupation of public squares and boulevards in Spain, Greece and Israel, through to the international Occupy movement – contained an '*immanent vanguard*, endowed with a power of immanent command', but where 'leadership' was 'distributed'. Groups and individuals, he convincingly shows, were often able 'to temporarily take on the role of moving things forward by virtue of coming up with courses of action that provide provisional focal points for activity' (Nunes 2012). He argues leadership, in these struggles, functioned similarly to Gilles Deleuze and Félix Guattari's discussion of the 'leader of the pack' (Nunes 2012). Drawing on the writer Elias Canetti's distinction between mass (or 'crowd') multiplicities and multiplicities of the packs, they argue, '[d]oubtless there is no more equality or any less hierarchy in packs than masses, but they are of a different kind. The leader of the pack… plays move by move, must wager everything every hand, whereas the group or mass leader consolidates or capitalizes on past gains' (Deleuze and Guattari 2004, 37). This is a phenomenon that resonates of course, in many ways, with notions of instant racallability and revocability of leadership often associated with workers' councils (e.g. Pannekoek 2003 [1948], 44–50), albeit radicalised and organised organically.[23]

How, then, can a *Realpolitik* operate in such a context? How can organisation be co-extensive with a spontaneity that is defined by a quintessential absence of consolidation and capitalisation? Again, Hardt and Negri's use, in particular, of Spinoza may be helpful here, especially in terms of their development of a distinct notion of 'institutionalisation'. Thomas Jefferson and Machiavelli, as well as Spinoza, are identified as contributing to a so-called 'minor line' within social theory that conceives *social conflict* as opposed to *social contract* as an adequate basis for the formation of institutions (Hardt and Negri 2009, 355). Whereas in the 'major line', with which Hobbes would again certainly be identified, 'your consent to the contract forfeits your right to rebel and conflict' – the centralised, disciplined model of party organisation that dominated in the 'classical Marxist' period, between Marx's death and the October Revolution of 1917, is an obvious example of such an approach – in the alternative conception, favoured by Hardt and Negri (2009, 355), however, 'the minor line accepts conflict as internal to and the constant foundation of society'.[24] Indeed, for Machiavelli and Spinoza, the democratic nature of social institutions depends upon remaining open to and being constituted by conflict (Hardt and Negri 2009, 356). '[O]ne of the main elements through which political existence takes form,' for Spinoza – 'similar in some ways to [Machiavelli]' – is 'between the two extremes of constitution and dissolution of the collective body' (del Lucchese 2009, 63).

If we accept that spontaneous social, political and economic struggles derive their form, in many ways, from conditions that are given – that there is, in other words, a strong degree to which the predominant 'will' within these movements is shaped by the contexts they emerge out of – and that, historically, the most efficacious forms of (self-)organisation have been co-extensive with these struggles (emerging from and acting back upon them), it is an organisational form along these lines which is likely called for today.

4.1 From immediate spontaneity to the historical uprisings of the multitude

It would certainly seem – at least initially, and on the basis of various accounts (e.g. Castells 2012; Mason 2012; Nunes 2012) – that the uprisings and protests that began in 2011 hint towards the emergence of (spontaneous) struggles whose structures, ethics and impulses demonstrate a capacity for decision and common action despite heterogeneity, and a dynamism in terms of the components that play a 'leading' role in the initiation or inspiration of political initiatives and projects. Perhaps an early measure or indication of any degree to which these spontaneous struggles have already begun 'reflecting back upon themselves' – constituting substantial, sustained (concrete utopian) efficacy – lies in an assessment as to whether they have variously been able to establish themselves not only as *immediate uprisings* but as *historical* ones, to borrow Alain Badiou's (2012, esp. 16–43) distinction. While the former rarely move beyond 'negation and destruction' (Badiou 2012, 25), the later contain the potential to produce 'enduring truth' (Badiou 2012, 21). In Badiou's account, historical uprisings describe a (seemingly) trans-historical model for success. When read from the perspective of Negri's Lenin, however, the *form* assumed by these uprisings is telling. Immediate uprisings – the term Badiou attributes to the urban riots in England in 2011 and, elsewhere, to the 2013 protests in Turkey, centred on Istanbul's Gezi Park – are said to be characterised by 'unrest among *a [particular] section* of the population'; they tend to be 'located in the territory of those who… [took] part', and to have spread '*not by displacement, but by imitation'*, itself occurring 'in sites that are similar, even largely identical, to the initial focal point' (Badiou 2012, 22–24, my emphasis).[25] The events described as historical uprisings – such as those in Tunisia and Egypt – in contrast, are said to have entailed 'extension [not only] by imitation' but also a 'qualitative extension', whereby 'a multiplicity of voices, absent or virtually absent from the clamour of an immediate riot' were articulated and transversal connections established across social spaces and strata (Badiou 2012, 33–35). Crucially, such events often involved the construction – or rather, the *occupation* – of 'an enduring central site', where 'composition… [stopped] being uniform', producing 'a unified representation in mosaic form' (Badiou 2012, 33–35).

Those uprisings that might have, or might yet, become 'historical' in this sense would seem to refer, then, to the becoming for-itself, the initiation of a potential politics of paradise, a concrete utopian project, that *exceeds* any discreet social group, no matter how heterogeneous – the precariat, the new working or educated middle classes. They are constituted *out and on the basis of* spontaneous struggles (Badiou's [2012, 22] 'immediate uprisings'), and represent a tentative project of political organisation and constitution – one whose boundaries remain open, inclusive, and expansive. To a degree at least, as Simon Critchley (2007, 103) has argued, '[p]olitics is always about nomination. It is about naming a political subjectivity and organizing politically around that name.' Today, multitude names what is already taking place.

Acknowledgements

I would like to thank Matthew Johnson for the invitation to submit an article examining the sociological and political relationship between the notions of 'precariat' and 'multitude', which has enabled me to clarify – at least for myself – the ways they might be brought into relation with one another. Thanks are also due to Emma Dowling as well as an anonymous reviewer for thoughtful feedback on an earlier draft.

Notes

1. On the (Euro)MayDay movement, see also my article, Trott (2005, esp. 222–224).
2. Although, as noted, Standing's (2011, 7–13) 'precariat' is generally described a discreet social group, he nevertheless similarly hints at the ways precariousness increasingly forms all modes of work and life today; or at least towards the tendential expansion of the precariat (e.g. Standing 2011, 16–17).
3. In delineating between precarity and precariousness in the introduction to her book, *Frames of War*, Butler (2009, 2–3) insists that the ontological components implied by the definition of the latter category 'is not to lay claim to a description of fundamental structures of being that are distinct from any and all social and political organization… The "being" of the body to which this ontology refers is one that is always given over to others, to norms, to social and political organizations that have developed historically in order to maximize precariousness for some and minimize precariousness for others… The more or less existential conception of "precariousness" is thus linked with a more specifically political notion of "precarity."' She suggests 'it is the differential allocation of precarity that, in my view, forms the point of departure for both a rethinking of bodily ontology and for progressive or left politics' (Butler 2009, 3). Isabell Lorey (2012, 13–37) takes up and develops these distinctions in her book, *Die Regierung der Prekären*.
4. On the growth of the 'shadow' or 'informal' economy, see Standing (2011, 6, 57, 11). Davis (2006, 178) claims the global 'informal working class' to be 'about one million strong'. He describes it as a class 'without legal recognition or rights' (Davis 2006, 175).
5. For Standing's discussion of denizenship and migration, see in particular Standing (2011, 93–102). On criminality, see Standing (2011, 13–16).
6. This work often includes activities like 'building websites, modifying software packages, reading and participating in mailing lists and building virtual spaces' (Terranova 2004, 74).
7. For an example of this argument, emerging from participants in the EuroMayDay network, see the call for the 2008 MayDay parade in Berlin here: http://maydayberlin.blogsport.de/rueckblick/mayday-2008/english-08/
8. There is insufficient space here to deal with Standing's (2011) discussion of the state in this regard.
9. Standing is honorary co-president of the Basic Income Earth Network (www.basicincome.org). For an overview of debates around basic income and its plausibility, see also Widerquist et al. (2005). The proposal has not been uncontroversial among left and critical theorists. See, for example Henninger (2007) and Therborn (2007); Raventós' (2007, 177–198), in his book, *Basic Income*, attempts to address a number of criticism advanced from across the political spectrum.
10. For Harvey's discussion of the connection between surplus product and urbanisation, see Harvey (2012, 5).
11. Standing's (2011, 171–178) account of the proposal echoes precisely such enthusiasm. A number of contemporary political theorists and recent social movements have, however, pointed towards (perceived) dangers entailed with demands and political programmes. John Holloway (2010, 8), for instance, suggests they can imply not only an acceptance of the externality of power to those who articulate them, but can also contribute to that power: 'converting our power-to into an external power-over.' (See also The Invisible Committee' [2009, esp. 112], *The Coming Insurrection*.) The dangers of demands were also widely debated among participants in Occupy Wall Street, as the anthropologist David Graeber (2013, 1–54) has documented.
12. For Marx and Engels' key polemics against utopianism, see *The Communist Manifesto* (Marx and Engels 1985 [1848], esp. 114–118) and Engels' *Socialism, Utopian and Scientific*.

13. Weeks' notion of what she calls the 'utopian demand' resonates in many ways with Žižek's (2013, 11) more recent description of the art of politics, mentioned above. She defines it as, 'a political demand that takes the form not of a narrowly pragmatic political reform but of a more substantial transformation of the present configuration of social relations; it is a demand that raises eye-brows, one for which we would probably not expect immediate success. These are demands that would be difficult – though not impossible – to realize in the present institutional and ideological context; to be considered feasible, a number of shifts in the terrain of political discourse must be effected' (Weeks 2011, 176).
14. The discussion of such questions is certainly not entirely absent from Standing's (2011) work. He points, for instance, towards some of the shortcomings in the EuroMayDay movement, the need to develop new forms of collective bargaining, and to projects like the Freelancer's Union in New York and the Self-Employed Women's Association of India (SEWA) (Standing 2011, 167–170). This is clearly not, however, his primary focus here.
15. For an introduction to this 'Italian school', see Wright (2002). On the notion of the 'social factory' in particular, see Wright (2002, 37–41).
16. Negri's reading of Lenin is historical materialist in the sense that he insists, as Hardt (2005, 15) notes, 'we must submit Lenin's thought to a Marxist analysis and trace its development through specific historico-political periods'.
17. On the distance between Negri and Althusser's readings of Lenin, see (Hardt 2005, 27–29).
18. The editors of Negri's *Revolution Retrieved: Selected Writings on Marx, Keynes, Capitalist Crisis & New Social Subjects* provide a helpful summary of this aspect of Negri's (1988a, 7) argument. (There is insufficient space here to discuss the crucial role, obscured by this account, played by women's and feminist struggles in the Fordist/Keynesian context.)
19. This is the manner in which it is also described by Hardt, Negri and Virno (e.g. Hardt and Negri [2004, 99–100], Hardt and Virno [2009, 2369] and Virno [2004, 21]).
20. Del Lucchese (2009, esp. 115–166) nevertheless points to a number of important parallels between Spinoza's concept and 'the people', or *popolo*, in Machiavelli's work.
21. It is in this sense that the people are identified with the sovereign, rather than the multitude, as Hardt and Negri (2009, 51) point out. Hardt and Negri (2009, 42–43) refer to the section of Hobbes' (1985 [1651]) *Leviathan* cited in the many body of text above in their discussion of his concept of the multitude.
22. See for instance paragraph six of chapter four in the *Political Treatise* (Spinoza 2000 [1677], 60).
23. Indeed, Virno (1996, 203) has suggested 'leagues,... councils, and... soviets – in short, the organs of nonrepresentative democracy' as concrete examples of 'political expressions to the "acting-in-concert" that... already always enjoys a publicness that is completely different from what is concentrated in the person of the sovereign... To representation and delegation, the Soviets [of the multitude] counterpose an operative style that is far more complex, centered on *Example* and *political reproducibility*.'
24. On the '[p]arty ideal' that dominated in the classical Marxist period, from Germany to Russia, see Lih (2005, 113).
25. Badiou's book was published prior to the protests around Gezi Park, although he used the description of the events as an 'immediate uprising' in a subsequent statement in support of the protests (e.g. http://cengizerdem.wordpress.com/2013/06/19/alain-badiou-on-the-uprising-in-turkey-and-beyond/). While his distinction between immediate and historical uprisings or riots is persuasive, his categorisation of various events along these lines is not always convincing. To cite just one example, he would appear to over-state, for instance, the homogeneity of the 2013 uprisings in Turkey, and hence their potential to have produced (or been able to produce) enduring 'truths'. For an alternative account of the social composition of the protests, by anthropologist Emrah Yildiz, see: http://www.jadaliyya.com/pages/index/12001/alignments-of-dissent-and-politics-of-naming_assem

References

Althusser, L. 2001. "Lenin and Philosophy." *Lenin and Philosophy and Other Essays*. Translated by Ben Brewster, 11–44. London: Verso.

Althusser, L. 2005. "Contradiction and Overdetermination." *For Marx*. Translated by Ben Brewster, 87–128. London: Verso.

Aronowitz, S., D. Esposito, W. DiFazio, and M. Yard. 1998. "The Post-Work Manifesto." In *Post-Work: The Wages of Cybernation*, edited by S. Aronowitz and J. Cutler, 31–80. New York: Routledge.

Badiou, A. 2012. *The Rebirth of History: Times of Riots and Uprisings*. Translated by Gregory Elliot. London: Verso.

Balibar, É. 1994. "Spinoza, The Anti-Orwell: The Fear of the Masses." In *Masses, Classes, Ideas: Studies on Politics and Philosophy Before and After Marx*, Translated by James Swenson, 3–37. London: Routledge.

Balibar, É. 2004. *'Droit de cité or Apartheid?' We, the People of Europe? Reflections on Transnational Citizenship*. Translated by James Swenson. Princeton, NJ: Princeton University Press.

BBC. 2013. "The Great British Class Survey – Results." *BBC Science*. Accessed April 3. http://www.bbc.co.uk/science/0/21970879

Butler, J. 2009. "Introduction: Precarious Life, Grievable Life." In *Frames of War*, 1–32. London: Verso.

Butler, J. 2011. "For and Against Precarity." *Tidal: Occupy Theory, Occupy Strategy* 1: 12–13.

Castells, M. 2012. *Networks of Outrage and Hope: Social Movements in the Internet Age*. Cambridge: Polity Press.

Critchley, S. 2007. *Infinitely Demanding: Ethics of Containment, Politics of Resistance*. London: Verso.

Davis, M. 2006. *Planet of the Slums*. London: Verso.

del Lucchese, F. 2009. *Conflict, Power, and Multitude in Machiavelli and Spinoza: Tumult and Indignation*. London: Continuum.

Deleuze, G., and F. Guattari. 2004. *A Thousand Plateaus: Capitalism and Schizophrenia*. Translated by Brian Massumi. London: Continuum.

Foti, A. 2004. "Mayday, Mayday: Euro Flex Workers Time to Get a Move On." *Greenpepper Magazine. Precarity Issue* 2: 21–27.

Graeber, D. 2013. *The Democracy Project: A History, a Crisis, a Movement*. London: Allen Lane.

Gray, A. 2004. *Unsocial Europe: Social Protection of Flexploitation?* London: Pluto Press.

Hardt, M. 2005. "Into the Factory: Negri's Lenin and the Subjective Caesura." *In The Philosophy of Antonio Negri: Resistance in Practice*, edited by T. S. Murphey and A.-K. Mustapha, 7–37. London: Pluto Press.

Hardt, M., and A. Negri. 2001. *Empire*. Cambridge, MA: Harvard University Press.

Hardt, M., and A. Negri. 2004. *Multitude: War and Democracy in the Age of Empire*. New York: Penguin.

Hardt, M., and A. Negri. 2009. *Commonwealth*. Cambridge, MA: Harvard University Press.

Hardt, M., and P. Virno. 2009. "Multitude." In *The International Encyclopedia of Revolution and Protest: 1500–Present,* 5, edited by I. Ness, 2369–2372. Malden, MA: Wiley-Blackwell.

Harvey, D. 2012. *Rebel Cities: From the Right to the City to the Urban Revolution*. London: Verso.

Henninger, M. 2007. "Doing the Math: Reflections on the Alleged Obsolescence of the Law of Value Under Post-Fordism." *Ephemera: Theory and Politics in Organization* 7 (1): 158–177. Accessed November 17, 2013. http://www.ephemerajournal.org/sites/default/files/7-1henninger.pdf

Hobbes, T. 1985 [1651]. *Leviathan*. London: Penguin.

Holloway, J. 2010. "Hope Moves Faster than the Speed of Thought." In *What Would It Mean to Win?* edited by Turbulence Collective, 7–9. Oakland, CA: PM Press.

The Invisible Committee. 2009. *The Coming Insurrection*. Los Angeles, CA: Semiotext(e).

Jameson, F. 2007. *Archaeologies of the Future: The Desire Called Utopia and Other Science Fictions*. London: Verso.

Lazzarato, M. 2012. *The Making of Indebted Man: An Essay on the Neoliberal Condition*. Translated by Joshua David Jordan. Los Angeles, CA: Semiotext(e).

Lenin, V. I. 1989 [1902]. *What Is to Be Done?* Translated by Joe Fineberg and George Hanna. London: Penguin.

Lih, L. T. 2005. *Lenin Rediscovered: What It to Be Done? In Context*. Chicago, IL: Haymarket Books.

Lorey, I. 2012. *Die Regierung der Prekären*. Vienna: Verlag Turia + Kant.

Marx, K. 1995 [1847]. *The Poverty of Philosophy.* Translated by H. Quelch. New York: Prometheus Books.

Marx, K., and A. Engels. 1985 [1848]. *The Communist Manifesto*. London: Penguin.
Mason, P. 2012. *Why It's Kicking Off Everywhere: The New Global Revolutions*. New York: Verso.
Montag, W. 1999. *Bodies, Masses, Power: Spinoza and His Contemporaries*. London: Verso.
Murphey, T. S. 2005. "Glossary." In *A. Negri Books for Burning: Between Civil War and Democracy in 1970s Italy*. Translated by T. S. Murphey, xxxii–xxxvii. London: Verso.
Negri, A. 1988a. "Keynes and Capitalist Theories of the State Post-1929." In *Revolution Retrieved: Selected Writings on Marx, Keynes, Capitalist Crisis & New Social Subjects – 1967–83*, 9–42. London: Red Notes.
Negri, A. 1988b. "Marx on Cycle and Crisis." In *Revolution Retrieved: Selected Writings on Marx, Keynes, Capitalist Crisis & New Social Subjects – 1967–83*, 47–90. London: Red Notes.
Negri, A. 1988c. "Crisis of the Planner-State: Communism and Revolutionary Organisation." In *Revolution Retrieved: Selected Writings on Marx, Keynes, Capitalist Crisis & New Social Subjects – 1967–83*, 97–148. London: Red Notes.
Negri, A. 2008. *Goodbye Mr. Socialism: Antonio Negri in Conversation with Raf Valvola Scelsi*. Translated by Peter Thomas. New York: Seven Stories Press.
Ness, I. 2005. *Immigrants, Unions, and the New U.S. Labor Market*. Philadelphia, PA: Temple University Press.
Ngai, P. 2005. *Made in China: Women Workers in a Global Workplace*. Durham, NC: Duke University Press.
Nunes, R. 2012. "The Lessons of 2011: Three Theses on Organisation." Accessed November 17, 2013. http://www.metamute.org/editorial/articles/lessons-2011-three-theses-organisation#_edn16
OECD. 2010a. "Chart LMF1.6B: Change in the Percentage Share of Women's Part-Time Employment Rates, 2000 to 2009." Accessed November 17, 2013. http://www.oecd.org/document/0,3746,en_2649_201185_46462759_1_1_1_1,00.html
OECD. 2010b. "Chart LMF1.5A: Gender Gap in Median Earnings of Full-Time Employees, 2008." Accessed November 17, 2013. http://www.oecd.org/document/0,3746,en_2649_201185_46462759_1_1_1_1,00.html
Olivera, O. 2004. *¡Cochabamba! Water War in Bolivia*. In collaboration with Tom Lewis. Translated by Tom Lewis. Cambridge, MA: South End Press.
Pannekoek, A. 2003 [1948]. *Workers' Councils*. Edinburgh: AK Press.
Perlin, R. 2011. *Intern Nation: How to Earn Nothing and Learn Little in the Brave New Economy*. London: Verso.
Raventós, D. 2007. *Basic Income: The Material Conditions of Freedom*. Translated by Julie Wark. London: Pluto Press.
Sassen, S. 2001. *The Global City: New York, London, Tokyo*. 2nd ed. Princeton, NJ: Princeton University Press.
Savage, M., F. Devine, N. Cunningham, M. Taylor, Y. Li, H. Johs, B. Le Roux, S. Friedman, and A. Miles. 2013. "A New Model of Social Class: Findings from the BBC's Great British Class Survey Experiment." *Sociology*, 1–32. doi:10.1177/0038038513481128.
Spinoza, B. 2000 [1677]. *Political Treatise*. Translated by Samuel Shirley. Indianapolis, IN: Hackett.
Standing, G. 1997. "Globalization, Labour Flexibility and Insecurity: The Ear of Market Regulation." *European Journal of Industrial Relations* 3 (7): 7–37. doi:10.1177/095968019731002.
Standing, G. 1999. "Global Feminization Through Flexible Labor: A Theme Revisited." *World Development* 27 (3): 583–602. doi:10.1016/S0305-750X(98)00151-X.
Standing, G. 2008. "Economic Insecurity and Global Casualisation: Threat or Promise?" *Social Indicators Research* 88 (1): 15–30. doi:10.1007/s11205-007-9202-7.
Standing, G. 2011. *The Precariat: The New Dangerous Class*. London: Bloomsbury Academic.
Terranova, T. 2004. *Network Culture: Politics for the Information Age*. London: Pluto Press.
Therborn, G. 2007. "After Dialectics: Radical Social Theory in a Post-Communist World." *New Left Review 43*: 63–114.
Trott, B. 2005. "Gleneagles, Activism and Ordinary Rebelliousness." In *Shut Them Down! The G8, Gleneagles 2005 and the Movement of Movements,* edited by D. Harvie, K. Milburn, B. Trott, and D. Watts, 213–233. New York: Autonomedia.
Virno, P. 1996. "Virtuosity and Revolution: The Political Theory of Exodus." In *Radical Thought in Italy: A Potential Politics*. Translated by Ed Emory, edited by M. Hardt and P. Virno, 189–209. Minneapolis: University of Minnesota Press.

Virno, P. 2004. *A Grammar of the Multitude: For an Analysis of Contemporary Forms of Life*. Translated by Isabella Bertoletti, James Cascaito, and Andrea Casson. Los Angeles, CA: Semiotext(e).

Weeks, K. 2011. *The Problem With Work: Feminism, Marxism, Antiwork Politics, and Postwork Imaginaries*. Durham, NC: Duke University Press.

Widerquist, K., M. A. Lewis, and S. Pressman, eds. 2005. *The Ethics and Economics of the Basic Income Guarantee*. Aldershot: Ashgate.

Wright, S. 2002. *Storming Heaven: Class Composition and Struggle in Italian Autonomist Marxism*. London: Pluto Press.

Žižek, S. 2013. "Trouble in Paradise." *London Review of Books* 35 (14): 11–12.

REPLY

Self-nomination and autonomy: a reply to Ben Trott

Timothy S. Murphy

Department of English, Oklahoma State University, Stillwater, OK, USA

This is a reply to:

Trott, Ben. 2013. "From the precariat to the multitude." *Global Discourse*. 3 (3–4): 406–425. http://dx.doi.org/10.1080/23269995.2013.876714.

Ben Trott's critique of Guy Standing's work and his proposal of an alternative to it, with which I am largely in agreement, are suspended between two identical citations of a passage from Simon Critchley: 'Politics is always about nomination. It is about naming a political subjectivity and organizing politically around that name'. Critchley's claim implies that the choice of names for a political subjectivity is a deeply significant act, that such names are not mere arbitrary signifiers but effective operational terms that have profound consequences for political action. That claim is easy enough to verify by glancing at sources as disparate as Betty Friedan's *Feminine Mystique* (1963, chap. 1), which helped to inaugurate the second wave of American feminism by 'naming the problem that had no name', and Louis Althusser's *Machiavelli and Us* (1999, 25–26), which analyzes the political consequences of the difference between the privileged subject named in the title of Machiavelli's *Prince* and the one named in the opening chapter of Marx and Engels' *Communist Manifesto*, the proletariat.

Additional examples would not be difficult to cite, but a moment's pause over the name proposed by Marx and Engels may allow us to formulate the terms for a response to and extension of Trott's critique of Standing. Marx, a student of Roman law, invented the name 'proletariat' by borrowing the ancient Roman word *proletarii*, which referred to the class of Roman citizens with little or no property whose only positive contribution to the defense and expansion of Roman society was their offspring, in Latin *proli*. Likewise, the members of Marx and Engels' proletariat had no property beyond their labor-power as a means for earning a living. Although Standing's name 'precariat' is clearly modeled on 'proletariat' and intended to serve a similar function, in one important way it actually constitutes a logical antithesis to Marx's name in that, whereas the name 'proletariat' is derived from an affirmative or productive property of the subject, its capacity to produce offspring (in the original Latin) or its capacity to labor (in Marx's neologism), the name 'precariat' is derived from a negative or privative property of the subject, its lack of socioeconomic stability or security. This is evident in the name's derivation from 'precarious', which is in turn derived from the Latin *precarius*, meaning 'begged for', and ultimately from *prex*, meaning 'prayer'. To put it another way, Marx's name emphasizes the active power of the political subject while Standing's emphasizes its powerlessness and passivity, to the extent that we could even say that Standing's name paradoxically turns the political subject into a political object that is acted upon but does not act for itself.

Although this may appear to be a rather pedantic linguistic distinction, I think it can help us to map a fundamental divide among contemporary left political theorists and militants that Trott's critique of Standing implies without discussing. That divide separates those thinkers who name contemporary political subjectivity negatively or privatively and those who name it affirmatively or productively. If Standing's notion of the precariat names it privatively, then so does Judith Butler's parallel emphasis on the modalities of precariousness that Trott mentions while fleshing out his account of Standing. A different version of privative naming can be found in Giorgio Agamben's influential work on *Homo sacer*, both the general theory of 'bare life' and the more specific figures of the sacred man who is 'outside both human and divine law' (1998, 73) and the *Muselmann* of Auschwitz, 'defined by a loss of all will and consciousness' (1999, 45). All these names focus on the subject's impotence, relative or absolute as the case may be, in the face of sovereign power. When Trott advocates the adoption of the name 'multitude', borrowed from Virno and Hardt and Negri (who themselves borrow it from Spinoza), to replace Standing's 'precariat', he implicitly takes the side of affirmative naming, since 'multitude' was chosen by those authors precisely because it emphasizes the productive power, however unorganized or potential, of the contemporary political subject. For Virno (2004, 52–66), the multitude is characterized less by its precariousness than by its linguistic inventiveness and its 'virtuosity', the latter term referring to its complex practical and cognitive skills (and also, I think, to what Machiavelli called its *virtù*, its capacity to create new value that was opposed to the expropriation of value, which he called *fortuna*).[1] For Hardt and Negri, as Trott notes, the multitude is essentially defined by its inclusive multiplicity, its radical internal self-differentiation, which is the source of its protean power to create new objects, affects, practices, institutions, and even forms of subjectivity. On this affirmative side of the divide, we should also place the work of other, primarily Italian thinkers like Franco 'Bifo' Berardi (2009a, 2009b), who names the contemporary political subject the 'cognitariat' in order to emphasize the productive power of what Marx called its 'general intellect', as well as others like Andrea Fumagalli (2007) and Carlo Vercellone (2006) who work in the area of cognitive capitalism.[2]

If this distinction is granted, then I would like to make the further claim that it helps to explain why and how, as Trott argues, the multitude constitutes a concrete utopian enterprise while the precariat remains an abstract one. If the defining characteristics that give the political subject its name are conceived as essentially privative, then the form of its effective political self-organization – or at least an organization that would aim to go beyond the piecemeal reform of those features of sovereign power that constrain it, toward a more thorough restructuring of capitalist society – is implicitly posited as deferred, virtual, or unimagined, and it can only be conceived and produced through a long and uncertain process of trial and error. If those defining characteristics are affirmative, productive sources of actual power, on the other hand, then as Trott argues in relation to Negri's analysis of Lenin, the form of political self-organization may be more readily constituted for the simple reason that the subject is, in however limited and unconscious a way, *already in the process of producing and indeed using* that organization as it expresses its productive power. There are undoubtedly dangers here, notably that of unwarranted subjective optimism regarding the ease with which the political subject can self-organize and that of mistaking productive activities that objectively reinforce capitalist exploitation for subversive activities that constitute self-organization,[3] but they are likely to be less damaging than the dangers that negative naming entails.

But although what name is used for the political subject is an important matter, even more important is the issue of who does the naming, not so much in the sense of who comes up with the name that is adopted as in the sense that for a name to be effective, it must be consciously adopted and used by the emergent political subject itself. In other words, effective political naming must be self-nomination. The entire history of the Marxist critique of positivist economic sociology follows from this insight, in that sociology divides the exploited class into unrelated layers and gives them names defined by their specific working conditions and access to property, while the single name 'proletariat' of Marxist theory aims to emphasize the continuities of exploitation that should unite them in struggle against their exploiters. Standing's own analysis, as Trott presents it, is partially guilty of such sociologism, which persists in the Great British Class Survey of 2013 as well (see Savage et al. (2013)). To adopt the name of one's exclusive layer as the name of one's political subjectivity is to choose a politics of division (and consequently conquest by the exploiting class), while to adopt an inclusive and affirmative name, the name of one's productive power, is to choose a politics of alliance (and consequently the multiplication of power that it makes possible), at least in principle.[4] Thus, it makes a difference whether a worker calls himself a proletarian or a non-guaranteed lower-middle-class wage earner. It also makes a difference whether collective action in the present is carried on by groups calling themselves precarians or multitudes. The self-nomination of the Occupy movement and its offshoots, 'We are the 99%', offers a compelling example that combines economic demands for redistribution of wealth with institutional demands for democracy.

This point could be made in purely linguistic terms by noting the apparent (but strictly speaking fictive) etymological convergence between self-nomination and autonomy. The Latin root of self-nomination is *nominatio,* meaning simply 'naming', while the Greek root of autonomy is *nomos*, meaning 'law' or 'rule'. (If the Greco–Latin hybrid 'auto-nomination' were admissible, the convergence with autonomy would be even clearer.) In short, it seems to me that political self-nomination is a necessary practical precondition – though perhaps not a sufficient one – for political autonomy. The fact that the theorists whom Trott endorses and whom I have ranged on the affirmative or productive side of the nominal divide all come out of the historical experience of the Italian Autonomia movement of the 1960s and 1970s, then, is not the result of chance. The history of that movement is precisely the history of struggles to name the new political subject and in so doing make it conscious of the power that it already possesses, so that it will be able to organize itself for more concerted political action. This focus on affirmative naming, on naming as power, is one important reason why, as Patrick Cuninghame has asserted,

> Today autonomism can be seen as a global network of alliances between occupied social centers and media activists in Europe, Zapatistas and Piqueteros in Latin America, Black Blockers in North America, cyber hacktivists in Japan, and autonomous workers, unemployed youth, students, dispossessed peasants, and urban squatter movements in South Korea, South Africa, … united in their disparity and diversity by the overriding principle and practice of autonomy from all forms of capitalist institution, authority, or power, but also along the lines of the autonomy of one section of the multitude from the rest in order to prevent their absorption by traditional socialist 'workers' centrality'… (Cuninghame 2010, 451)

Trott's argument confirms the practical importance of appropriately naming and thereby further empowering this hydra-headed subject of contemporary left militancy.

Notes

1. On Machiavelli's terminology, see Negri (1999, chap. 2).
2. See also Fumagalli and Mezzadra (2011).
3. John Holloway and Ida Dominijanni, among others, have forcefully articulated these dangers; see Holloway (2005, 164), and Dominijanni (2005, 32).
4. This is not to say that a privative name cannot produce substantive political effects – consider, for example, the protests against evictions and utility cutoffs in South Africa, in which militants of black and Indian descent worked together under the slogan 'We are the poors' (cited in Hardt and Negri (2004, 135–136)). The key to success in this case, though, was less the privative name itself than the opposition between the inclusive multiplicity of 'the poors' and the exclusiveness of traditional racial identities: 'We are not Indians, we are the poors! We are not Africans, we are the poors!'

References

Agamben, G. 1998. *Homo Sacer: Sovereign Power and Bare Life*. Translated by Daniel Heller-Roazen. Stanford: Stanford University Press.

Agamben, G. 1999. *Remnants of Auschwitz: The Witness and the Archive*. Translated by Daniel Heller-Roazen. New York: Zone Books.

Althusser, L. 1999. *Machiavelli and Us*. Translated by Gregory Elliott. New York: Verso.

Berardi, F. 2009a. *Precarious Rhapsody: Semiocapitalism and the Pathologies of the Post-Alpha Generation*. Translated by Arianna Bove, Michael Goddard, Giuseppina Mecchia, Antonella Schintu, and Steve Wright. London: Minor Compositions.

Berardi, F. 2009b. *The Soul at Work: From Alienation to Autonomy*. Translated by Francesca Cadel and Giuseppina Mecchia. Los Angeles, CA: Semiotext(e).

Cuninghame, P. 2010. "Autonomism as a Global Social Movement." *Working USA: The Journal of Labour and Society* 13 (December): 451–464.

Dominijanni, I. 2005. "Rethinking Change: Italian Feminism Between Crisis and Critique of Politics." *Cultural Studies Review* 11 (1): 25–35.

Friedan, B. 1963. *The Feminine Mystique*. New York: Norton.

Fumagalli, A. 2007. *Bioeconomia E Capitalismo Cognitivo: Verso Un Nuovo Paradigma Di Accumulazione*. Rome: Carocci.

Fumagalli, A., and S. Mezzadra, eds. 2011. *Crisis in the Global Economy: Financial Markets, Social Struggles, and New Political Scenarios*. Translated by Jason Francis McGimsey. Los Angeles, CA: Semiotext(e).

Hardt, M., and A. Negri. 2004. *Multitude: War and Democracy in the Age of Empire*. New York: Penguin Press.

Holloway, J. 2005. *Change the World Without Taking Power: The Meaning of Revolution Today*. London: Pluto Press.

Negri, A. 1999. *Insurgencies: Constituent Power and the Modern State*. Translated by Maurizia Boscagli. Minneapolis: University of Minnesota Press.

Savage, M., F. Devine, N. Cunningham, M. Taylor, Y. Li, J. Hjellbrekke, B. Leroux, S. Friedman, and A. Miles. 2013. "A New Model of Social Class: Findings from the BBC's Great British Class Survey Experiment." *Sociology* 2013: 1–32. http://soc.sagepub.com/content/early/2013/03/12/0038038513481128.

Vercellone, C., ed. 2006. *Capitalismo Cognitivo: Conoscenza E Finanza Nell'epoca Postfordista*. Rome: ManifestoLibri.

Virno, P. 2004. *A Grammar of the Multitude*. Translated by Isabella Bertoletti, James Cascaito, and Andrea Casson. Los Angeles, CA: Semiotext(e).

RESEARCH ARTICLE

Breaking the heartland: creating the precariat in the US lower rust belt

Joseph J. Varga

Labor Studies Department, Indiana University Bloomington, Eigenmann Hall, Bloomington, IN, USA

This article uses the context of the struggle over antiunion legislation in Indiana to explore the decomposition of the New Deal working class, and the emergence of a more precarious class of workers in the lower rust belt of the United States Midwest. Through an examination of workers in three economic sectors in Southern Indiana (consumer durables, mineral extraction, and light or high-tech manufacturing), the article traces the historical processes by which wageworkers in this region have been dispossessed of workplace rights and security, and how worker power has diminished. This decline of worker's rights and labor market security has brought about the composition of a new, more precarious class of workers. The emergence of this precariat is changing the political, social, and cultural landscape of the region of the country long known as the 'heartland'.

Introduction

Indiana is located in the region of the United States long referred to as the 'heartland', geographically located in the lower Midwest. The state is situated between the upper south and the Great Lakes industrial 'rust belt', so-called for its decaying factories abandoned in the era of global trade, beginning in the late 1970s. Indiana prides itself on moderation, and on a mixed economy, with great stretches of farmland interspersed by heavily industrialized areas. While parts of the state are dominated by rural, conservative politics, Indiana also boasted, in the 1960s and 1970s, some of the highest rates of unionization in its industrial workforce (Hirsh, McPherson, and Vroman 2001). Like other areas of the rust belt, Indiana, by 2010, had experienced severe declines in union membership that accompanied industrial job loss.

On 3 February 2012, Indiana became the second industrial state in the United States, and the 23rd overall, to pass legislation that criminalized mandatory representation fees in unionized workplaces. Such laws are typically referred to as 'right to work' (RTW) laws. Indiana did not go RTW without a political struggle. In the run-up to the vote in 2012, union officials and members waged a concerted campaign against passage of the legislation. In South Central Indiana, an area deeply affected by industrial job loss and plunging union density, the White River Valley Central Labor Council (CLC), led by CLC President Jackie Yenna, spearheaded the anti-RTW effort. Early on in the fight, in late 2010, Jackie gave his views on the situation facing Indiana's workers: 'First the jobs went, then the communities fell apart, then the schools all went to hell, then we voted in these

Republicans. We can't let them take our union rights away; it's the last damn thing we got!'[1] Yenna was expressing what many believed to be true: that the right to collective bargaining was the last thread that working people tenuously grasped in the long shift from the security of the New Deal labor regime. The relative security of Indiana's industrial workforce emerges under Fordist production models in concert with legal protections for collective bargaining that stem from the National Labor Relations Act (NLRA) of 1935. That security is transformed into the flexible workplace of the post-Fordist models of accumulation that come to define the work environment of the new century (Jessop 1992; Harvey 2007).

In this article, Yenna's statement about collective bargaining being the 'last damn thing we got' is put to the test through a preliminary examination of three key industrial sectors in South Central Indiana: consumer durables, extractive industries, and light or high-tech manufacturing (HTM). Through an examination of specific segments within these three sectors, the article charts the creation of the flexible or precarious labor market formed by the transition to post-Fordist models of production and deindustrialization, and charts how the dispossession from Indiana workers of hard-won labor market securities has created the conditions that British Sociologist Guy Standing has termed 'precarity' (Standing 2011). Precarity here can be understood as generational insecurity combined with an unmoored politics that produces an unpredictable situation of class re-alignment and political reformation.

Consequences of this shift to a precarious working class can be seen in the demise of the fragile New Deal coalition that emerged between labor unions, progressive organizations, and the Democratic Party in the post-World War II period, 1946–1980 (Milkis and Mileur 2002; Leuchtenberg 2001). A key element in the breaking of that coalition has been the creation of a more flexible or precarious labor market, where workers are forced to compete with each other and with global labor over scarce employment and benefits (Craypo 1997; Crump and Merrett 1998; Alderson 1999; Wallace and Fullerton 2003). For the United States, labor market security and working class prosperity result from two processes: the Fordist production model, with its concomitant vertical integration of firms, Taylorist models of workplace organization, and rising wages for the industrial workforce, and the NLRA of 1935. The NLRA, and the subsequent amendments and case law that stem from the legislation, provided the legal vehicle for mass unionization and the consolidation of working class political influence (Glyn 1990). The subsequent demise of the political power of organized labor under new modes of flexible, or post-Fordist accumulation strategies, beginning in the mid-1970s, marks a period of wage stagnation and increasing labor market insecurity for US wageworkers (Vidal 2011). This period of post-Fordist accumulation, 1980–2010, witnesses the emergence of a new class of US workers, more precarious and politically unstable then their postwar predecessors.

Breaking the heartland

The development of a relatively secure and prosperous working class in Southern Indiana did not happen overnight, nor did it happen by chance or market forces. The processes of uneven geographic development created the network of factories, mines, quarries, supply chains, and government-funded infrastructure that led to the literal creation of a regional aggregate of wageworkers (Cowie 1999; Nelson 1995; Harvey 2006, 2007). Likewise, the demise of working class prosperity in the region has been an uneven process that has occurred not through the invisible hand, but rather through purposeful, historically located actions (Hansen 2001; Western and Rosenfield 2011). The heart of the lower rust belt working class, what propelled its prosperity and pumped its lifeblood, was a combination of investment capital and working class organization, acting in uneasy, sometimes warring, concert to produce a prosperity and stability that characterize industrial labor relations in the period between 1946 and 1980.

Until the Second World War, Southern Indiana was predominantly an agricultural region, though the extractive industries of coal and limestone were vital components of the regional economy (Ayer 1963). The postwar era brought an influx of industry to the region, including such manufacturing stalwarts as Whirlpool in Evansville, General Motors (GM) in Bedford, General Electric (GE), Otis Elevator, and Radio Corporation of America (RCA) in Bloomington (Cowie 1999, 60–65). As southern workers emigrated in during the war years and newly trained workers increased in number, South Central Indiana experienced the gradual creation of a concentrated postwar working class that, while never homogenous, was identifiable and regionally specific. Further, while South Central Indiana had experienced labor struggles, wageworkers employed in manufacturing did not dominate the economy until after the relocation of the above-mentioned firms (Peckham 2003).

Increasing industrial production, along with the protections afforded workers by New Deal legislation, led to the development of a relatively secure working class in Southern Indiana. The combination of legislation, labor union political influence, protective regulations, and restrictions on capital flows and relatively high marginal rates of taxation, among other factors, led to the secure labor system of the postwar era. As Daniel Nelson, in his study of Midwestern labor conditions notes, 'Stability was the notable theme of day-to-day industrial relations' (Nelson 1995, 155–157). As American corporations concentrated capital in an effort to control global profits, they sought labor peace, or at least accord, with labor unions that placed an emphasis on job control. Importantly, the postwar period was marked by not only labor's gain of an increasing share of profits through wage and benefit packages, but increasing influence over shop-floor conditions. 'The end of the foreman's unilateral authority to assign, discipline, and fire workers' marked the period as a high point of worker control (Nelson 1995, 159). These gains were increasingly tied to the support organized labor received in its increasingly influential relationship with the Democratic Party. As Nelson states, by the end of the 1950s, labor's alliance with the Democrats was 'firm and flourishing' (Nelson 1995, 160).

In short, Midwestern and South Central Indiana industrial workers had reason to feel secure. The key factors that led to labor market security, measured in rising living standards, long-term employment, stable communities, and next-generation economic and social mobility, formed the basis of what Guy Standing terms 'industrial citizenship' (Standing 2011, 10–11). Standing lists seven forms of labor market security that resulted from a combination of factors that coalesce in the postwar period to form a relatively stable working class. For the US, this is the heart of the New Deal labor regime, a combination of progressive legislation, industry and corporate planning and cooperation, protection and subsidy for domestic industry, labor aggression and militancy, and a tenuous social consensus based on a rising standard of living (Davis 2000).

The seven forms of labor market security, according to Standing, that combine to form the Fordist model of accumulation exemplified in the US by the New Deal labor regime, are enumerated below. For the purposes of this study, these seven forms of security are what solidify the New Deal labor regime working class, whose relative prosperity as both producers and consumers formed the backbone of postwar Fordist accumulation. It is the dispossession of these securities over time that produces the precariat:

(1) Labor market security: Included here is some state commitment in varying forms to full employment. Also included are tariff, duties, and direct and indirect subsidies that protect domestic jobs.
(2) Employment security: This security refers to protections in place once employment is attained, such as protection against arbitrary dismissal, dismissal based on protected categories, and protection from global market forces.
(3) Job security: Job security differs from employment security in that it provides skill protections and opportunities for upward mobility on the job or employment site. It includes internal promotion practices, stability of job description and duties, and protection against technological obsolescence and de-skilling due to technological processes.
(4) Work security: Included here are real and enforceable safety and health regulation, periodically updated to meet conditions. It also includes protection against hostile environments, unreasonable demands and changes, and compensation to employees for both injury and inconvenience (shift differentials, staggered start times, payment for work attire).
(5) Skill reproduction security: An often-overlooked aspect, this includes on-the-job training, outside education, and opportunities for apprenticeship and skill acquisition.
(6) Income security: A protected, adjustable guarantee of adequate, stable income in employment and between employment including safety net provisions, pensions, wage indexing, and progressive taxation to fund supplements while reducing inequality.
(7) Representation security: Workers possessing collective voice and union rights in the workplace with concomitant political and social power maximized through collective effort and consensus, combined with the ability to collectively represent class interests while promoting general issues that favor working people.[2]

Taken together, these measures of worker protection resulted in the rising share of profit received by US workers, along with the political and social power achieved through high rates of unionization. Each measure of labor security has a historical trajectory that is deeply embedded, in the case of the US working class, in the long struggle waged by American workers from the beginning of the industrial era through the New Deal and into the present (Lichtenstein 2002). Each aspect of security works alongside the others, and none is fully possible without the other. For example, the protection against arbitrary dismissal, or employment security, in the US system of 'at-will' employment is impossible to imagine without the protections gained through collective representation both at the shop and political level. Likewise, job security and macro-level labor market security work in tandem, where macro-level subsidies, tariffs, and other industry supports provide the density of employment opportunities that allow for internal job securities.

The maintenance of these levels of security for those in the wage labor market relied upon several interdependent factors prevailing in the postwar period, and lasting, with variations, until the mid-1970s. They can be summarized as the following: a working class with enough influence to elect politicians favorable to their interests and to forcefully advocate for the maintenance of security; a political class with some interest in maintaining protections for domestic labor markets and industries, and bound in a dependent relationship on the support of workers achieving levels of security; and, while more ambiguous, the maintenance of security depends on a business class at least partially committed to the health of domestic industries.[3] For Indiana, the repeal of the 1957 RTW law, and the fact that overall union membership and union density increased while the law was in effect, exemplify the strength of organized labor in the postwar period.

Dispossession

South Central Indiana provides an excellent case study for both the growth of a prosperous postwar working class, and the emergence of a post-Fordist precariat. The industrial belt, ranging south of Indianapolis through Terre Haute, Evansville, Bloomington, Columbus, and New Albany, experienced high rates of unionization in the Fordist period, 1946–1973 (Hirsh, McPherson, and Vroman 2001). The area contained a sizable, somewhat militant, union movement that achieved higher wage and benefit levels than non-union counterparts in bordering southern states, while producing the products that comprised the American Dream of material success for postwar America. Console RCA televisions, GE refrigerator/freezers, and Westinghouse and Whirlpool washer/dryers were just some of the products produced in the region, almost all of which are currently produced elsewhere, or are obsolete. As with other industrial regions of the United States, Indiana experienced peaks of union density, and a narrowing of wealth gaps between 1950 and the early 1970s. As well, as with other industrial regions, the 1970s witnessed efforts by firms to seek ways to either maintain or increase profit rates. While studies such as Jeff Cowie's work *Capital Moves* have demonstrated that the capital flight in the face of declining profits is not a new phenomenon, the period beginning in the late 1970s does constitute, for many scholars, the end of the New Deal regime of lessening inequality and rising share of profits accruing to wageworkers, especially those in labor unions. While the first major work on this era of deindustrialization, Bluestone and Harrison's *The Deindustrialization of America,* appears in 1982, Southern Indiana would experience its period of industrial job loss somewhat later, mainly in the 1990s (Cowie 1999; Bluestone and Harrison 1982). While Indiana had been losing industrial jobs in the 1980s, the signing and implementation of the North American Free Trade Agreement in 1994, vigorously opposed by Indiana workers and legislators from both parties, accelerated the process (Starks 2003; Robey 1999). For Southern Indiana's industrial working class, this period, between 1980 and 2000, marks the full advent of post-Fordism, and the transition to precarity.

The flight of industrial jobs from Southern Indiana, like many other regions, has not been abrupt, but has been rather a slow, inexorable process conducted unevenly over a long period. As companies slowly relocated production facilities, local communities, politicians, and unions made efforts to keep the jobs in place, often sacrificing hard-won security in return for employment that was always tenuous, and often times temporary. The result of this process was the increasing loss, or dispossession, of rights and securities for Indiana workers (Craypo and Cormier 2000). As companies used the threat of relocation to extract concessions from workers and their unions, they also used the same threats to extract tax breaks, subsidies, and political favors from the local and national political class, undermining over time the influence that workers had built through the political system. The result, by the turn of the new century, was the flexible workforce sought by capitalist firms: skilled, educated, without union protection, and in debt. As Don Mitchell notes, 'In capitalism, deindustrialization and capital flight *make sense*' (Mitchell 2004, 766).

For Southern Indiana, the process of dispossession described above, where workers formerly operating under a relatively stable regime of labor laws and job security are slowly dispossessed of workplace rights, takes place unevenly, and at different rates in different locations. While I do not argue that Indiana workers operated in a labor utopia of guaranteed work and perpetual stability, the labor regime that emerged out of the struggles of the first half of the twentieth century in the United States constitutes a unique historical period for Indiana and other industrial workers in the Midwest. In general, it is fair to say that in the region comprising Southern Indiana's industrial belt, the average worker, without secondary education, and often with the right connections, had certain reasonable expectations for employment security in the period leading into the 1990s (Crump and Merrett 1998, 497–498). Providing they were in good health and stayed clear of disciplinary issues, workers could expect a job that paid above the prevailing hourly wage; employment with a company whose products were protected and subsidized; a segment of the political class whose term in office was dependent in part on the relationship with the workers' unions; opportunities for advancement and skill improvements within the workplace; protection on the job against arbitrary treatment and unsafe conditions; and a social safety net maintained through a progressive tax system (Dark 1999).

The withdrawal of labor rights in Indiana, as with other states, has accelerated with the emergence of an aggressively antiunion Republican faction centered on organized resistance to health care reform and the presidential administration of Barack Obama. While battles in Washington DC garnered most of the media attention, new Republican majorities in Indiana and other state-level governments pushed through antiunion agendas along with tax cuts, school privatization, restrictions on reproductive health, voting rights, and reductions in social safety net provisions. In Indiana, a veto-proof Republican majority in the State Assembly, elected in the 2010 midterm backlash against the Affordable Care Act, passed new rules promoting private school vouchers and new restrictions on women's health clinics while also passing RTW and pushing for further restrictions on project labor agreements and local living wage provisions.

In the following section, this article looks briefly at three key sectors of the South Central Indiana economy: consumer durables, extractive industries, and light or HTM. I will do so by focusing attention on three companies and their workforces: GE in Bloomington, Indiana Limestone in Oolitic, and Printpack, also in Bloomington. Each sector and employer provides examples of how workers, dispossessed of one or more of the seven forms of labor security, are placed into the flexible regime of the neoliberal labor market. The loss of security not only threatens the existing living standards of current employees, but also limits or outright eliminates opportunities for the incoming generation of workers. It is workers in these limited circumstances who comprise today's precariat, and whose position within the contemporary political and social environment is equally uncertain, and volatile. The examination of these three employers highlights how industrial job loss and global competition result not just in lower wages and benefits, but the loss of basic mechanisms for upward mobility, community stability, and social cohesion.

Consumer durables: General Electric workers

In 1985, Bloomington, Indiana's West Side manufacturing district was home to RCA, Thompson Electronics, and GE, a formidable lineup of producers of large, expensive durable consumer products. GE's production facility arrived in Bloomington in 1965, and together with the other manufactures mentioned, constituted the major employers of the South Central Indiana working class in the Bloomington area (Cowie 1999, 57–69). In that same year, 1985, the big manufacturers employed over 6000 union members, who worked under contracts that included wage and benefit packages that exceeded local averages (Conover, Kinghorn, and Slaper 2007). Union contracts also included safety and job classification clauses, and provisions for job security, seniority, retraining, and skill upgrading that made employment relatively secure (Phillips 1987). In 2012, after a long period of industrial job loss, outsourcing, technological displacement, and productivity gains, RCA/Thompson has left the area, while GE maintains a rump of its former work force. Union jobs in the durables sector number approximately 450. There has been no subsequent growth in unionized employment in other sectors, and the three unions that covered the bulk of the 1985 workforce, the International Brotherhood of Electrical Workers (IBEW), Communication Workers of America (CWA), United Electrical Workers (UE), barely maintain a presence in the area (IDWD 2013).

At what could be considered the peak of its productive capacity in the mid-1970sto 1997, GE enjoyed market domination in the area of large kitchen appliance production. For workers in Bloomington, and in GE's nearby industrial center in Louisville, Kentucky, this market dominance meant abundant jobs at different skill levels. It also meant that the company, through its capacity for research and development, and its possession of industry knowledge, could continually introduce new and improved product lines. These new lines meant plant expansions at existing facilities, with more jobs available. It further meant that new skills were needed among sectors of the unionized workforce. For the Bloomington workforce, market stability meant constant production of GE's flagship product, the side-by-side refrigerator (Immelt 2012). At peak production in the 1970s through 1990s, GE wageworkers at the Bloomington facility could expect steady wage increases, above-market benefit packages, and the opportunity to move both laterally and vertically in the production process.

As GE joined the trend of moving production facilities to sources of cheaper labor, the Bloomington plant suffered major job loss. From a peak of 3400 members of their collective bargaining unit in 1997, members of IBEW local 2025 were down to 504 active workers by 2012. Along with the obvious problems of job loss, benefit reductions, tiered workforces, and lack of bargaining power, GE workers faced the loss of job and skill reproduction security. As manufacturing processes became increasingly dispersed, GE workers who previously would have been afforded opportunities to train for new roles in the production process often saw those roles either offshored or broken into component parts, a modern day de-skilling that severely reduced opportunities for skill upgrades and shop-floor advancement. For GE wageworkers, particularly those just entering the workforce, loss of job and skill reproduction security reduced their options, both at GE and in the larger labor market (Hauptmeir and Greer 2012).

Local 2025 President Carven Thomas reports that over the 13-year period 1997–2010, the Local has managed to hold on to some benefits, but pressures from GE in negotiations, including both implicit and explicit threats to close the facility, have forced concessions that have made the job less attractive, especially for younger workers. While union members are still eligible for tuition reimbursement to Ivy Tech, Indiana's community college, the extensive training program once available has been lost. In 1997, the GE facility in Bloomington included a full on-site training center in partnership with Ivy Tech and Vincennes College. There, workers could attain Associates Degrees in Mechanical or Electrical Engineering, allowing eligible workers to move to different positions in the production process. The training program was especially geared at women and minorities, who were under-represented in the more skilled positions at the plant. GE workers were also paid time and a half for any mandatory training that took place after their regular shift. Another key loss was the hourly employee safety committees, as skill upgrades made workers eligible for these positions.[4]

According to both Thomas and Jackie Yenna, who worked at GE for 48 years before his retirement in 2012, the loss of on-site training and skill upgrades makes the job less attractive and hurts overall morale and solidarity. For Yenna, part of the attraction of the job was the ability to move up through the system and acquire new skills: 'If I thought I was going to be driving in screws for 40 years in 1965, I'm not sure I would have stayed. But I knew I could move up, and I did'.[5] The lack of mobility now means that workers are stuck in the assembly line positions that are the least desired and result in repetitive motion injuries and wear and tear on the body. Thomas reports that workers are held in these positions for much longer, and often get discouraged and seek work elsewhere. He also reports that workers leaving GE depart without the skills the workforce once acquired through training programs. Workplace solidarity has been further eroded by the implementation of a tiered wage contract in 2010, the result of the Louisville plant agreeing to one earlier, and Bloomington being classically 'whipsawed' into accepting. These factors make the job less attractive, and make the Local appear less effective, causing Thomas and other union leaders to worry about the effects of the new RTW law, which will include Local 2025 members in 2015.

The ramifications of the loss of job and skill reproduction security run deep and are entwined with the loss of other forms of labor market security. As manufacturing jobs vanished, and training programs withered, workers entered the job market without transferable skills. As well, those with skills that once paid high wages increasingly find that wage levels do not match their expectations. While the period between GE's arrival in Bloomington and the beginning of industrial job loss, 1965–1985, cannot not be considered a worker's utopia, the hallmarks of the peak periods of production for GE were also a period when GE line workers could look forward to ever-increasing product lines and consequent skill upgrades. These upgrades not only served to improve the negotiating position of both individual workers and the bargaining unit as a whole, but also provided those workers who chose to change employers with transferable market skills that could command livable wage and benefit packages. The eventual erosion of labor market protections for production jobs diminished the opportunities for skill upgrades, while whipsawing meant that new production lines might never come. The loss of these two forms of labor market security not only effected individual workers' ability to secure a living wage, but also decreased the generational reach of labor union politics, as opportunities for new groups of workers who opted not to attend college were greatly restricted.[6] As more unskilled and semi-skilled workers lacked the opportunity that union shops provided in the areas of skill upgrades and job classification changes, their political loyalties became potentially unmoored to a work-centered, union-oriented politics, the very process of precariatization (Wallace and Fullerton 2003).

Extractive industries: Indiana limestone

South Central Indiana has two main regions of extractable commodity products that play a key role in the regional and state economy. One is the coal region that runs south of Terre Haute and crosses both the Illinois and Kentucky borders. The other is the unique limestone belt that runs from 20 miles south of Indianapolis, through Bloomington, and terminates just south of Bedford, in Lawrence County. Limestone extraction is an old industry, and part of the identity of the region. Local homes, businesses, and especially town and county buildings are constructed from it, and the stone has been used in famous structures from the Empire State Building to the Pentagon. In the 'belt', as it is known, few families do not have a member, friend, or acquaintance that has not been connected to the industry in some fashion (Ferrucci 2005). The 1978 film Breaking Away, in which the children of limestone workers faced a bleak future as the industry struggled and jobs were scarce, in part, formed Southern Indiana's cultural image.

The limestone industry in the region has been buffeted by market forces for its entire existence. It has experienced peaks and valleys based on the changing trends in building design and the fluctuating prices of competing building materials. For the local families that controlled the quarries from the mid-1800s to the end of the 1900s, the industry has experienced the ups and downs of the larger economy, as limestone tends to be viewed as a luxury material. For the limestone workers, their allies in the struggle for a decent living and labor security have been their own skills, their communities, and the relative uniqueness of the product. Their enemies have been shifting fortunes of the building industry, recessions, and technological advancements that have steadily eliminated human input in the quarrying and cutting processes. For the mostly male workforce that quarries, cuts, moves, and fabricates the stone, labor market security has always been tenuous, but has at times provided a better than area average living for 'cutters' and their families.

For Indiana workers in the limestone belt, control and input into working conditions is crucial. Much of the labor in the industry involves the movement of large pieces of quarried stone. Injury and death are constant worries, and most experienced limestone quarries and fabricators recognize the value of strict safety enforcement and the need for coworkers who are experienced, trained, and know their role in the processes. The chances of injury and death are greatly increased when the pursuit of short-term profit, often driven by shifting market conditions, can cause employers to increase pressure on the workforce to speed up or cut corners from normal, safe practices. Over time, most of the Southern Indiana quarries experienced either unionization of union drives. At present, the majority of wageworkers in the limestone belt are not organized, but industry workers agree that the 'union effect', the threat of organizing, improves conditions for workers at all mills, including the pressure on employers to provide safe conditions.[7]

In the past decade, a new player has emerged on the limestone scene and posed new challenges for both the industry and workers. Equity capital companies have found the old family owned quarries, with their fixed sources of material, aging, and expensive equipment, and skilled yet not too highly paid workforce, as prime targets for acquisitions, mergers, restructurings, and resales at profit.[8] For the quarry workers and stone cutters at Indiana Limestone in Oolitic, Indiana, the financialization of their industry, a relatively new phenomenon, is already having profound effects on their security. The company had been family owned for over 100 years, and many of the workers had generational relationships with the firm, or with other limestone quarries in 'the belt'. Workers at Indiana Limestone were unionized, and had been for over 40 years, organizing during a period of union activity in the quarries in the 1960s. While relations with the company were never perfect, the union, Carpenters Local 8093, had struck only once, in the 1980s, and long-time members describe the relationship with the company as amicable if not friendly. Many union members noticed a change in the company when Resilience Capital Partners (RCP) acquired it in 2010.[9]

RCP is an investment capital firm that specializes in buying distressed or marginally profitable enterprises, and eventually reselling at profit. RCP moved into the limestone belt with its purchase of Victor Oolitic, a competitor of Indiana Limestone that had been purchased and placed in bankruptcy by equity capital firm Audax Group. After the acquisition of Oolitic in 2009, RCP purchased Indiana Limestone in 2010 and began to make changes that the company deemed necessary to increase the profitability and resale value of the company.[10] While the company expresses no antiunion positions in its publicity releases or descriptions, its stated goal when purchasing a company is to increase the company's value over the short term, a process that often requires reductions in labor costs.[11]

Carpenters Local 8093 members began to notice changes on the shop floor shortly after RCP purchased the company. They noted pressures to speed up work procedures, more confrontational attitudes from new supervisors and management personnel, increased incidences of disciplinary write-ups for lateness and absence, and an exertion of control over work assignments by the new management team. For the workers on the floor at Indiana Limestone, these changes represented an assault on forms of control they had achieved through years of struggle and negotiation with ownership. For members of Local 8093, workplace and shop-floor control were considered the major advantages of collective bargaining, as their pay scale actually lagged behind several local competitors. Many in the workforce cited what they felt was an increased 'lack of respect' for the difficulty of the work they performed and a lack of appreciation for the skill and experience it took to perform the job safely. Finally, in the lead – up to contract negotiations in summer 2011 – members of Local 8093 noticed two developments: an increase in speedup pressure to build inventory and a further increase in confrontational behavior from management.[12]

The demands for givebacks and concessions, for Local 8093 members, were less about wages and benefits, and more about their own ability to negotiate working conditions and standards that secured input, decent treatment, and shop-floor safety. A majority of Local 8093 members were male, married, with families, and were often the sole earner in the household. Fear of loss of work time to injury, loss of bodily function and permanent disability, or loss of work time due to disciplinary action, constantly loomed over a workforce who faced rising prices, loss of purchasing power and household wealth, and increased liabilities for health insurance and other costs. For many of the Local 8093 members interviewed, the loss of control over the workplace was as or more important than their benefit package, and many suspected that acceding to company demands was the initial step in the eventual loss of their union and workplace.[13]

Specifically, RCP and Indiana Limestone proposed changes in basic seniority rights in job duties and layoff procedures, alterations in just-cause standards for discipline and dismissal, and reductions in excused absences. One of the main sticking points for the union was the company's proposal to do away with meetings of the union–management safety committee, which met regularly to deal with and update shop-floor safety and work procedures. Local 8093 members considered the safety committee to be the key mechanism through which they maintained safe conditions in the face of demands for speedups and increased production. The company proposal also included increased health contributions and a wage freeze, but the work rules were the major point of contention. Local 8093 members reported that they already made slightly less per hour than mill workers in Indiana Limestone's area competitors, but considered that a fair trade-off for their increased ability to effect control over the work process through their union.

The giveback demands resulted in Local 8093 unanimously authorizing a strike in November 2011. The basic demands of the company, sensing weakness in the union, were for concessions in work rules, safety and health procedures, and job assignments and classifications. For members of Local 8093, issues of shop-floor control, the ability to resist management imperatives, and the need to have a direct voice in the daily operation of the mill were as important as wage and benefit packages. Indiana Limestone management recognized that if the workforce could be stripped of its basic rights to workplace protections in these categories, many members would likely come to the conclusion that being a member of the union was not to their benefit, as workers in other quarries received equivalent wage scales without union representation. Without a union representing its workers, Indiana Limestone would make a much more attractive resale package for RCP.

Local 8093 engaged in 2-month strike that resulted in bitter feelings on both sides, public recriminations, picket line incidents, and an eventual agreement that seemed to satisfy neither side. While Local 8093 members believe they won the strike, their eventual contract did include some of the concessions over safety and workplace rules. While most members of Local 8093 expressed satisfaction with the outcome of the strike and the new contract, they also expressed a general apprehension that the battle was far from over. With a new RTW law meant to weaken the union position, new technologies taking more work roles, and a company determined to reduce costs and enhance the resale value of their 'product', Local 8093 members were anything but secure in the aftermath of the strike. Several workers interviewed for this article expressed serious doubt that their children, the next generation, would work in the limestone industry, or, if they did work in the 'belt', that they would not be able to maintain even the marginal standard of living available to them.[14]

High-tech: Printpack

As the process of deindustrialization limits employment options in certain types of manufacturing, new forms of employment emerge. As discussed below, many workers find employment in the service sector, but another trend touted by economists and labor market experts is HTM. In fact, the slow jobs recovery in the industrial sector following the 2007–2008 recession has been led, in part, by new and returning jobs in hi-tech (Fishman 2012; Nolan 2010a, 2010b). The sector is loosely defined and even the Bureau of Labor Statistics give no definitive meaning to the term, but it generally refers to companies that utilize advanced computer and technologically sophisticated processes to produce innovative or 'next generation' products in any given field (Helper, Krueger, and Wial 2012). Printpack, Inc. with its corporate headquarters in Atlanta, considers itself to be in this category in the field of plastic and chemical-based packaging for foods.[15] In 2001, Printpack opened a new production facility in Bloomington, Indiana, located in space once occupied by Independent Packaging, in a facility in the heart of Bloomington's then-fading consumer durables industry. While the jobs provided by Printpack were needed in the area, the price Bloomington and Monroe County paid for those jobs illustrates the difficulties of the withdrawal of item one in Standing's list, basic labor market security, leads to the erosion of other forms of security as well. The story of Printpack's quest for tax breaks is an illustration of this process.

At the time of its decision to locate a production facility in Bloomington, Printpack was an established leader in the area of plastic packaging. The Atlanta-based firm, started in 1956, had 25 facilities in eight states, and locations in Mexico and England. It employed 4400 workers company-wide, had total sales of 1.3 billion dollars, and boasted that it was 'the second largest flexible plastic manufacturer' in the United States. Printpack uses sophisticated manufacturing techniques to produce plastic packaging that allows for long-term shipping and storage of perishable food items. Most of its production process is supervised by skilled managers and engineers, while the production line jobs require only a basic education and some training. For the Bloomington region, still reeling from the loss of RCA, and the downsizing of Otis Elevator and GE, the arrival of Printpack, with its 150 manufacturing jobs, while hardly a replacement for the losses, was a welcome event.

Buffeted by the processes of industrial job flight, and desperate to maintain job levels, the City of Bloomington welcomed Printpack to the area, despite some misgivings. The symbolic nature of a new company occupying part of the old, dying manufacturing location, along with the 150 jobs, was too much to turn down. In spite of questions regarding the environmental problems caused by the plastic packaging process, Bloomington and Monroe Councils both found it difficult to deny location and tax abatements to the new company. In an irony not lost on local environmentalists, Printpack's location was directly opposite the Superfund site on Curry Pike that had been home to the regions notorious industrial polluter, Westinghouse (Greene 1995). The Westinghouse site had been the location of a long-running dispute between local environmentalists and those advocating for less regulation in order to attract jobs. As of this writing, the former Westinghouse site sits vacant, still unfit for even industrial use.

Printpack's occupation of the Independent Packaging site followed the company's purchase of Independent in 2001. Independent Packaging had recently received 10-year tax abatement from the City of Bloomington in exchange for guarantees regarding jobs and local investment in plant and equipment. Printpack agreed to abide by the existing agreement it had inherited and started its stay in Bloomington under a tax abatement agreement. The company has maintained its presence since, with over 150 manufacturing jobs paying between 14 and 17 dollars per hour, with a high-deductible, high premium health care package. While Printpack has been a good corporate citizen, contributing to local charitable causes, questions have been raised by the environmental impact of their production processes (Fyall 2009c). Given the area's recent experience with Westinghouse, the industrial pollution question was a high priority for many citizens of the city and county, but the pressure to attract jobs easily outweighed environmental concerns.

Having welcomed the company with open arms in 2001, Bloomington officials were surprised and disappointed when Printpack announced that it would close its production facility in late summer of 2009. However, before announcement of the plans to close the existing facility had been made public, the company had already purchased a parcel of land in a green space located within a Tax Increment Finance District a mere half-mile from the Curry Pike plant. The new facility on West Vernal Pike had already undergone architectural planning, and was to be a state-of-the-art production facility. Inexplicably, as land was being cleared for new construction, the company informed the city and county that they intended to move production from the Bloomington plant to 'Mexico or Tennessee' unless the city and county agreed to new tax abatements and incentives (Fyall 2009a).

As work on Printpack's new facility continued, Monroe County's heavily Democratic County Council debated the issue of tax abatements. While council members expressed concerns, the majority voiced approval of the extension of abatements throughout the debate. A minority of voices on the County and City Council and the Economic Development Corporation (EDC) expressed publicly their opposition to new tax breaks. County council member Julie Thomas was perhaps the loudest and most persistent voice in opposition to the plan, but her objections were often overwhelmed by the 'jobs' mantra coming from other members, best expressed by Council member Marty Hawk: 'That's Russian roulette with local jobs. I'm not willing to play' (Fyall 2009b). In spite of the fact that Printpack had already purchased new land, the threat of job loss overwhelmed objections like those expressed by EDC member Greg Travis, who pointed out that tax abatements in Increment Finance zones punished taxpayers not in the Tax Increment Financing (TIF) by forcing them to subsidize development with little or no return. Travis and Thomas both agreed that Printpack's decision to purchase property meant that the company intended to stay, and that the tax abatement was not necessary nor would it help the area in general. Travis further points out that he found no credible evidence that abatements 'have any meaningful effect on economic development'.[16]

The decision to extend new tax abatements to Printpack in 2009 can be traced to the dispossession of income security for workers in the Monroe County region. As economic and political pressures cause local governments to extend such tax breaks to selected industries and employers, they must either make such breaks revenue neutral by increasing revenue elsewhere, or decrease outlays for public good and services. Consequent increases in revenue can mean higher taxes on individuals and families, or cuts, restrictions, and lack of improvements in school funding, infrastructure repair, social safety provision, first responders, and other public services. For Indiana, the increased pressure to shift revenue burdens has led to a State constitutional limit on property taxes, increased use of tax breaks for business, and subsequent increases in sales taxes and fees, which shifts the burden to working families. As Louise Story documented in an investigative report for *The New York Times*, municipalities often do not receive the promised economic benefits from tax breaks, and just as often experience revenue decreases that lead to service cuts (Story 2012). In addition, revenue decreases have led to poor safety net provision in the state, and a decrease in public funding for vital educational institutions. To take just one example, state funding for Indiana University has decreased from over 70% in the 1980s to just fewer than 25% by 2012, causing higher tuitions which make attendance difficult if not impossible for working class families.[17]

Lack of protection for domestic manufacturing, brought on in part by the diminishing influence of unions in the political system, results in the 'whipsawing' effect for both workers and local governments, with negative effects in the areas of taxes, school and infrastructure support, community stability, and the integrity of the political process (Zullo and Mukherji 2011). As cities like Bloomington suffered increasing job loss, pressure on local officials to replaced lost employment at any cost increased. The process of whipsawing, where workers in certain locations are forced to make concessions under the threat of losing new production to cheaper facilities, has a similar effect on municipalities. While Printpack did keep 150 or so jobs in its facility in Bloomington, there was no guarantee that the employees were local taxpayers. When infrastructure, local services, environmental degradation, and other factors are subtracted, the cost to the city may wind up exceeding the benefits of the local jobs preserved.

Beyond the economic and tax issues, cities and towns suffer from a form of democratic deficit when subjected to whipsawing. When companies like Printpack exert pressure on local councils, particularly during hard economic times, the public perception that corporate power trumps the public interest can be magnified, leading to political apathy, shifting political allegiances, and even political extremism. As council member Thomas pointed out during the Printpack debate in 2009, it was equally important to look out for the 'best interests of the people of the county' and to 'look out for county taxpayers' as it was to preserve jobs. Given the public pressure to create a favorable business environment, local councils feel pressure from business interests to override public concerns, leading to representatives elected by the majority to appear to be acting in the minority interest. Both Thomas and Travis confirmed the heavy presence of pressure to approve Printpack's abatements in spite of the low return anticipated in an objective assessment of the benefits.[18]

The problems of industrial blackmail and tax abatements result from the dispossession of labor market security. The loss of protection and subsidy for domestic industry and the proliferation of new trade pacts opening up manufacturing to global competition decrease the ability of municipalities to make objective judgments on decisions that have long-lasting ramifications for area workers. Tax abatements that do not benefit the entire region and population can mean decreased funding for schools, parks, city services, and an increase in factors such as environmental degradation (Story 2012). Further, accepting that any job is better than none often opens areas to low-wage, often dangerous manufacturing. These factors can contribute to the deterioration of working class communities, and to a decrease in the kinds of family and community stability that produce generational upward mobility. For small cities such as Bloomington, the loss of tax revenue has already led to cuts in services for the economically vulnerable and in the privatization of city jobs, where private contractors pay lower wages with few benefits.

Conclusion: precarity

This study of three sectors of the South Central Indiana economy demonstrates the interrelated and long-term trajectory of the process of dispossession. As macro-level political support was withdrawn from labor unions and domestic industries beginning in the 1970s, and the post-Fordist model of accumulation spread throughout the Midwest, formerly secure workers were dispossessed of hard-won rights, such as the right to job security, safety protections, skill training, and protections from arbitrary treatment. For South Central Indiana workers, dispossession has included a decrease in political influence for labor unions, decreased access to higher education and job training, erosion of local budgets and social provision, and the rise to power of political actors who are openly hostile to organized labor, and the interests of the working class and working poor. As union influence and membership have diminished, many working class residents have embraced this new politics. When the assault on union rights began in the Indiana legislature in 2010, much of the work for antiunion forces had already been accomplished. Union membership was already at historically low levels, and the political influence of labor, while still considerable, was ultimately impotent in the face of the RTW campaign.

For Indiana, passage of a RTW law was only the latest link in a long chain of dispossession dating back to at least the 1980s. Beginning with the corporate attempt to halt the falling rate of profit, a process that emerges as forms of financialization (Marazzi 2010; Boyer 2000), the long search for the spatial fix had slowly yet inexorably transformed the region from a desired location for manufacturing to a landscape transformed by deindustrialization, decreasing union membership, diminished working class political influence, and finally, the creation of a new, more precarious work force, unmoored from the politics of the New Deal coalition. The erosion of labor market security dispossessed Indiana workers of basic expectations in the workplace and community, expectations that had formed the backbone of the upwardly mobile Indiana working class in the post-World War II period.

For workers in the three sectors examined here, the dispossession of labor market securities has affected their ability to influence workplace conditions, affect the political system, improve skills and mobility, and provide for secure, prosperous communities. While no utopia, the relative security that workers achieved as they took possession of workplace rights in the postwar period reproduced a stable working class whose politics, while never monolithic, was somewhat cohesive in its support of the maintenance of labor market securities. As the steady erosion of labor market securities has dispossessed workers of these same workplace rights, older workers seek new forms of political allegiance, and newer members of the working class, deprived of the stability of good-paying, stable manufacturing work, join the new precariat, piecing together work, family, and community under pressures never faced by previous generations. With this new precarity come new political alliances, unmoored from the maintenance of labor rights characteristic of the New Deal coalition and the Fordist mode of accumulation. The most obvious political manifestation is the rise of working class participation in movements such as the Tea Party, and in the overt hostility expressed toward the national Democratic Party by former unionized wageworkers (Levinson and Texeira 2013).

Notes

1. Jackie Yenna, President, White River Valley Central Labor Council. Interview by author. Bloomington, Indiana, 17 November 2010.
2. I take the categories directly from Standing's book, but add some explanatory features to fit the case studies of the US workplace.
3. The case of the passage of an antiunion right to work law in Indiana in 1957 is a good example of the era's uneasy cooperation between business and organized labor. The law was promoted by mainly rural representatives, while the heads of major industries in the state, including the influential Cummings Manufacturing in Columbus, opposed the law, believing that it would cause unrest among the unionized labor force.
4. Carven Thomas, President IBEW Local 2249. Interview by author. Bloomington, Indiana, 12 and 13 March 2013.
5. Jackie Yenna, General Electric employee. Interview by author. Bloomington, Indiana, 12 March 2013.
6. See notes 4 and 5.
7. Based on extensive interviews with workers from three area limestone companies on 12 September 2010 (Bloomington, Indiana), 24 November 2011 (Oolitic, Indiana), 10 December 2011 (Oolitic, Indiana), 2 February 2012 (Bedford, Indiana), 23 March 2012 (Bloomington, Indiana), 10 July 2012 (Bedford, Indiana), and 15 August 2012 (Bedford, Indiana). The companies are Indiana Limestone Company, BG Hoadley and Sons, and Victor Oolitic Stine Company. The workers preferred to remain anonymous, unless otherwise noted.
8. The information on Resilience Capital Partners is drawn mainly from the company's own promotional material and trade publications. Company representatives refused to participate in interviews for this article.
9. Jerry Banks, Tim Spreen, and Ron Watson, officers, Carpenters Local 8093. Interview by author, Bedford, Indiana, 10 July 2012.
10. 'Resilience capital partners completes acquisition of Indiana Limestone Company'. *PR Newswire.* 16 November 2010. http://www.prnewswire.com/news-releases/resilience-capital-partners-completes-the-acquisition-of-indiana-limestone-company-108441734.html
11. 'Resilience capital partners aquires Indiana Limestone'. *Cutting Edge.* December 2010. http://bluetoad.com/publication/index.php?i=55742&m=&l=&p=7&pre=&ver=flex
12. See note 9.
13. See note 9.
14. Dusty Amstutz, Mike Fish, Ron Watson, various 8093 members. Interview by author, Bedford, Indiana, 2 February 2012.
15. On Printpack's self-presentation as a high-tech company, see their website: http://www.printpack.com/
16. Gregory Travis, interview by author, Bloomington, Indiana, 9 November 2012. Julie Thomas interview by author, Bloomington, Indiana, 12 November 2012.
17. For a good review and breakdown of Indiana and state funding for higher education, see: http://www.inthepublicinterest.org/article/iu-purdue-expect-state-aid-continue-falling.
    Christopher (2011) is a great account of the loss of public funding for higher education in California and overall.
18. See note 16.

References

Alderson, A. 1999. "Explaining Deindustrialization: Globalization, Failure or Success." *American Sociological Review* 64 (5): 701–721 (October 1999).

Ayer, H. M. 1963. "Hoosier Labor in the Second World War." *Indiana Magazine of History* 59 (2): 95–120 (June 1963).

Bluestone, B., and B. Harrison. 1982. *The Deindustrialization of America: Plant Closings, Community Abandonment, and the Dismantling of Basic Industry*. New York: Basic Books.

Boyer, R. 2000. "Is a Finance Led Growth Regime a Viable Alternative to Fordism? A Preliminary Analysis." *Economy and Society* 29 (1): 111–145 (February 2000).

Christopher, N. 2001. *Unmaking the Public University*. Boston, MA: Harvard University Press.

Conover, J., M. Kinghorn, and T. Slaper. 2007. *A Look Inside the Bloomington Economy*. Bloomington, IN: Indiana Business Research Center, June 2007.

Craypo, C. 1997. "The Impact of Changing Corporate Strategies on Communities, Unions, and Workers in the U.S." *Journal of Law and Society* 24 (1): 10–25 (March 1997).

Craypo, C., and D. Cormier 2000. "Job Restructuring as a Determinant of Wage Inequality and Working Poor Households." *Journal of Economic Issues* 34 (1): 21–42 (March 2000).

Crump, J. R., and Christopher D. Merrett 1998. "Scales of Struggle: Economic Restructuring in the U.S. Midwest." *Annals of the Association of American Geographers* 88: 497–516. (September 1998).

Cowie, J. 1999. *Capital Moves: RCA's Seventy-Year Quest for Cheap Labor*. Ithaca, NY: Cornell University Press.

Dark, T. 1999. *The Unions and the Democrats: An Enduring Alliance*. Ithaca, NY: Cornell University Press.

Davis, M. 2000. *Prisoners of the American Dream: Politics and Economics in the History of the U.S. Working Class*. New York: Verso Press.

Ferrucci, K. 2005. *Limestone Lives: Voices from the Indiana Stone Belt*. Bloomington: Indiana University Press.

Fishman, C. 2012. "The Insourcing Boom." *The Atlantic Magazine*, December.

Fyall, C. 2009a. "Printpack to Close Plant, But May Stay in Monroe County." *Herald Times Bloomington*, August 27.

Fyall, C. 2009b. "No Printpack Officials Attend Tax Break Hearing." *Herald Times Bloomington*, September 2.

Fyall, C. 2009c. "Printpack Wins Tax Break for New Plant." *Herald Times Bloomington*, October 7.

Glyn, A. 1990. "Productivity and the Crisis of Fordism." *International Review of Applied Economics* 4: 28–44.

Greene, L. 1995. "The PCB Mess in Bloomington, Indiana." *Synthesis/Regeneration* 7–8 (Summer 1995).

Hansen, S. B. 2001. "The Impact of a Low-Wage Strategy on State Economic Development." *State Politics and Policy Quarterly* 1 (3): 227–254 (Fall 2001).

Harvey, D. 2006. *Spaces of Global Capitalism*. New York: Verso.

Harvey, D. 2007. *A Brief History of Neo-Liberalism*. London: Oxford University Press.

Hauptmeir, M., and I. Greer. 2012. "Whipsawing: Organizing Labor Competition in Multinational Auto Companies." *ILERA*, July.

Helper, S., T. Krueger, and H. Wial. 2012. "Locating American Manufacturing: Trends in the Geography of Production." *Metropolitan Policy Program*, Brookings Institution 2012.

Hirsh, B. T., D. McPherson, and W. Vroman. 2001. "Estimates of Union Density by State." *Monthly Labor Review*, July 2001, Bureau of Labor Statistics.

Immelt, J. 2012. "The CEO of GE on Sparking an American Manufacturing Renewal." *Harvard Business Review*, March.

Indiana Department of Workforce Development (IDWD). 2013. *Major Employers for Monroe County*. http://www.hoosierdata.in.gov/major_employers.asp?areaID=105

Jessop, R. 1992. "Fordism and Post-Fordism: A Critical Reformulation." In *Pathways to Industrialization and Regional Development*, edited by M. Storper and A. J. Scott, 42–62. New York: Routledge.

Leuchtenberg, W. 2001. *In the Shadow of FDR: From Harry Truman to Barack Obama*. Ithaca, NY: Cornell University Press.

Levinson, A., and R. Texeira. 2013. "Why the Democrats Still Need the White Working Class." *New Republic*, June 5.

Lichtenstein, N. 2002. *State of the Union: A Century of American Labor.* Princeton, NJ: Princeton University Press.
Marazzi, C. 2010. *The Violence of Finance Capitalism.* New York: Semiotext(e).
Milkis, S., and J. Mileur. 2002. *The New Deal and the Triumph of American Liberalism.* Amherst: University of Massachusetts Press.
Mitchell, D. 2004. "Geography in an Age of Extremes: A Blueprint for a Geography of Justice." *Annals of the Association of American Geographers* 94: 764–770.
Nelson, D. 1995. *Farm and Factory: Workers in the Midwest, 1880–1990.* Bloomington: Indiana University Press.
Nolan, B. 2010a. "WestGate Industrial Park Near Crane a Success Story for Three Counties." *Herald Times Bloomington*, August 29.
Nolan, B. 2010b. "Visteon Plant Repurposed Into High-Tech Business." *Herald Times Bloomington*, August 29.
Peckham, H. H. 2003. *Indiana: A History.* Champagne: University of Illinois Press.
Phillips, S. 1987. "At G.E. Plant, Familiar Fears." *The New York Times*, July 28.
Robey, J. S. 1999. "Civil Society and NAFTA: Initial Results." *Annals of the American Academy of Political and Social Science* 565: 113–125 (September 1999).
Standing, G. 2011. *The Precariat: The New Dangerous Class.* London: Bloomsbury Academic.
Starks, B. 2003. "The New Economy and the American Dream: Examining the Effect of Work Conditions on Beliefs About Economic Opportunity." *The Sociological Quarterly* 44 (2): 205–225 (Spring 2003).
Story, L. 2012. "As Companies Seek Tax Deals, Governments Pay High Price." *The New York Times*, December 1.
Vidal, M. 2011. "Reworking Postfordism: Labor Process Versus Employment Relations." *Sociology Compass* 5 (4): 273–286.
Wallace, M., and A. Fullerton 2003. "Workers' Earnings in the New Economy." *Sociological Forces* 36 (1): 7–27 (February 2003).
Western, B., and J. Rosenfield 2011. "Unions, Norms, and the Rise of Wage Inequality." *American Sociological Review* 76 (4): 513–537.
Zullo, R., and K. Mukherji. 2011. "Regional Employment Effects of Motor Vehicle Industry Job Loss in Michigan Counties: 2001–2008." *Institute for Research on Labor Employment and the Economy*, February.

REPLY

Breaking the heartland: creating the precariat in the US lower rust belt: a response to Joseph J. Varga

Angela Wigger

Radboud University Nijmegen, The Netherlands

This is a reply to:

Varga, Joseph J. 2013. "Breaking the heartland: creating the precariat in the US lower rust belt." *Global Discourse.* 3 (3–4): 430–446. http://dx.doi.org/10.1080/23269995.2013.859877.

Joseph J. Varga's 'Breaking the heartland' makes a very important and astute contribution to understanding the socioeconomic processes that have led to the emergence of precariat in the 'lower rust belt' of Southern and Central Indiana. The demise of employment conditions is particularly interesting as back in the 1960s and 1970s, unionizations rates were one of the US' highest in what is also known as the Lower Midwest. Alongside a profound de-industrialization of the region in the time between the 1980s and 2000, the number of unionized workers has dropped dramatically – well before the adoption of anti-union legislation in 2012, or what has been euphemistically disguised as 'right to work' laws.

Varga reveals the incremental yet far-reaching dispossession of hard-won labor security rights in three industrial sectors characteristic for the area: consumer durables, extractive industries, and light and high-tech manufacturing. On the basis of Guy Standing's seven macro- and micro-level labor security indicators, Varga shows that the creation of the precariat has become manifest in an overall employment insecurity, not only through flexible contracts and neoliberal wage compression but also through the loss of basic mechanisms for upward job mobility, skill acquisition, and safety rights, as well as workplace and shop floor control. The strength of Varga's analysis lies in outlining the particularities of the three industries, their importance for overall employment in the area, and the subsequent changes that have led to increased precariousness. The analysis is empirically well sustained and builds, amongst others, on unique evidence gathered from interviews with the workforce of companies in the three industrial sectors.

Varga locates the observed precariatization trajectories against the broader context of the transition from post-war Fordist to post-Fordist accumulation strategies and the resulting de-composition of the New Deal working class as political force. As we learn from Varga's article, a longitudinal analytical perspective is indispensible here. Precariousness does not immanently become visible, but takes shape through interrelated and long-term processes of dispossession of labor security rights. Importantly, the pace and ferocity, as well as the timing in which labor security rights were and continue to be dismantled, has been uneven in the wider area of Central and South Indiana. As Varga shows, it is precisely this unevenness that is co-responsible for the broader loss of collective political organization and social and cultural cohesion that characterizes the precariat more generally. The 'breaking' of the heartland, as mentioned in the title, is hence epitomized in the dissolution of traditional alliances between (organized) labor, progressive forces, and the Democratic Party.

Analyses, like that of Varga, which link seemingly isolated regional and industrial-sector level trajectories to wider structural changes of capitalist accumulation strategies are to be welcomed, particularly as the emergence and rise of the precariat elsewhere might follow similar patterns. Although the article makes an important contribution to critical research, Varga's presentation of the rise of the precariat is at times overly descriptive, while the actual mechanisms or conditioning factors that underpin the creation of flexible and more precarious labor are mentioned in passing only. Only through understanding the mechanisms at play, however, can the precariat as a 'class-in-the-making', as Standing (2011, 155) has labeled it, become 'a-class-for-itself' and define its terrain of emancipatory politics. Different yet interconnected mechanisms that have played into the emergence of the precariat can be abstracted from Varga's contribution, nonetheless. In what follows, I will try to highlight and expand on these mechanisms a bit more.

In the case of the consumer durables sector, Varga links the deskilling and job loss to global competitive pressures and the ensuing relocation of production to cheap labor areas, leaving the remaining GE workforce in Bloomington with dispersed and increasingly dull production steps, decreased access to higher education, and no meaningful career prospects, both for contemporary employees and the incoming generation alike. Varga hinges here on an important yet frequently overlooked condition in the creation of precariousness, namely that capitalist competition has probably never been harsher and more encompassing in scope than today. In fact, the labor security rights of the post-war era, or what has been generally referred to as capitalism's Golden Age in the industrialized world, have been established at a time when capitalist competition in the US has been predominantly 'co-respective' with often implicit agreements not to compete on prices (see Crotty 2008; Bowles, Gordon, and Weisskopf 1990, 75–76). Until the 1960s, US companies, moreover, faced no noteworthy competition from abroad. Competition only intensified in the 1970s, when European and Japanese companies mimicked US corporate management styles and further developed US production technologies, with the effect that cheaper products and services penetrated US markets. The rise of export-oriented Asian low-cost competitors eventually increased competitive pressures massively. As Marx ([1887] 1965, 626) observed well over a century ago, '[t]he battle of competition is fought by cheapening of commodities. The cheapness of commodities depends, all other circumstances remaining the same, on the productivity of labour [...]'. Thus, the permanent competitive battle to reduce costs implies that the prices of competitors can only be undercut by a further exploitation of labor, and in a wider sense also nature. In other words, the devaluation and depreciation of labor through unpaid overtime, worsening working conditions, wage depression, or redundancies, as well as the much more subtle dispossession of labor security rights that Varga has identified on the basis of Guy Standing's work, is intimately related to increased capitalist competition. The consumer durables sector analyzed by Varga engenders all the above-mentioned features but in particular the attempt to increase productivity through fragmenting the labor process and outsourcing production to cheap labor and low tax areas.

In the case of the lime stone sector, Varga links the loss of workplace control and overall deteriorating working conditions to changes in the ownership structures. Interesting here is that the commodification of companies through mergers and acquisitions induced by financial market players goes paired with attempts to increase the value of a company in the short term by speeding up the production process and ignoring safety standards – in addition to wage repression. Here, it is important to keep in mind that the scale and speed of mergers and acquisitions has been unparalleled in the years prior to the outbreak of the current crisis. For example, in 2006, eight of the ten worldwide largest mergers ever were concluded. The acquisition and selling of companies has been strongly speculative in nature, boosted by ongoing processes of financialization and the emergence of (new) financial players, such as private equity, hedge funds, and other institutional investors, which had attracted huge amounts of liquidity to finance mergers and corporate buyouts. In 2007, private equity firms were estimated to be responsible for more than 20% of all global merger activity (see Wigger 2012). As Varga shows for the lime stone sector, the actual goal of the private equity has been not real economic production but to exploit speculative arbitrages and resell the company with a profit, and this has major repercussions for labor security rights. Or to quote Marx ([1847] 1975, 134–135) once more, there 'are even phases in the life of modern nations when everybody is seized with a sort of craze for making profit without producing. This speculation craze which recurs periodically, lays bare the true character of competition [...]'.

In the case of the high-tech sector, Varga highlights yet another element, namely corporations in deindustrialized areas using the exit option as a blackmail strategy for corporate tax abatements and a tolerant stance vis-à-vis environmentally polluting practices. As Varga illustrates well, this not only erodes local budgets with great consequences for the provision of welfare and education but also severely undermines democratic decision-making.

The question why the creation of the precariat in Indiana has brought politicians such as from the Tea Party into power that demise organized labor and the working poor, and more generally whether the precariat is indeed a dangerous class as Guy Standing has suggested, remains unanswered by Varga. Here again it might help to understand the detrimental downsides of capitalist competition. In the presence of a reserve army of unemployed and precarious work forces, competition not only pits capital against labor but also labor against labor. Competition by definition divides more than it unites, and as Varga shows in his analysis, this backfires on solidarity and the organizational power of labor.

References

Bowles, S., D. M. Gordon, and T. E. Weisskopf. 1990. *After the Wasteland: A Democratic Economics for the Year 2000*. Armonk, NY: M. E. Sharpe.

Crotty, J. 2008. "If Financial Market Competition Is Intense, Why Are Financial Firm Profits so High? Reflections on the Current 'Golden Age' of Finance." *Competition & Change* 12 (2): 167–183.

Marx, K. 1965 [1887]. *Capital Volume 1*. Moscow: Progress Publishers.

Marx, K. 1975 [1847]. *The Poverty of Philosophy*. Moscow: Progress Publishers.

Standing, G. 2011. *The Precariat: The New Dangerous Class*. London: Bloomsbury Academic.

Wigger, A. 2012. "The Political Interface of Financialisation and the Regulation of Mergers and Acquisitions in the EU." *Journal of European Integration* 34 (6): 623–641.

RESEARCH ARTICLE

Precarity of place: a complement to the growing precariat literature

Susan Banki

Department of Sociology and Social Policy, University of Sydney, Sydney, Australia

This article suggests that our current understandings of precarity are insufficient to describe the specific challenges of noncitizen living. It offers a counter concept that is related, but distinct from precarity: 'precarity of place'. The term, far from being focused on the way precarity manifests itself in the workplace, instead focuses on the challenges of physical residence for migrants and the tightrope-like nature of migrant life. The article draws several parallels between the growing literature on what I call 'labour precarity' and 'precarity of place', including its origins in colonialism and neoliberalism, its nebulous class quality, and social movement responses. Drawing on examples from Burmese migrant populations in Thailand, the article posits that 'precarity of place' be considered in conjunction with, but separated from, our current understandings of (labour) precarity.

Introduction

The growing precarity literature offers some valuable ways of thinking about both the roots of and responses to precarity, whether defined existentially, economically, or intersubjectively. As the terms 'precariat', 'precarious', and 'precarity' grow ever more popular in the academic literature, it should also be noted that the term, in its eagerness to encompass all those who experience precarity, fails to properly capture the challenges of one of its subset populations: that of noncitizens.

Rather than discard the term altogether, this article incorporates elements from the precariat literature and offers a counter (sub)concept: 'precarity of place'. The article reviews the precarity literature and then argues for the importance of a separate term for 'precarity of place', as differentiated from labour precarity, noting how the concepts are uneasily aligned, that is, they complement each other but offer clearly distinct experiences to their victims. The article turns to an example from the Global South to illuminate similarities and differences between the two concepts, drawing on Burmese migrant populations in Thailand, and concludes with suggestions for future research, both theoretical and empirical.

Precarity and the precariat

The notion of precarity describes the condition of being vulnerable to exploitation because of a lack of security. Precarity suggests the *potential* for exploitation and abuse, but not its certain presence. Thus precarious work is not the fact of consistent unemployment, but the looming threat, and perhaps frequent fact, of it. Precarity of residence does not suggest imminent deportation from a country, but its very real possibility. Similarly, social precarity does not describe an absence of supportive networks, but the potential for their dismantling. The literature has made frequent reference to the fact that precarity of one kind may aggravate other precarities. For example, precarious legal status affects the ability to secure stable work. Social networks are weakened when people are uprooted. And an unstable work environment can stem the ability to develop relationships, as those in precarious situations lack the social infrastructure to create networks and lack the confidence and financial resources that much socialising requires (Goldring and Landolt 2011).

The intellectual founders and forerunners of precarity comprise Bourdieu, who articulated the term in 1998, Foucault, Habermas, Hardt and Negri, and Arendt (Standing 2011, 2). It has further been explored by Butler, whose treatment of the notion delves into our understandings of self-sovereignty (and its lack) and suggests a communal approach to nonviolence that encourages a repositioning of not only our ethnic and racial frames, but our human ones (relative to nonhumans) (2006). This philosophical positioning of the term sowed the seeds for an empirically grounded concept, of which precariat is the result.

The precariat, referred to by Standing as 'globalisation's child' (2011, 5), is not necessarily part of the 'working class' or the 'proletariat' but instead consists of social 'classes' on either side of the proletariat – both highly educated and motivated creative workers struggling to find secure employment, on the one hand, and a *lumpen proletariat*-minus-stability, on the other hand. Each 'type' of precariat class member faces different challenges, although the first certainly has more freedom and flexibility than the second.

Precarious work, which since the 1970s has become nearly a universal phenomenon, is defined by Branch and Hanley as employment that is 'uncertain, unpredictable, and risky from the point of view of the worker' (2011, 569). They argue that the nature of such work is felt particularly acutely by low-skill and low-wage workers (2011). Fantone reminds us that precariousness is an inherent feature of capitalism and although it is more pronounced in western, post-Fordist capitalist cities recently transformed by globalisation and information technologies, in colonial cities hyperexploitation of labour, particularly women's domestic labour, has always been the norm (2007, 10).

Despite the lengthy history of the precarious nature of capitalism, the precariat movement only relatively recently found its wings in the stirrings of the Milan May Day 2001 protest and subsequent EuroMayday protests starting in 2005, which challenged the tenets of globalisation through creative and symbolic repertoires of contention. The movement demands universal rights for workers (Doerr 2010, 4), free migration policies, and a universal basic income (Dean 2012, 356) (also known as a 'citizenship income', 'a form of welfare [allowing workers] to choose which professional path to pursue and what to produce' (Galetto et al. 2007, 111), which would ensure the 'right to decent work' enshrined, in Dean's interpretation, in Article 23[1] of the Universal Declaration of Human Rights (2012, 357)).

Most commonly the precarity literature refers to insecurity in the workplace, and Standing's oft-cited work on the precariat details seven forms of labour security that are absent in the condition of precarity (2011, 10). Yet the notion of precarity has theoretical traction elsewhere, as the examples above and the literature below indicate, and other works have expanded the understanding of the term to include a lack of security in other areas of how we manage day to day, such as debt and indebtedness (Ross 2008), access to legal documentation (Goldring and Landolt 2011), gender norms (Brah 2002; Abrahamson 2004; Fantone 2007), and 'other aspects of intersubjective life, including housing, debt, and the ability to build affective social relations' (Neilson and Rossiter 2005, n.p.).

Critiques and variations of the use of precarity as a term have emerged along with its increasing popularity. These include charges of US-centrism (Lee and Kofman 2012), which this article tries to correct by a focus on the Global South. There has also been considerable debate on the 'newness' of precarity as a condition of work or a structural feature of a social class (Mitropoulos 2005). As part of the history of capitalism, many people around the world have, after all, been subject to unreliable, unprotected and poorly paid work conditions for centuries; the contemporary 'naming' of the precariat arguably comes about through the cultural capital of the middle classes enabling them to name their conditions as their standards of living decompose and they become exposed to the risks that are routine for so many other workers.

Indeed, as precarity has increasingly encompassed a greater number of actors – the poor, the rich, the creative, the human, the animal, the worker, the temporary worker, the nonworker, the migrant, and the refugee – there is real concern that its essence has been diluted. Yet there are populations for which the underlying concept of precarity is useful, because it describes both the roots of precarity in global systems and its outcomes in creating differentiated types of sufferers. Specifically, this article argues, there is value to capturing a subset of the precariat: that of non-citizens, who experience 'precarity of place'.

Precarity of place

The precarity of noncitizens is particular, and at the same time, it aligns closely with broader concepts in the precariat literature. Yet 'precarity of place' deserves its own analysis because, as the extensive migration literature notes, our current global system is organised around units of nation states, and it is primarily from these units, and national governments, that our rights accrue. Arendt famously related those with no state to those with no rights ([1951]1979). While the introduction of an international human rights regime makes individuals subjects of *humanity* and not *nationality*, in practice, it is sovereign governments that protect (or fail to protect) these rights. Even without using rights language, we can argue that membership in a group proffers benefits, and that in our current international system, the body that controls the distribution of the vast portion of benefits that can render our lives better (and less precarious) is the state.

Denizenship, just short of citizenship, suggests that the state can offer a suite of rights, in effect, picking and choosing the rights they want to protect and the services they want to offer (see, e.g., Hammar 1990). Even post-national membership positions the state as the actor that distributes rights and benefits, though in this scheme, not on the basis of nationality but according to other categories – rights of residents, workers, and so on (Tambini 2001; Standing 2011, chapter 4; Soysal 2012). That the state should be the benefactor of privileges when membership is not defined by nationality requires deeper examination. For example, arrangements between Thailand, Burma, Cambodia and Laos to register migrant workers, or arrangements between India, Nepal and Bhutan to permit access to higher education and the ability to open bank accounts permit cross-national benefits and rights that are tied to regional location, not national ones. Yet it is national governments, examining residence, that proffer the benefits of these regional programmes.

While the artifice of national membership remains salient, there is a physical, place-based importance to these rights and benefits given by the state. Physical removal reflects a call to explore 'the spatial linkages between the "*hurt and the hurter*"' (Waite 2009,

427). It is *physical* residents who walk or drive on the roads, or otherwise use a place's infrastructure. It is *physical* residents who require health services; whether they are permitted to use such services legally is another question, but this does not stop residents of all levels of membership from needing such services by having children, getting sick, and dying. It is *physical* residents who engage in 'acts of citizenship' (Isin 2009, 368), for example, lobbying politicians directly or participating in demonstrations that require physical presence to produce 'an interruption and transformation of the political' (Nyers 2011, 141).[1] And it is *physical* residents whose lives prop up the lives of other residents: through legal work, undocumented work, child care, elderly care, and simple, daily interactions. In short, the *physical* residence of persons represents a key aspect of how our world is shaped and coloured, as does, of course, the physical removal of persons. As Bauböck has noted, a rethinking of public philosophies of citizenship lets us imagine that those who live in a place, and thus have a stake in the future of that place, are represented in the polity (2008). Thus, the permission to remain in one's physical place is perhaps paradoxically at the core of a concept of national assignment of privileges and benefits. 'Precarity of place' describes the absence of such permission and can be defined as *vulnerability to removal or deportation from one's physical location.*

Several caveats are necessary. First, in this article, removal and deportation is considered out of a national space, with national boundaries, but it is clear that the definition could be used to apply to other types of precarity of place. Here, to enrich our understanding of the term, we will focus solely on vulnerability to deportation from a country, by a national sovereign government. Second, this definition clearly suggests a continuum, on which citizenship sits on one end. On the other end is the noncitizen who lacks appropriate documentation and connections to safely remain. 'Appropriate' documentation is an important modifier, because, as noted by Goldring, Berinstein, and Bernhard (2009), the mere possession of documents is not sufficient to mitigate a precarious existence. Third, this definition, which speaks merely of physical location, may appear to be less than capacious, but that is precisely the point: as the subsequent empirical section will reveal, the simple fact of vulnerability to deportation and removal has wide-reaching implications, such as a fear of accessing public transportation, social spaces, and public offices.

Why precarity?

Thus precarity of place – vulnerability to removal from a country – deserves our attention. But why, if the concept of the precariat originated to describe precarious work, is it useful in this context? In other words, why not use a different term, such as insecurity, that does not focus primarily on labour? In sum, the two types of precarity share five compelling elements. These elements are (1) similar root causes; (2) the tightrope-like nature of both; (3) similarly ambiguous social and economic class identification; (4) varied methods of collective action; and (5) the importance of social networks to both. In this section, the two types of precarity are named as 'labour precarity' and 'precarity of place' in order to differentiate them.

First, the roots of both labour precarity and precarity of place are external, and, at their source, stem from the colonial legacy and neoliberal economic forces. Fantone suggests the link between colonialism and our current use of labour in exploitative and precarious ways (2007, 10). That is, colonialism's exploitation of people and resources created enduring imbalances in the global system whose consequence is consistent efforts by former colonial powers to maintain supremacy by reducing labour costs and devaluing labour rights, leading to a rejection of secure jobs and careers in many sectors. Likewise, neoliberalism's emphasis on capital and capital's need for low-cost workers produces precarious working conditions.

The hefty literature on the link between neoliberal economies, globalisation, and precarity will not be reviewed here; a fine summary by Arnold and Bongiovi notes:

> Global scale transitions and transformations shape the increasing precariousness of work.... The growing power and reach of global capital has exceeded the ability of nations and labor movements to regulate it, exacerbating inequality and precarious work. Numerous labor trends have been associated with neoliberal globalization, including a decline in attachment to employers, an increase in long-term unemployment, growth in perceived and real job insecurity, increasing nonstandard and contingent work, risk shifting from employers to employees, a lack of workplace safety, and an increase in work-based stress and harassment. The lack of public and private investment in skills and development is accompanied by a lack of access to schooling, where women and ethnic and racial minorities disproportionally bear the brunt of these disadvantages. (2013, 290)

Precarity of place is related to these same forces. The imbalances that both colonialism and neoliberalism have wrought, and the extreme movement of capital as part of the neoliberal agenda, have fuelled seasonal and temporary work, facilitating an 'economic logic' migrant labour (Sassen 2001, 34). As Standing has noted, 'capital welcomes migration because it brings low-cost malleable labour' (2011, 103). In fact Standing devotes considerable attention to explaining how undocumented migrants both fuel the neoliberal engine and are its primary victims. 'Too many (socioeconomic) interests benefit from an army of illegal migrants, and too many populists depict attempts at legalisation as eroding the security of the citizenry' (2011, 91). Put another way, the unequal flow of labour and capital across borders creates not only migrant populations, but the deprivation that underpins many of the world's current conflicts. As such, migrants of all kinds can be similarly made precarious by globalisation (Castles 2010). And it is widely known that colonialism lies at the root of many of the conflicts that have produced today's flows of forced migrants, most of whom lack appropriate documentation when they cross borders (Chimni 1998).

The second similarity refers to the tightrope-like nature of precarity, the anxiety of 'teetering on the edge' (Standing 2011, 20). Thus precarity is the condition of 'not quite, not yet'. That is, not quite poverty-stricken, not yet impoverished.[2] Similarly, precarity of place describes the condition of not quite homeless, not yet deported or detained. For many populations living in refugee camps, for example, a thatched roof above their heads suggests a physical shelter, but at the same time, the threat of deportation looms if authorities find something awry. With very limited recourse for legal protection, refugees such as these teeter on the edge: not quite forced to flee once again, not yet safe from scrutiny by host authorities. This teetering quality has both practical implications (e.g., difficult to plan the future) and psychological ones, and affects the kinds of choices that people make in everyday life. A broad swath of literature has asserted the profound psychological effects of uncertain understandings about our futures, in particular, the deeply damaging effects of indefinite detention (Silove and Steel 1998; Steel et al. 2006; Silove, Austin, and Steel 2007).

The third similarity that the two concepts of precarity share is the difficulty to identify its members with traditional understandings of class and status. Uncertain labour may fall mainly to low-skill and low-wage workers (Branch and Hanley 2011, 597), but it is also associated with other categories of insecure workers of varying skill-levels, such as skilled 'permatemps' in the food industry (Elcioglu 2010, 123) and artists (Bain and McLean 2013). This is why Standing has referred to the precariat as a 'class in the making' (2011, 7). Labour precarity describes those who are not necessarily part of the 'working class' or the 'proletariat' but instead includes both skilled workers struggling to find secure employment, on the one hand, and lower-skilled and inexperienced workers, on the other hand. Similarly, migrants experiencing 'precarity of place' cross borders with a variety of skill sets, education, and experience. Reinforcing this, it has been noted that migration

> is formed by heterogeneous rather than unitary social networks, possessing distinct personal and social resources, having differential human and social capital, migrating under disparate circumstances, and expressing significant local, regional, political, cultural and religious differences. ... [Migrants thus often have] dissimilar political and economic opportunities and constraints. (D. Smith 1997, 243)

The two types of migrants that Abrahamson identifies – unskilled (who mostly find jobs in the service industry in global cities) and skilled (often those who have chosen exile from a restrictive country) (2004, 49) – offer a useful starting frame for dividing precarious populations, although this division requires further differentiation, because in both migrant and refugee populations, one finds skilled and unskilled populations. For the purposes of this article, it is sufficient to note that precarity of place makes victims of all groups.

One of the implications of this heterogeneity of victims, as it were, is that collective action among mobilisers for both populations (those experiencing labour precarity and precarity of place) will take on forms informed by the motivations and needs of each, a point that has been made in the transnational social movement literature (Tarrow 2005; Brees 2010; Banki 2013b). Labour precarity activists, as noted, have developed significant 'repertoires of contention' to make rights claims about wages, work safety, and employment stability (De Sario 2007). These can be colourful, playful affairs, laden with symbolism, such as the Chainworkers, an Italian activist group, who created San Precario, patron saint of the precariat, and took his effigy on tour throughout the country (Vanni and Tari 2005). Or it may be sombre demands for change. At the University of Sydney, sessional teachers working on short-term contracts set up a temporary, open-air office in the quadrangle to demonstrate the temporary, unresourced nature of their employment (http://www.nteu.org.au/blog/University-of-Sydney-39/tag/Mark%20in). Because migrants who leave countries with economic and political problems are often forced into situations of precarity, engaging in activism in the host country – to better one's rights where one lives, or to the place where one might return – has considerable appeal. But in the case of precarity of place, mobilisation is very much tied up with the political opportunity structures available in the host country (Tilly 1978; Burgerman 2001; Tarrow 2005).

Finally, there is an increasing recognition that social networks can serve to mitigate both labour precarity and precarity of place. Arnold, citing the Institute of Sustainable Development for the South of Vietnam (2009), argues that 'commune networks' of rural-urban migrants from the same area of the countryside facilitate trusting environments, allow people to share skills, experience, and material goods. Further, Legal Aid Centres in Vietnam have recognised the importance of such networks and are now seeking to deliver legal information through these networks (Arnold 2013, 481). Bain and McLean point to artists' collective social spaces in Canada to respond to marginalisation and insecurity (2013). Similarly, one of migrants' greatest protection against removal and detention is the knowledge and assistance of informal community networks (Banki 2006).

Empirical examination

In this section, the situation of migrants from Burma living in Thailand is examined through the lens of precarity of place. This population was chosen deliberately as an attempt to expand the precarity literature to non-citizen populations of the Global South. As will be clear, those vulnerable to deportation and removal from Thailand cannot easily be slotted into the 'undocumented' category. Indeed, they possess a range of statuses and types of documentation, which, while not the subject of this article, has been widely explored in both academic (M. Smith 1997; O'Kane 2007) and policy literature (Caouette and Pack 2002; Human Rights Watch 2004). Whether registered, in possession of refugee identification, or with no documentation whatsoever, migrants from Burma offer a clear example of how labour precarity and precarity of place are uneasily aligned.

Burma, also known as Myanmar, was a military dictatorship for four and a half decades, referred to as a 'pariah' nation by human rights organisations (Human Rights Watch 1999). In 2011, however, the country began a period of political and economic reform. A semi-civilian government, packed with former military serving as ministers, replaced military rule (Human Rights Watch 2012; ICG 2012a). While the next general elections scheduled for 2015 present the possibility of a significant shift to a majority of seats held by the National League for Democracy (NLD), observers contend that obstacles for adequate representation of the range of interests and parties will remain (ICG 2012b). There are heated debates about the genuineness of the reform (Altsean 2012; Lintner 2012; Selth 2012), but scholars concur that the changes are more than cosmetic. While some internal changes are evident, those who left the country due to decades of political and economic instability have not returned to Burma. For these migrants, return to Burma is not yet on the horizon; structural faults of a political, economic, and social nature take a long time to repair even in the most optimistic of scenarios.

Today, there are an estimated 2 million undocumented migrants in Thailand from Burma (UNHCR 2013). This includes 83,033 refugees (TBC 2012, 8) – recognised by the Royal Thai Government (RTG) as 'displaced persons fleeing fighting' (Laungaramsri 2003). While the classic differentiation between migrants and refugees is meant to suggest that the refugees were forced to flee and the remainder moved willingly, in reality, data on the two populations have rarely reflected reality. In Thailand, for example, the figure mentioned above should not suggest that the 83,000 are the only ones in danger nor that the latter are simply seeking economic opportunity; they merely represent the ways in which the RTG and the international humanitarian community try to make sense of those populations experiencing precarity of place.

The refugee and migration literature is replete with discussions about the difficulty of differentiating between the two populations and the significant grey area in which most migrants fall (e.g., Castles 2004). This discussion will not be repeated here, except to say that Burmese migrants in Thailand very much follow the path of *mixed migration*, that is, the heterogeneity of migrant populations makes it impossible to tag an entire group with one set of experiences (e.g., Caouette and Pack 2002). Further, migrants come with mixed motivations that emerge at different temporal and spatial locations. It is thus difficult to identify one group with respect to the other. In this section, both populations are referred to as migrants, except where a differentiation in labelling is necessary.

Just as colonisation and globalisation play a role in creating the conditions that produce precarious work in Thailand (not the subject of this article, but see Arnold (2005) for an excellent summary), so too do they produce precarity of place. Numerous analyses of Burma's dual struggles for independence and autonomy point to its colonial history and a poor transitional period as the source of the country's myriad ethnic rifts, emphasis on military power, and inability to heed the results of its 1990 election (Silverstein 1998; Lang 2002; Fink 2009). These occurrences have led to outflows of Burmese migrants and refugees for decades, first documented by border groups who noted ethnic minority populations fleeing across the border into Thailand as early as 1984 (TBBC 2004). Exacerbating these conditions, and leading to further undocumented migration across the Thai–Burmese border, are globalising forces in Southeast Asia that (1) attract Burmese migrants to work in Thai factories that produce for multinational corporations (Arnold and Bongiovi 2013); and (2) have opened the door for extractive industries to engage in exploitative labour in Burma, thus increasing outflows by those migrants fleeing human rights violations. For example, the Yadana gas pipeline, a project of French Total, US Chevron, Thai PTTEP, together with the Myanmar Oil and Gas Enterprise, has been extensively documented as contributing to widespread human rights violations, including forced labour, and subsequent migration from the country (Earthrights International 2009).

Migrants from Burma in Thailand come from a wide spectrum of social and economic class continua, just as, globally, the labour precariat do. Those with *education and skills* are the smaller group, and primarily comprised (1) refugees from urban areas of Burma with political leanings, who have worked as activists to effect change in Burma over the past 20 years; and (2) rural ethnic minorities from Burma who have been trained as medics or midwives or pharmaceutical assistants in camps or on the Thai–Burmese border by international aid organisations.[3] The former group, with excellent English and polished writing skills, and the recipients of myriad human rights/capacity building trainings (MacLean 2004; Egreteau 2012), are by and large dependent on overseas advocacy organisations to pay their salaries. As has been argued elsewhere, the 'logic of the activist' suggests that those with skills sometimes choose to remain gainfully and meaningfully employed, *even if it means they face precarity of place* (Banki 2013a). Thus relatively well-paid job opportunities that mitigate labour precarity still present fearful challenges to living, residing, and communicating, placing the dangers of precarity of place in stark relief.

The presence of *unskilled* migrants in Thailand working in fishing and seafood processing, garment factories, construction, and as domestic workers is well documented, including both the legal challenges they face and the civil society organisations that have emerged to protect them (Arnold 2005; Pearson et al. 2006). Thailand's immigration policies for migrant workers has been equally well covered in the policy literature; since 1992 the RTG has formed and reformed policies (ad hoc at the start) to manage the inflow of unskilled workers (Chantavanich, Vungsiriphisal, and Laodumrongchai 2007). Since then, registration programmes to formalise the work of migrants, and subsequent criticisms of these programmes, have come one after another. The earliest efforts to register migrants were called 'no more than a yearly relaxation of the immigration law' (Chantavanich, Vungsiriphisal, and Laodumrongchai et al. 2007, 5). The 2003 Memorandum of Understanding (MoU) that the RTG signed with Burma (as well as Laos and Cambodia) to attempt to legalise workers began the process of ensuring both rights and obligations of legal workers, but implementation has been slow because of high registration fees and the presence of corrupt officials and employers (Human Rights

Watch 2010, 72–78). Extensions of the deadlines have done little to quell the concern of potential registrants, who continue to fear threats of deportation (Schearf 2013). Most relevant to this article, it has been noted that this registration process, even for those who completed it, did not assure protection against arrest:

> A registered worker's status always remained *illegal, pending deportation* due to original irregular (i.e. illegal) entry, despite the legal permission to work, and restrictions on freedom of movement were extensively applied and extensive social protection denied to these workers. The cumbersome nature of registration processes has always ensured both workers and employers rely on unregulated brokers to formally register and this significantly results in debt bondage. (Hall 2012, 6) (italics in the original)

Thus registration that workers hoped would resolve their labour precarity appears to be of little use in addressing the issue of precarity of place. The example clearly delineates the difference between labour precarity and precarity of place, and the importance of differentiating between the two. It also supports the contention that there are no 'bright boundaries' between legality and illegality (Goldring, Berinstein, and Bernhard 2009, 256).

The precarity of place experienced by migrants from Burma has a tightrope-like quality, in that migrants are still in residence, but living fearfully, and changing their quotidian behaviour. A July 2013 raid in Chiang Mai, Thailand, for example, instilled fear in migrants from Burma's Shan state in such a way that they stopped going to work and avoided going out publicly. One ethnic Shan migrant noted that 'There is fear among migrants as police check every day on all the streets' (Nyein 2013). The inability to be mobile – to move from one place to another – is exactly what characterises those who experience precarity of place. Because a modicum of safety is only plausible with no movement outside the place of shelter, it is argued here that the element of mobility ought to be vested with great significance. Thus, as an implicit corrective to our earlier definition of precarity, we must also acknowledge that precarity of place occurs when one becomes vulnerable to deportation simply because one moves from one place to another, or is physically in a public space. Mobility, then, is deeply linked with precarity's 'teetering on the edge' quality.

Related to mobility is the ability to mobilise. For Burmese migrants in Thailand, precarity of place and its associated discontent provide the motivation for collective action, but these are likely to vary based on what is permitted by the RTG. Following a crackdown on public events like demonstrations in Thailand in 2000, the coordinator of Altsean-Burma, a civil society organisation seeking to effect change in Burma, noted that activists sought out other means to promote awareness about human rights violations in Burma (such as low-key events, and the production of publications in English, Burmese and ethnic languages) (AFP 2000). More recently, a migrant activist who writes about continuing problems in Burma from inside Thailand noted that while the RTG knows of his organisation's existence, his office could be 'raided at any time'. In order to remain in Thailand, he noted, he changes the location of his office frequently.[4] For this migrant and others who similarly engage in underground activism, precarity of place and precarity of labour intersect, because activism provides employment. Thus, the balancing act of locating safe spaces to live while also operationalising a human rights campaign is a response to both kinds of precarity.

Finally, given that the threat of deportation to Burma is real, and that mobility is restricted for those experiencing precarity of place, it comes as no surprise that networks are critical for Burmese migrants. That migrant networks are an integral response to precarity is intuitive as well as documented, and are often transnational in nature. Support in the form of shelter, food, and other economic resources, as well as the sharing of information on employment or government restrictions, is commonplace among Burmese migrants, as research on Karen refugees demonstrates (Brees 2010; Lee 2012). And scholars have noted that women migrants from Burma, for example, work through social networks to respond to trauma in transformative ways and use transnational advocacy to challenge notions of sovereignty in Southeast Asian nation states (O'Kane 2007). For migrants from Burma who have no documentation, networks allow the unmobile to sit tight when crackdowns arise. Networks cannot mitigate precarity entirely, but they can stop deportation in the short term. As one migrant noted, 'When the police are active, the others from Burma are the only thing that stand (sic) between me and the police. I can't leave my house, so they do it for me.'[5]

This section has grounded with empirical examples the theoretical assertion that labour precarity and 'precarity of place' are related, but separate phenomena. An examination of migrants from Burma in Thailand demonstrates that there is significant overlap between the two types of precarity, that they stem from similar sources (colonialism and neoliberalism), and that they produce similar kinds of differentiated victims, of varying skills levels. While both types of precarity have activist components, those experiencing 'precarity of place' also find themselves limited by host government restrictions that shape the modes and strategies of activist campaigns. And while networks are important for both types of precarity, and share some similar traits (e.g., sharing of information), in the former instance it is used to fight the structures that have imposed precarity, while in the latter, a more direct mitigation of precarity of place is attempted by networks.

This empirical examination has also laid bare the ways in which mobility and precarity are related. For the labour precariat, mobility becomes a tool by which employment can be obtained, a 'mode of subjectification' (Lorey 2010, 3) by which movement is required in order to remain on a teetering tightrope. For Burmese migrants experiencing precarity of place, however, mobility is a luxury that is dependent on the policies and practices of host governments or local officials. This confirms research on the ethnic Karen from Burma in Thailand, where mobility has the potential to unlock refugees from 'spatial incarceration' (Lee 2012, 266). While the relationship between precarity and mobility is intuitive, it is not well theorised. But the examples above make clear that mobility is so crucial to mitigating precarity that it ought to be accorded the same status as political economists give to development. Rather than Sen's suggestion that we consider *development as freedom* (1999), we might well consider *mobility as freedom.*

Conclusion

This theoretical and empirical examination of precarity has offered a spatial and political counter concept to current understandings of precarity. The term 'precarity of place' focuses on the challenges of being migrants and the tightrope quality of noncitizen life. The article draws several parallels between the growing literature on 'labour precarity' and the term offered here, 'precarity of place', including its origins in colonialism and neoliberalism, its nebulous class quality, and social movement responses. While the article focuses on those displaced across national borders, the term may also be theoretically useful for other populations experiencing precarity of place: internal migrants, those displaced by climate change, or those dispossessed of their land. These populations, as well as others, are similarly vulnerable to removal and hence deserve consideration.

There are theoretical and practical implications of a clearly defined understanding of precarity of place. First, the term draws together the related literatures of precarity, forced migration, membership and denizenship, and, at this initial stage, notes not only the human rights implications, but the basic quality of life issues associated with permission to reside. In theoretical terms, this is a valuable nexus that holds rich possibilities for exploration. Second, precarity of place acknowledges that the state's ability to remove individuals from their territory, while an important component of sovereignty, has the potential to develop a 'class' of individuals, whose needs and goals could directly challenge that very sovereign power. Third, the term suggests the importance of mobility as a necessary element of residence.

Further research is of course needed to explore the concept. Two suggestions are offered as a way forward: first, efforts to bring together the conceptual understandings of precarity – the existential, the labour-related, and precarity of place – would be most welcome in providing future theoretical avenues to grasp the difficulties of instability, uncertainly, and insecurity.

Second, further empirical research on migrants and refugees could better delve into questions of removal, *refoulement* (forced return) and detention – those who are subject to it, what the responses have been, and these effects. There are of course studies that have begun this examination, but it is not systematic, and there is limited focus on the Global South. A cross-country or longitudinal study of precarity of place, establishing links between threats of removal and other quality of life issues, would be welcome and highly valuable.

Notes

1. In the political arena, physical absence can be manipulated by those who physically remain. Burman notes that in Montreal the names of arrested and deported activists continue to reverberate and circulate, and be 'memorized by opponents of secret trials and arbitrary state detention powers' (2006, 280).
2. I thank Sharni Chan for the term 'not quite, not yet'.
3. The number of Burmese skilled migrants has decreased rapidly in Thailand in the past few years, for two reasons: first, the process of resettlement, whereby a small group of countries of the Global North have agreed to move and offer citizenship to large portions of the camp refugee population, have drained the camps of their best educated and skilled residents (Banki and Lang, 2008). Second, recent changes in Burma have encouraged some, but not all, of the activists on the border to return to Burma to engage in Burmese civil society directly, from the inside (Naing, 2012).
4. Interview with ethnic Sgaw Karen male refugee activist, May 2013, via Skype.
5. Interview with female Burmese migrant, January 2013, Thailand.

References

Abrahamson, M. 2004. *Global Cities*. New York: Oxford University Press.

AFPAAFP. 2000. *Myanmar's 8/8/88 Uprising To Be Marked Quietly After Rebel Sieges*. Paris: Agence France-Presse.

Altsean, B. 2012. *Not All That Glitters Is Gold: Burma's Facade of Reform*, 1–42. Bangkok: Altsean-Buram.

Arendt, H. [1951]1979. *The Origins of Totalitarianism*. New York: Harvest.

Arnold, D. 2005. "Exploitation in Global Supply Chains: Burmese Migrant Workers in Mae Sot, Thailand." *Journal of Contemporary Asia* 35 (3): 319–340.

Arnold, D. 2013. "Social Margins and Precarious Work in Vietnam." *American Behavioral Scientist* 57 (4): 468–487.

Arnold, D., and J. R. Bongiovi. 2013. "Precarious, Informalizing, and Flexible Work: Transforming Concepts and Understandings." *American Behavioral Scientist* 57 (3): 289–308.

Bain, A., and H. McLean. 2013. "The Artistic Precariat." *Cambridge Journal of Regions, Economy and Society* 6 (1): 93–111.

Banki, S. 2006. "The Triad of Transnationalism, Legal Recognition, and Local Community: Shaping Political Space for the Burmese Refugees in Japan." *Refuge* 23 (2): 36–46.

Banki, S. 2013a. "Urbanity, Precarity, and Homeland Activism: Burmese Migrants in Global Cities." *Moussons* 22 (2): 35–56.

Banki, S. 2013b. "The Paradoxical Power of Precarity: Refugees and Homeland Activism." *Refugee Review* 1 (1): 1–20.

Banki, S., and H. Lang. 2008. "Difficult to Remain: The Impact of Mass Resettlement." *Forced Migration Review* 30: 42–44.

Bauböck, R. 2008. *Stakeholder Citizenship: An Idea Whose Time Has Come?* 1–13. Washington, DC: Migration Policy Institute, Migration Policy Institute.

Brah, A. 2002. "Global Mobilities, Local Predicaments: Globalization and the Critical Imagination." *Feminist Review* 70: 30–45.

Branch, E. H., and C. Hanley. 2011. "Regional Convergence in Low-Wage Work and Earnings, 1970–2000." *Sociological Perspectives* 54 (4): 569–592.

Brees, I. 2010. "Refugees and Transnationalism on the Thai-Burmese Border." *Global Networks-a Journal of Transnational Affairs* 10 (2): 282–299.

Burgerman, S. 2001. *Moral Victories: How Activists Promote Multilateral Action*. Ithaca: Cornell University Press.

Burman, J. 2006. "Absence, "Removal," and Everyday Life in the Diasporic City Antidetention/ Antideportation Activism in Montréal." *Space and Culture* 9 (3): 279–293.

Butler, J. 2006. *Precarious Life: The Powers of Mourning and Violence*. London: Verso Books.

Caouette, T. M., and M. E. Pack. 2002. *Pushing Past the Definitions, Migration From Burma to Thailand*. Washington, DC: Refugees International.

Castles, S. 2004. "The Factors That Make and Unmake Migration Policies." *International Migration Review* 38 (3): 852–885.

Castles, S. 2010. "Understanding Global Migration: A Social Transformation Perspective." *Journal of Ethnic and Migration Studies* 36 (10): 1565–1586.

Chantavanich, S., P. Vungsiriphisal, and S. Laodumrongchai. 2007. *Thailand Policies Towards Migrant Workers From Myanmar*. Bangkok: Asian Research Center for Migration (ARCM), Institute of Asian Studies, Chulalongkorn University.

Chimni, B. S. 1998. "The Geopolitics of Refugee Studies: A View From the South." *Journal of Refugee Studies* 11 (4): 350–374.

Dean, H. 2012. "The Ethical Deficit of the United Kingdom's Proposed Universal Credit: Pimping the Precariat?." *The Political Quarterly* 83 (2): 353–359.

De Sario, B. 2007. "'Precari Su Marte': An Experiment in Activism Against Precarity." *Feminist Review* 87 (1): 21–39.

Doerr, N. 2010. "Politicizing Precarity, Producing Visual Dialogues on Migration: Transnational Public Spaces in Social Movements." *Forum: Qualitative Social Research* 11 (2): 1–27.

Earthrights International. 2009. *Total Impact: The Human Rights, Environmental, and Financial Impacts of Total and Chevron's Yadana Gas Project in Military-Ruled Burma (Myanmar)*, 1–107. Chiang Mai: EarthRights International.

Egreteau, R. 2012. "Burma in Diaspora: A Preliminary Research Note on the Politics of Burmese Diasporic Communities in Asia." *Journal of Current Southeast Asian Affairs* 31 (2): 115–147.

Elcioglu, E. F. 2010. "Producing Precarity: The Temporary Staffing Agency in the Labor Market." *Qualitative Sociology* 33 (2): 117–136.

Fantone, L. 2007. "Precarious Changes: Gender and Generational Politics in Contemporary Italy." *Feminist Review* 87: 5–20.

Fink, C. 2009. *Living Silence in Burma: Surviving Under Military Rule*. London, NY: Zed Books.

Galetto, M., C. Lasala, S. Magaraggia, C. Martucci, E. Onori, and F. Pozzi. 2007. "A Snapshot of Precariousness: Voices, Perspectives, Dialogues." *Feminist Review* 87: 104–112.

Goldring, L., C. Berinstein, and J. K. Bernhard. 2009. "Institutionalizing Precarious Migratory Status in Canada." *Citizenship Studies* 13 (3): 239–265.

Goldring, L., and P. Landolt. 2011. "Caught in the Work–Citizenship Matrix: The Lasting Effects of Precarious Legal Status on Work for Toronto Immigrants." *Globalizations* 8 (3): 325–341.

Hall, A. 2012. *Myanmar Migrant Workers: Briefing and Recommendations*. Bangkok: Mahidol Migration Centre, Institute for Population and Research.

Hammar, T. 1990. *Democracy and the Nation-State: Aliens, Denizens and Citizens in a World of International Migration*. Aldershot: Avebury. Accessed September 12, 2013. http://www.nteu.org.au/blog/University-of-Sydney-39/tag/Mark%20in

Human Rights Watch. 2010. *From the Tiger to the Crocodile: Abuse of Migrant Workers in Thailand*, 1–116. New York: Human Rights Watch.

Human Rights Watch. 1999. *Human Rights Watch World Report 1999: Burma*. New York: Human Rights Watch.

Human Rights Watch. 2004. *Out Of Sight, Out Of Mind: Thai Policy Toward Burmese Refugees*, 1–47. New York: Human Rights Watch.

Human Rights Watch. 2012. *Human Rights Watch World Report 2012: Burma*. New York: Human Rights Watch.

Institute of Sustainable Development for the South of Vietnam. 2009. *Research on Social Networks of Migrant Workers in Bien Hoa Industrial Zone: Study of Dormitory Workers in Long Binh Ward, Bien Hoa City*. Ho Chi Minh City: Institute of Sustainable Development for the South of Vietnam, Centre for Research and Consultancy for Development, Dong Nai Labour Union, Labour Union Legal Aid Centre.

International Crisis Group (ICG). 2012a. *Myanmar: Storm Clouds on the Horizon*, 1–31. Jakarta/Brussels: International Crisis Group (ICG).

International Crisis Group (ICG). 2012b. *Reform in Myanmar: One Year on*, 1–20. Jakarta/Brussels: International Crisis Group (ICG).

Isin, E. F. 2009. "Citizenship in Flux: The Figure of the Activist Citizen." *Subjectivity* 29 (1): 367–388.

Lang, H. 2002. *Fear and Sanctuary: Burmese Refugees in Thailand*. Ithaca, NY: Southeast Asia Program, Cornell University.

Laungaramsri, P. 2003. "Ethnicity and the Politics of Ethnic Classification in Thailand." In *Ethnicity in Asia*, edited by C. Mackerras, 157–173. Hove: Psychology Press.

Lee, C. K., and Y. Kofman. 2012. "The Politics of Precarity Views Beyond the United States." *Work and Occupations* 39 (4): 388–408.

Lee, S. K. 2012. "Scattered but Connected: Karen Refugees' Networking in and Beyond the Thailand-Burma Borderland." *Asian and Pacific Migration Journal* 21 (2): 263.

Lintner, B. 2012. "The Limits of Reform in Myanmar." *Asia Times*, January 18.

Lorey, I. 2010. "Becoming Common: Precarization as Political Constituting." *Eflux Journal* 17. Accessed January 25, 2014. http://www.e-flux.com/journal/becoming-common-precarization-as-political-constituting/

MacLean, K. 2004. "Reconfiguring the Debate on Engagement: Burmese Exiles and the Changing Politics of Aid." *Critical Asian Studies* 36 (3): 323–354.

Mitropoulos, A. 2005. "Precari-Us." *Mute–Culture and Politics After the Net* 1 (29): 88–96.

Naing, S. Y. 2012. "Exiled Dissidents Return to Push for Reform." *The Irrawaddy*, September 6.

Neilson, B., and N. Rossiter. 2005. "From Precarity to Precariousness and Back Again: Labour, Life and Unstable Networks." *The Fibreculture Journal* 5: 70–89.

Nyein, N. 2013. "Thai Police in Chiang Mai Arrest 200 Burmese Migrant Workers." *The Irrawaddy*, July 4.

Nyers, P. 2011. "No One Is Illegal Between City and Nation." *Studies in Social Justice* 4 (2): 127–143.

O'Kane, M. 2007. "Blood, Sweat and Tears: The Political Agency of Women Activist-Refugees of Burma." *Intersections* 15. Accessed January 21, 2014. http://intersections.anu.edu.au/issue15/okane.htm

Pearson, E., S. Punpuing, et al. 2006. *The Mekong Challenge–Underpaid, Overworked, and Overlooked: The Realities of Young Migrant Workers in Thailand*. Bangkok: International Programme on the Elimination of Child Labour, International Labour Organization.

Ross, A. 2008. "The New Geography of Work Power to the Precarious?." *Theory, Culture & Society* 25 (7–8): 31–49.

Sassen, S. 2001. *The Global City: New York, London, Tokyo*. Princeton, NJ: Princeton University Press.

Schearf, D. 2013. "Thailand Extends Migrant Worker Registration Deadline." *VOA*, January 18.

Selth, A. 2012. *Assessing Burma's Reform Program. the Interpreter*. Sydney: Lowy Institute.

Sen, A. 1999. *Development as Freedom*. Oxford: Oxford University Press.
Silove, D., P. Austin, and Z. Steel. 2007. "No Refuge From Terror: The Impact of Detention on the Mental Health of Trauma-Affected Refugees Seeking Asylum in Australia." *Transcultural Psychiatry* 44 (3): 359–393.
Silove, D., and Z. Steel. 1998. *The Mental Health and Well-Being of on-Shore Asylum Seekers in Australia*, 1–35. Sydney: Psychiatric Research and Teaching Unit.
Silverstein, J. 1998. "The Evolution and Salience of Burma's National Culture." In *Burma: Prospects for a Democratic Future*, edited by R Rotberg, 11–32. Washington, DC: Brookings Institution Press.
Smith, D. 1997. *Third World Cities in Global Perspective: The Political Economy of Uneven Urbanization*. Oxford: Oxford University Press.
Smith, M. 1997. "Burma's Ethnic Minorities: A Central or Peripheral Problem in the Regional Context?." In *Burma: The Challenge of Change in a Divided Society*, edited by P. Carey, 97–128. New York: St. Martin's Press.
Soysal, Y. N. 2012. "Citizenship, Immigration, and the European Social Project: Rights and Obligations of Individuality." *British Journal of Sociology* 63 (1): 1–21.
Standing, G. 2011. *The Precariat: The New Dangerous Class*. London: Bloomsbury Academic.
Steel, Z., D. Silove, R. Brooks, S. Momartin, B. Alzuhairi, and I. Susljik. 2006. "Impact of Immigration Detention and Temporary Protection on the Mental Health of Refugees." *British Journal of Psychiatry* 188: 58–64.
Tambini, D. 2001. "Post-National Citizenship." *Ethnic and Racial Studies* 24 (2): 195–217.
Tarrow, S. 2005. *The New Transnational Activism*. Cambridge: Cambridge University Press.
TBC. 2012. *Programme Report July– December 2012*, 1–210. Bangkok: TBC.
TBBC. 2004. *Between Worlds: Twenty Years on the Border*, 1–120. Bangkok: Thailand Burma Border Consortium (TBBC).
Tilly, C. 1978. *From Mobilization to Revolution*. Reading, MA: Addison-Wesley.
UNHCR. 2013. *2014 UNHCR Country Operations Profile – Thailand*. Accessed August 18. http://www.unhcr.org/cgi-bin/texis/vtx/page?page=49e489646
Vanni, I., and M. Tari. 2005. "The Life and Deeds of San Precario, Patron Saint of Precarious Workers and Lives." *Fibreculture* 5: 1–7.
Waite, L. 2009. "A Place and Space for a Critical Geography of Precarity?." *Geography Compass* 3 (1): 412–433.

REPLY

Some thoughts on 'precarity of place': a reply to Banki

Wanda Vrasti

This is a reply to:

Banki, Susan. 2013. "Precarity of place: a complement to the growing precariat literature." *Global Discourse.* 3 (3–4): 450–463. http://dx.doi.org/10.1080/23269995.2014.881139.

Susan Banki's piece introduces the concept 'precarity of place' to stand alongside the more traditional 'labour precarity' and, thus, offers a more nuanced, one might say 'intersectional', understanding of the nature of uncertain life in these times of neoliberal globalization. The greatest problem with the concept of precarity, as Banki already notes, is that it has never been able to provide a satisfactory language for describing life in the core and the periphery of global capital. Are flexible workers in the North, who lack security in the workplace, are hounded by personal debt, and cannot hope to ever acquire all the fabled comforts of the American Dream, *precarious*, whereas workers in informal markets of the Global South or in the new 'satanic mills' of export processing zones are best described as *poor*? What is the difference between the two, conceptually and experientially? The final word (or any word really) on the subject still remains to be written.

Banki does not solve her puzzle. Instead, she directs her attention to a different vector of precarious existence, namely residence and locality, and in so doing reminds us that the developed and the developing world are never quite as distinct as we would like to believe. The marker of the neoliberal phase of capital accumulation is not only a certain measure of globality (or integration) to circuits of production and distribution, but also the coexistence of seemingly contradictory processes, such as neoliberalism and colonialism. Certainly, these are enduring features of capitalism, but in its accelerated phase, we find a sharpening of special asymmetries of power and resources ('uneven development') and a much greater contrast and contact between what we know as the 'developed' and 'developing' parts of the world. Undocumented migrants, driven out by conflict or natural disaster, 'teetering on the edge' of post-industrial economic hubs, unseen and unwanted yet crucial for the reproduction of our standard of life are a case in point: core and periphery can exist inside one another or alongside each other. More than that, capitalism always needs an 'outside', whether it is the colonies, the domestic sphere, the global lumpenproletariat or various forms of dissent to feast upon. There spaces of unregulated exploitation and the sexual and racial division of labour that go along with them are what allow capital to maintain a legal face under the mantle of liberal democracy.

But the interest of Banki is not exactly in how 'capitalism survives through the production of space' (Harvey 2003, 87). Rather, she approaches this subject from the bottom-up. She devises the concept 'precarity of place' to understand how migrants and refugees experience the spatial (and legal, social, economic) asymmetries that make up global capital flows. The distinctive feature of this experience is, as Banki explains it, the 'looming threat' of deportation. 'Precarity of residence does not suggest imminent deportation from a country, but its very real possibility' (1). Banki is very clear about the minimalism of this definition. 'Precarity of place' is not about deportation or detention per se (the threat of vulnerability realized), nor is it about the struggle to obtain rights and residency permits (vulnerability overcome), nor the inability to emigrate or cross borders (vulnerability denied). It is the in-between state of permanent vulnerability, of living in a state of limbo with no papers and no end in sight. 'Precarity of place' occurs in residency, in *physical* residence, to be precise.

As we already know from undocumented migrant struggles in North America and Europe in recent years, to reside in a country without papers (or the correct kind of papers) is a form of social death. It is belonging with all the responsibilities (and more), of making a living, paying bills, respecting the law, learning the language, yet without any of the rights. The result is a complex mesh of invisible borders at all junctions of everyday life. Etienne Balibar (2002) has argued that the border is 'world-configuring', not just territorial, referring to the way in which borders proliferate even inside a sovereign territory to keep out the undocumented, the poor and the delinquent from various state services and infrastructures. Banki's minimalist definition of 'precarity of place' is perfectly attuned to this reality although it approaches it from the other end. 'Vulnerability to removal or deportation from one's physical location' (4) is what bars access to services, housing, jobs and even informal social and solidarity networks, such as those described by Banki in her case study of Burmese migrants in Thailand. Just like in the case of labour precarity, precarity of residence, defined as the fear of deportation, is once again an effective tool of governmentality to reduce the redistributive mandate of the state and instil an ethos of individual responsibility (based on fear).

I salute Banki's seemingly narrow focus. In privileging residency over citizenship, and access to specific services, sites, infrastructures and communities over legal legitimation and inclusion into a polity, as a proper measure of belonging, 'precarity of place' begins to draw the contours of a social justice politics for our time. It is the physical residence of people that gives shape to the world we inhabit. 'It is *physical* residents whose lives prop up the lives of other residents: through legal work, undocumented work, child care, elderly care, and simple, daily interactions' (3), a point made clearly in the French documentary, *We Work Here! We Live Here! We Stay Here*. I believe we can find here the foundations of a transnational ethics of care and hospitality that runs counter to the opportunistic impulse of exploiting spatial asymmetries and the global division of labour in the spirit of capitalism.

Banki does not go that far, but I believe 'precarity of place' could be an extremely useful analytic tool for strengthening a politics of sanctuary. Just like basic income is the favoured conclusion of most conversations about labour precarity (ours not being a world where wage labour is a sufficient measure of worth or mode of redistribution anymore), so sanctuary could be the appropriate response to residential precarity. The activist group No One Is Illegal defines a sanctuary city as 'one where all people, regardless of immigration status, can live without fear of detention or deportation' (http://toronto.nooneisillegal.org/). Same with basic income: it is a wage paid out to all people regardless of their contribution to the productive economy. Just like in a post-Fordist economy based on the debt of creativity, collaboration and communication, it becomes impossible to measure people's contribution to work (what about the work of producing life, for instance?), it is also impossible to measure who contributes to a city and who doesn't. As Banki rightfully recognizes, 'those who live in a place, and thus have a stake in the future of that place' (3) should be, if not properly included or represented, then at least protected by the polity.

My only suggestion is that the concept be further strengthened to better fit an intersectional research agenda by including greater attention to differences of race, gender and class. Further, it could be made into a 'moving' concept, that is, used to understand how different migrants gain access to various services or cross various borders depending on how they are positioned within the intersectional matrix. In other words, 'precarity of place' ought to be understood as a moving scale rather than a fixed marker. A female migrant of colour will have greater difficulties 'residing' in a place, for instance, than a male worker from Eastern Europe, even if both lack necessary documentation. And finally, and relatedly, greater attention could be paid to the sexual division of labour and how this intersects with and reinforces the global division of labour. Patriarchy and colonialism are related parts of the hidden foundation of capitalist civilization and 'precarity of place' phenomena are bound to reflect that.

References

Balibar, Etienne. 2002. *"What Is a Border?" Politics and the Other Scene*, 75–86. London: Verso.
Harvey, David. 2003. *The New Imperialism*. Oxford: Oxford University Press.

RESEARCH ARTICLE

Precarious work, entrepreneurial mindset and sense of place: female strategies in insecure labour markets

Hanna-Mari Ikonen

School of Social Sciences and Humanities, University of Tampere, Tampere, Finland

This article discusses the uncertainty of working life by providing a viewpoint of one individual's experience of it. The article argues that entrepreneurship and employment are forms of income that are not separate from each other; instead, in precarious labour markets, individuals can alternate between the two. An entrepreneurial mindset and practices are required from the self-employed and employees alike, but neither form of livelihood ensures a permanent income. Though in different ways, the process of precariatisation touches many groups of people, and the varying alternatives for navigating this situation are deconstructed here. The analysis discusses how surviving precarious labour markets and uncertain income requires a lot of endurance and self-governance as illustrated by an in-depth interview with a woman who lives in a remote area. The analysis also proves that the opportunity to remain in a place of residence and establish a sense of belonging has a significant impact on an individual's ability to experience everyday pleasure and permanence, especially when everything else around them is changing in ways over which they have little control.

Introduction

Unpredictability and inconstancy are characteristic of contemporary labour markets. This precarious situation affects not only work but also other areas of life. As old institutions are losing their ability to provide stability, reliability and predictability, and as companies outsource their operations and agency work increases, individuals are left to their own devices. In such situations, everyone is supposed to assume an entrepreneurial attitude and take care of their employability themselves. One way out is to create their own work as entrepreneurs. Entrepreneurship is not, however, a simple or a permanent solution for employment, as is demonstrated in this article.

Another alternative for finding work in a world of changing work trajectories is relocation. However, migration is not an option for everybody; in fact staying put may be an important way of tolerating uncertainty. Therefore, this article explores the question of 'placeness'. Based on previous studies, it is evident that a sense of place influences the choices people make; a place is a limitation but it also provides resources, emotional or other (Eyles 1985; Heikkilä 2011; Ikonen 2008, 2012; McDowell 1999; Relph 1986; Tolonen 2005; Tuan 1977; Varis 2005). However, the emotionally laden meaning of place has not been significantly addressed in studies on employment and precarity. Actually, placeness and settling down have been seen as opposite conditions to an ideal figure of the current spirit of capitalism (Boltanski and Chiapello 2007). In addition to the concept of a sense of place, I work with the concept of an entrepreneurial mindset, which, in turn, is deduced from critical discussions on working life research that highlights individuality, potentiality, agility, flexibility and readiness to steer employment more than industriousness, loyalty and formal qualifications (Adkins 2008; Adkins and Jokinen 2008; Atkinson 2010; Boltanski and Chiapello 2007; du Gay 1996; Jokinen et al. 2011; Mäkinen 2012; Ross 2009; Standing 2011; Veijola and Jokinen 2008; Vähämäki 2009).

Neoliberal time takes various forms. For example, Will Atkinson (2010) points out that even though de-standardisation of careers and several job shifts really have taken place, they are remarkably driven along class tracks. In Atkinson's study on worker reflexivity, those who were 'dominant', i.e., had economic and cultural capital, were more capable of perceiving their changed work trajectories as an opportunity to downshift for a while, start something totally new or concentrate on something they had always wanted to do. Even the 'dominated' told about negotiating and taking active decisions – since they were familiar with the reflexivity discourse – but social mobility was scarce as the class-related material pressures hindered their options (Ibid.). Insecurity, precarity and in-work poverty were also examined by Jeremy Morris (2012), who studied how Russian male industrial workers see permanent, 'normative' employment as insecure. In a post-Soviet Russian context, a lack of control over work processes and overemphasised self-regulation make the work feel precarious, while compensatory social assets can be found in blue-collar networks of solidarity. These networks provide class-rooted alternatives to wage labour, such as opportunities for entrepreneurialism in the lay sense of the term, other informal jobs and, importantly, a shared feeling of self-dignity. However, the social capital of these networks remains marginal, which indicates the salience of class in debates about precarity (Ibid.).

Equipped with these notions on the new economy, I focus on the porous line between wage work and entrepreneurship, as well as on variety in entrepreneurship, which I think needs deconstruction. Even in the contemporary era of self-entrepreneurialism, emphasis must be put on class position, gender and geographical place, as these aspects, among many others, affect self-employment – or lack of it. My case study in particular is intended to add to the discussion about the interface between place and entrepreneurship in precarious times. In this article, I address the question of what it's like to inhabit the no-man's land between employment and entrepreneurship in a specific spatial context and illustrate it using a tangible interview example. I seek strategies for concretely managing and mentally tolerating the uncertainty of this paradoxical situation and provide an understanding of the social and spatial context behind those strategies. The empirical data for this article consists of one interview, which is part of a more extensive collection that includes a survey and interviews regarding the work and everyday life of female entrepreneurs in rural areas in Finland (Ikonen 2008, 2012). This particular interview gives a voice to a divorced mother of two children, who lives in a remote rural area and balances between being an entrepreneurial cobbler and working part-time in shoe sales. Of course, there is not one definitive experience of the precarious worker and people have different capabilities to manage uncertainty. It is also difficult to predict the movements of neoliberal labour markets and globally affected local economies. Therefore, the analysis shows common phenomena in work and the economy in a context.

The article continues by reviewing the entrepreneurial ethos with the core idea that entrepreneurship is not separate from employment or other kinds of livelihoods. The concept of an entrepreneurial mindset describes their more and more common junctions. One objective is to open the discussion on the connections between entrepreneurship and employment in the rapidly changing demands of working life. Then, the emotionally laden sense of 'placeness' and the regional context of a remote area in Finland are discussed. Thereafter I introduce the interview data. When analysing it, I discuss the paradoxical means of controlling the uncertainty of work, and expand upon the significance that place of residence has in the uncertain situation. Finally, I conclude with a number of uncertainties and ways of managing them in the state of being between wage work and entrepreneurship, and consider opportunities and threats from a wider working-life perspective.

Demand for an entrepreneurial mindset and the precarious entrepreneur

Regarding contemporary working life, the article makes two claims: (1) maintaining a strict divide between wage-work and entrepreneurship prevents us from seeing the reality of working life, and (2) supposing entrepreneurs to be a certain kind of group and not deconstructing that group prevent us from seeing the real accomplishments of entrepreneurial activities. Therefore, we begin by trying to understand the societal contexts for the entrepreneurial mindset and the gnawing insecurity that comes with it.

The ideological push towards entrepreneurialism has been continuing for quite some time. The demands for assuming an entrepreneurial mindset come from the ideology of neoliberalism, or the related concepts of advanced liberalism, turbo capitalism, knowing capitalism and the new spirit of capitalism (on the grouping of these terms, see du Gay and Morgan 2013, 2). The rationalities these modes of capitalism provide have taken a hold of governments, institutions and organisations, which now echo the salience of entrepreneurship, marketisation and choice (Ibid.). For example, Tony Watson (2009) states that neoliberal arguments about an entrepreneurial culture permeated the United Kingdom in the 1990s, when it became widely accepted that entrepreneurial values as such were important and that they made attaining added value and speeding up economic growth possible (also du Gay 1996; Obgor 2000). Even in Finland, entrepreneurialism is widely seen as the saviour of the post-capitalist country – as an unavoidable development when the state cannot or does not want to look after its citizens' welfare as it used to under free global competition. Entrepreneurial rhetoric has even found its way into tangible political measures.

There seems to be no end in sight for the pervasive spirit of entrepreneurialism. Citizens are encouraged to be active and take responsibility. For example, there is pervasive use of the term 'lifelong learning', which refers to a self-reflexive and proactive attitude that should empower a person in the neoliberal labour market (but there is little discussion of how this is actually not equally accessible or beneficial to everybody, see Atkinson 2010). The demands are not necessarily put forth directly; instead people internalise control, responsibility and internal entrepreneurship without their autonomy being formally interfered with (Miller and Rose 2008). Other researchers have talked about these elements in terms of enterprising self (Rose 1992) and self-subordination (Vähämäki 2009).[1] Individuals are given responsibility for issues and changes they can hardly influence. In this context, the need to tolerate and manage uncertainty applies to virtually all forms of work, even though it is traditionally more familiar to small business owners.

This leads to the entire working life and all forms of work becoming imbued with the ideology of entrepreneurialism, which, however, proves to be very special and exclusive. Hans Pongratz and Günter Voss (2003) use the term 'employee-entrepreneur' or *entreployee* (in German *Arbeitskraftunternehmer*) to describe the employee who manages himself or herself in an entrepreneurial manner. The employee takes responsibility for matters that used to be the employer's obligation. He or she manages his or her working time, the contents and quality of his or her work and networks, independent of time and place. Nevertheless, these requirements and practices do not directly lead to the independence traditionally associated with entrepreneurship: the company's profit objectives ultimately set the conditions.

Undoubtedly, there are positive sides to the formation of the character of an entreployee, such as changing from a passive worker into an actor who creates opportunities for himself or herself and who can utilise these acquired skills when working for other employers. An individual who can commercialise and market his or her skills can take advantage of the new labour markets (Ibid, 6–8). The problem is that these skills and jobs are only available to a limited group of people with certain classed capital, and similar efforts do not create the same results for everyone (Peltokoski 2012; Standing 2011).

Neither entrepreneurship nor an entrepreneurial attitude as such are totally alien to the working classes, less privileged or dominated (whichever term we use). Quite the opposite, in fact: for Finnish rural yeoman, for instance, making a living has required the adoption of a hard-working, opportunistic attitude, and craftspeople have independently controlled their work processes from beginning to end as well. What is new is that more and more individuals end up as entrepreneurs suddenly, involuntarily, temporarily and due to a lack of other possibilities. Accordingly, people in various situations with various backgrounds may find themselves as entrepreneurs. That is why 'groups of precarious workers, consisting of many subjectivities, *precarious people*, offer a more comprehensive repertoire of lives than the currently available majority group's models, such as employee/entrepreneur/student' (Meriläinen 2011, 160). Both the lowest end of the service economy (where people carry out routine tasks) and the highest end (which includes the creative classes of the knowledge-intensive economy) may meet with the radical uncertainty about the future, transience of employment contracts and uncertainty regarding social security benefits. Because of their different background capitals, they are differently equipped to treat their changed trajectories (Atkinson 2010), but the system of capitalist exploitation touches them all. Nevertheless, precariousness is especially a threat on the lower levels of the labour division hierarchy, where flexibility of working life means discontinuous incomes and poverty (Peltokoski 2012, 98).

Fixed-term employment and changing work trajectories do not necessarily lead to precarity and a feeling of uncertainty. Likewise, being precarious does not automatically lead to becoming an entrepreneur. However, for some, when the only predictable things are uncertainty and change, the wish to manage one's own life leads to viewing self-employment as an attractive option (Ross 2009, 6). Yet, self-employed people have rarely been seen to have something in common with precarious workers, which means that their experiences have largely been overlooked when studying uncertainty and temporariness. At least in Finland, the institutionalised working life research has so far focussed on normative employment and given less attention to the emerging issues in the working life. Therefore it is time to have a look at the differentiated processes, practices and motives of entrepreneurship.

In relation to class, this article defines entrepreneurship as a socially stratified category that has to be deconstructed, in contrast to its automatic social construction as middle class.[2] Nowadays, the entrepreneurial status does not dictate the entrepreneur's social class, which would include economic opportunities, education, tastes and consumption behaviour. The status of entrepreneurship changes in a precarious world where everyone should possess an entrepreneurial attitude, and when people become entrepreneurs as a result of outsourcing and being encouraged to become freelancers. Thus, the backgrounds, tastes and other indicators of social class become even more mixed among the category of entrepreneurs.

Connecting a sense of place and a remote place

Research often overlooks the characteristics of local labour markets, not to mention the fact that people do not always look for work in large cities, even though they may be willing to commute dozens of kilometres in their local area. Job opportunities and requirements set for employees are, in other words, coloured by the place in which they live (McDowell 2009; Tolonen 2005; Varis 2005). How does a place shape the range of jobs and an individual's choices then? Theoretically, according to Doreen Massey (1994), for example, places are constellations of certain physical characteristics, history, economy and culture and are therefore all different. However, places are not closed entities and do not have endogenous, essential identity; places are unique exactly because of mutual relations with other places. A global economy and its logics build places. There is inequality in how suitable and attractive a particular place is seen for economic activity, and inequality in terms of various indicators of social well-being (Ibid., 50–51). Different social groups and individuals are positioned in very distinct ways in relation to flows of capitalist production: some people initiate movement, others are more imprisoned by it (see Skeggs 1997, 2004 about the necessity of staying put and how it is connected to class in her argumentation). Thus, categories such as class, gender and ethnicity define a person's experience of a place, but in a very complicated way.

The feelings of insecurity and unsettledness in the middle of a hastened capitalist flux can lead individuals to resist changes to the peace and quiet of a certain locality that provides them with a strong sense of place. Massey (1994, 146–173) warns against seeing places as romanticised and static (and maintained as such by women's labour) as it sometimes has been seen. However, I argue here that being strongly connected to a place can be empowering. In accordance with what Massey ponders, I suggest that people's feelings about a place are a result of direct or indirect interacting with other people who see that place in a different way. Similarly, in interaction with other places – bigger, far away or in other ways different – one can attain an enhanced feeling of placeness. Empowered by this extroverted, conscious sense of place, one is equipped to meet unavoidable changes and can successfully respond to rather than deny them.

To come closer to the material context of this study on work and entrepreneurship in a place, it is worth noting that regional development acts in Finland rest largely on the hope of entrepreneurship. When structural problems of remote areas (such as the decrease of agriculture and basic industry and demographic changes towards the majority of elderly people) have continued for a long time and governmental safety nets have been loosened, the remaining people of working age (as well as potential new residents) are encouraged to acquire a livelihood as entrepreneurs.[3] Ideally, an individual's sense of place and regional development acts are in harmony; in any case both ways of imagining the place exist simultaneously.

Data and method

Entrepreneurs and employees are often studied at only one moment in time, which can make the respondent's entrepreneurship or employment seem more stable than it actually is. The respondent interviewed for this article was followed over a longer period of time. The analysis is initially based on the interview conducted in 2009. In addition, the thoughts expressed by the same respondent in a previous interview seven years earlier provide a backdrop for the analysis. The interview is further complemented by data from a survey that targeted 132 women entrepreneurs who work in the rural Northern Karelia and Tampere regions of Finland. Of this data, 18 interviews with women entrepreneurs were selected to provide a background for this article. Also included are the data from later follow-up interviews with the same women (with the exception of two who could not be contacted). Based on these previous survey data and interviews, I was aware of the respondents' backgrounds, life situations, ideas concerning their place of residence and experiences as entrepreneurs. The follow-up interviews focused on updating the information and discussing the overall changes. The interviews covered three wider themes applied to each respondent's situation at the time of the interview: the women's work situation and whether it was entrepreneurship or another activity; their relationship with their place of residence and the practices related to this; and questions pertaining to gender, for example, the significance of gender in work-related practices and a family's internal way of working.

The woman who was selected as the subject of this article is an example of the uncertainty of the times and of individual careers, and of how individuals try to manage the uncertainties and what potential futures they hope to gain for themselves. Her first interview provided a background; with this interview I show how employment is not permanent. The respondent shares the situation of the other interviewed women entrepreneurs, in that she has made work-related decisions and choices based on what is possible in her place of residence and what she considers to be the best for her family. Some other respondents, too, are living between entrepreneurship and other forms of earning a living.

I review the entrepreneur's interview specifically from the perspective of experiencing change, its impacts and management. Experience and management of one's own life path and setting its past, present and future in a societal narrative context can be viewed with narrativity (e.g. Herman 2009). Catherine Kohler Riessman (2001) summarises that narratives construct people's identity, make experiences comprehensible and illuminate the intersection of biography, history and society. At the same time, the narrative and the narrator are born again (and again) when the story is told. According to Paul Ricoeur (1991), narratives weave together heterogeneous elements in a story and individual stories into wider social narratives. Therefore, the narrative analysis method is suitable for an interview that evaluates one's own present state in relation to the past and future working life. My interviews did not essentially aim to tell stories; the narrative is only a method of thinking that steers the analysis. I draw attention to what the respondent chooses to say about her situation and how she understands her opportunities and herself as an actor. Nevertheless, in this article I focus only on certain themes and not much on the way the narrative is expressed. Steered by my research questions, I highlight the theme of work-related uncertainty.

In the cobbler's shoes

The 45-year-old female respondent used to run a cobbler's shop. The business is currently on a hiatus and she works part-time elsewhere. The reason for the pause in business is that she was taken ill due to physical exhaustion caused by the intensive pace of work, which finally manifested itself as physical pain in the hands and made her unable to work. She divorced a few years earlier. One of her children has moved out and is studying elsewhere, and the other one still lives at home and attends comprehensive school. She has not considered and does not want to consider moving away from the area, even though suitable jobs are hard to find where she currently lives. The family home is very important to her: it was built by her grandfather and she grew up in it. Today, and in the near future, she wants her children to have a place to which they always feel they can return. In the future, the children may be able to use the house as their home or as a summer cottage, and it may also be possible to work from there again as an entrepreneur.

Since putting her business operations on hold, the respondent has worked in various positions in the service industry, including in a grill café and as a cook at a service station. At the time of the interview, she was employed part-time in a shoe shop. The respondent has made tentative plans to start the business again by making leather products and selling them during the Christmas season. If this were to happen, she would have to put strict limits on her work by not necessarily accepting all orders and not imposing too strict deadlines on herself. She enjoyed all elements of working as a cobbler and managing the overall operations independently, but wished the bigger picture had been more controllable. Getting supplies, designing the products, handling customer service and making the products should all fit into a normal working day and generate enough income, but combining the running of the business in all its elements with life's other demands was difficult. This is often an issue for female entrepreneurs in particular.

Culmination of uncertainty and the struggle of control

Leaving entrepreneurship behind, moving to a new situation, evaluating the consequences of these actions and contemplating the future dominate the follow-up interview. The move away from entrepreneurship was not a carefully considered, final and fully satisfactory decision. This is what the respondent says about her current situation and how she found herself in it:

> R: Well it [pausing the business] happened because I got this sudden illness first, and they thought it was something caused by work stress. Then they took some more tests and it wasn't that after all. And then I got the long sick leave. And then, to give it a go, I tried shoe repairs, and it just didn't work anymore, my body couldn't take it anymore, full-time.
>
> Q: Yes.
>
> R: So then I started applying for other jobs and that's the road I'm still on. So I still have it [the business], because I didn't want to close it down completely or put it away, perhaps one day I can still get back to it or at least work somewhere else part-time and then on my own part-time. To make a full day of it.
>
> Q: Yes. Where do you work now?
>
> R: Well now I work at the shoe shop.

Intensive schedules and long days already emerged as themes in the first interview; at the time the respondent did not talk about them as her own negative experiences but mentioned comments from other people. The respondent says that her current situation is temporary, although she does not know how long it will last and in what format she can put her plans into action in the future. She evaluates her options spontaneously. The words 'being on that road still' describe the temporariness, sense of being side-tracked and the idea that in some sense she is expecting to arrive. She has taken short-term jobs in the immediate past and will perhaps do so in the near future, but 'now' her job is to be a sales assistant in a shoe shop. Her thoughts and identity are still those of a cobbler entrepreneur's, because that was work she enjoyed. She cannot stay in the present, because her current job is temporary. It is this very precariousness that leads to the compulsion of forecasting the future, but as unpredictability is inherent in the future, the situation is fragile and continuously prone to unexpected changes. Tolerating uncertainty and planning the future must take place concurrently.

In the following excerpt, the respondent assesses what it's like to be an employee as opposed to an entrepreneur:

> R: Otherwise I really like it: all the stress that comes with your own business is gone, working the long hours and never being able to take any time off or anything, so this is luxury now. But being part-time, financially and economically it's a complete disaster . . . But then mentally and otherwise, it's good, and you notice that the professional . . . the know-how is really good there too.

She thinks it is positive that she is able to utilise her previously acquired skills in the current job (cf. Standing 2011, 121–124). Being able to hold on to her professional identity gives her a feeling of control and of having previously achieved something important, even though the emphasis on the current job's easiness hints at underused capacity. The current situation highlights the fact that the part-time sales assistant job does not get her enough money. As a crafts entrepreneur, she had a low income but there was still the opportunity to generate more income through the business. In a labour-intensive field, this meant long and stressful days, which weighed heavily on her health and were compounded by all of the other non-work-related responsibilities of everyday life. Questions pertaining to economic opportunities limit her choices and the available options. As setting up the cobbler business was a solution to the challenges of trying to balance difficult work hours with childcare, it seems that she has gone from one paradox to another, and it does not seem that there are many means with which to manage the situation. Even though she is an active agent in her own life, as called for by the demands of the current labour market, being able to achieve this requires her to continuously find a balance between a living wage, well-being and the limits of endurance.

The paradox of easy work

When asked whether the respondent would prefer entrepreneurship or employment in an ideal situation, she explains what would be her terms for choosing entrepreneurship. It is interesting to note the type of employment against which she compares entrepreneurship. A job that is realistic would be working-class employment that requires relatively few skills, is poorly paid and not very challenging (cf. Atkinson 2010; Peltokoski 2012, 98). It is easy compared to middle-class jobs that are knowledge-intensive and permeate across time and place, and it is also easy compared to self-employment. Considering the respondent's background, her current employment is unusually independent (cf. Morris 2012). The supervision is not continuous and visible. This can make even a job that is too easy more likeable. There are also limits to the job's independence and entrepreneurialism, which means that she is not expected to perform tasks that create feelings of inadequacy and uncontrollability (as more demanding employment or entrepreneurship could do).

> Q: [...] if you could choose completely freely, in an ideal situation, would you rather be self-employed or work for someone else?
>
> R: I'd be self-employed, run the cobbler's shop, no doubt about it. Yes I would. I mean if I knew that I could do it in the eight hours, to make it work, the system, and it would bring in enough money to live on without having to worry all the time about whether there will be

enough money and also the clients would really come and get their stuff and pay for them on time. So yes, absolutely, I would choose it. Yes.

Q: Yes.

R: But this is easy now, I've seen both sides, working for someone else, I've done that my whole life, and then had my own shop and my husband has always had his own business. I've seen the ups and the downs, the good and the bad, everything. So, well, it's so easy to work for someone else, you just take care of your own hours and do your job well and get to have your holiday. It's so easy. It's easy in that sense. But then running your own business, it's the independence, that's my thing. But that's why I like working in the shoe shop, because my employer and the shoe factory are in the [neighbouring town], they have another shop there, and I take care of this one on my own and work the sales alone. So I am independent here, too. So in that sense to me being able to work independently is also a good form of being sort of an entrepreneur.

Independence is on the one hand an absolute requirement – employees should work like an entreployee who is responsible for his or her self, own work and employment – and on the other hand a distant dream: do they trust me enough to let me do things my way? Even apparent independence is not always allowed. Linda McDowell (2009) states that people in the growing area of service work, home care and nursing are lacking, the daily, immediate supervision. It is the very independence of work that motivates the employees, because a lack of strict control is not usual in lower-income working-class jobs. Independence is, of course, to some extent illusory; even a shoe shop has to be run according to executive orders.

What is thought to be a temporary and easy part-time job enables a more versatile everyday life than being self-employed and trying to continuously scrape together a living. On the one hand, she puts herself in the intentional, middle-class *downshifter's* position where people slow down and withdraw from career competition (e.g., Chhetri, Stimson, and Western 2009; Ikonen 2010). On the other hand, she speaks with an apologetic tone because the phase with the easy job is thought to be abnormal. She is always ready to take on more demanding work as soon as she feels well enough. In reality, her days are filled with things to do, and she admits to being afraid of being stuck. In the background is the concern over job fitness; she says she knows people who no longer want to go to work after not having to do it every morning. The respondent thinks it is self-evident that she has to take responsibility for always being employable. I interpret this as entailing an internalised concept of an ideal Finnish citizen, worker and rural resident, and an industrious, self-sacrificing woman and middle-class ideal of femininity in the vein of Beverly Skeggs (2004), against which the working-class woman is compared. Striving towards a middle-class ideal transforms into a form of internalised control (Lahikainen and Mäkinen 2012).

The paradox of loyalty

The interview involves lots of orientation towards the future because the current situation is known to be temporary. When talking about her tangible plans for the future, the respondent uses rhetoric that emphasises loyalty.

Q: What are your plans now?

R: Well if they ask me to work more in the autumn, then of course I'll do it because I've promised I would.

She intends to help during the summer holiday season and afterwards in the shoe shop, even though actual contracts have not been made. The employee is loyal to the employer. This attitude is at odds with the flexible knowledge workers' orientation towards individual careers due to organisations treating them as disposable workers (Gherardi and Murgia 2013), but which is also contrary to the working-class rebel against employers who do not any more provide reliability they used to (Morris 2012). The interviewee's speech takes the perspective of a loyal helper: she has even recently been substituting for other employees in the job she had prior to working in the shoe shop, so that the other employees 'could take their holidays'. Even when the business was on a hiatus and she was working in other jobs, she still expressed kindness and kept promises: she supervised a man's traineeship in her shop so that 'we [sic] were able to finish his course properly'.

To some degree, being loyal is worthwhile to her because in her insecure but easy wage work, there is the opportunity to separate work and leisure. Of course, her loyalty does not guarantee reciprocal loyalty. It is typical of women to be flexible, adjustable and go the extra mile for their clients. Loyalty and thinking of others can lead to small work opportunities that can help with income, but they can become a drain and prevent one from taking significant steps to improving one's own situation.

The interviewee recognised her own entrepreneurial style even in the first interview conducted at the beginning of the 2000s. I called the narrative about it an interpretation repertoire of doing well, which included being committed and trustworthy. At the time she was motivated by her enthusiasm, new skills and emerging professional pride and thought that she could make it without taking any time off. Later the job turned into a struggle in terms of keeping up with deadlines she had loyally promised, coping and making a living. Now she recognises with more clarity where she went wrong. She should have created time and space for herself, closed to the customers, not been so hard on herself and not so proud of being able to serve everyone. One should not give everything of oneself because thorough craftsmanship is no longer rewarded, as is deduced for example by Sennett (2006) and Vähämäki (2009). Maintaining boundaries, rather than overlapping functions, could be the key to job fitness (Jokinen 2010, 50).

Permanence provided by place in the midst of uncertainty

Characteristics of place (restrictions, an outsider could say) combined with her family situation, influenced the decision to set up a business. The entrepreneur trained herself, changed careers and became an entrepreneur in order to be able to take care of her children with more flexibility than when taking them to two different day-care centres at times dictated to her and set in advance. There are limited day-care facilities within a convenient distance in rural areas if your working hours are different from normal office hours. This made the respondent's whole life seem like one big childminding arrangement. She also hoped to be able to take care of the maintenance work and repairs required for the terraced house. These were her responsibilities even before the divorce because her husband spent weekdays away. Now the situation has changed in terms of her 'charges', but she still signifies the combination of working part-time and being a mother in a positive way. She was unable to control her working pace as an entrepreneur, now that she is an employee she has more time for the children. She also has more time to dedicate to the repairs and maintenance of the old house than she did when working from home. Place and motherhood go hand-in-hand throughout the interview and quite evidently throughout the years: both affect the practices of entrepreneurship.

Both the first and the second interviews reveal that work is subordinate to remaining in her place of residence. Staying put is not interpreted in any way as being forced.[4] The will to stay in the place of residence has also been noted in the interviews conducted for the project on casualisation and precariousness in Northern Karelia. In them, the respondents even feel guilty for not being willing to relocate to southern Finland (Heikkilä 2011, 45). They worry about being active enough because they are unwilling to leave, but at the same time they feel that place gives them a sense of permanence that work does not provide. Staying put is often a question of necessity, claims Skeggs (1997, 2004), among others: those with the best incomes can leave and move around, whereas the working classes must stay put. In the Finnish rural context, combined with gender aspects, this holds true. For rural men in particular, staying put is connected with a misery of sorts, especially for an unmarried adult male who lives with his parents. Statistics prove that men stay and women leave (Rural Development Programme 2007, 5), and men in remote areas have fewer qualifications and less social mobility than women who move (in Ireland: NíLaoire 2001). In contrast, from a global perspective, in order to avoid becoming disadvantaged some people are forced to leave their homes and move, for example by seeking work in cities or abroad (such as Estonian construction workers in Finland). Thus, place and spatiality are indirect ways of talking about social classes: where we are from, where we live and whether we leave or stay define us (Keith and Pile 1993; Tolonen 2005).

The cobbler does not want to be among those who leave. She has wanted to stay in her home 'ever since she was small', and there is 'no way she is leaving'. Emotional attachment to place is a human emotion for which there is not necessarily a rational explanation, except that 'it must be something in the water' (Eyles 1985, 126). Edward Relph (1986) writes about an authentic attitude to place. He divides this attitude into a conscious and unconscious sense of place. The unconscious feeling of being inside and belonging is widely present in my interviews. For example, the cobbler talks about place as 'her own little world' and uses this metaphor to make a distinction from the world outside where her entrepreneur husband worked. She talks about the husband being out and about several times by saying, for example, that her 'husband works in the outside world all week'. She voluntarily limits her 'own world' to the size of her house: an area that is emotionally significant.

An explanation of the significance of place can be sought from the perspective of assets and resources: the respondent describes her choice to stay put as a resource. She has been able to, not forced to, stay in her childhood home and still be an active agent in her life as a worker and a mother. She can take care of the house on her own. Her own house is an achievement, which she wishes to underline perhaps as a sign of being proper and respectable (Skeggs 1997) because 'a family in the little cottage is not a problem family' according to Finnish housing rhetoric (Uimonen 2008, 128). The house is also a tangible resource because it has previously offered, and perhaps will offer again, the premises for practising a livelihood.

Conclusions and discussion: network of uncertainties and control

Uncertainty in the respondent in the state of 'in-betweenness' is caused by the paradox that there is either too much work (when self-employed) or too little work (as an employee at the shoe shop) to ensure a sufficient livelihood, because work is available in short, temporary patches. If she were to continue as an entrepreneur, she would have to think about how to prevent the entrepreneurship from depleting her strength and health. It is possible that she now knows her limits better and does not slavishly follow requirements set by others or by her for herself. This skill could give a sense of being in control in uncertainty. Likewise, the respondent valuing her professional skills and liking her job generates a feeling of being in control. The wage work is also easy because at the end of the day you can leave it behind. Control strategies include the knowledge of being able to live alone in the beloved house.

The former cobbler sees potential to improve her income and sustain survival strategies in that the children are about to leave the nest (which can give her the strength to relaunch entrepreneurship), and because the extension of employment has been promised for the summer holidays. It is possible that she will work in one short, temporary job after another, which to the respondent is a better alternative than having no work at all. She is loyal to accepting the short, temporary contracts in a flexible manner. On the one hand, she refuses to see the challenges caused by the place and local economy, but on the other hand she does not have to, since there seems to be enough work as a cobbler. It is nevertheless possible that the remote area where she lives will fall further into economic decline, in which case there would be fewer employment opportunities available. The demand for Finnish-made shoes may further decline and people may need or want fewer repairs in a disposable culture. Therefore, considering the respondent's work and education history, the outlook for employment or entrepreneurship opportunities may not, after all, be very good, and the process of precariatisation may continue.

Illustrated by the respondent's narration, I have tried to give a shape to the changes in the labour markets, local economies and personal valuations that have a critical effect on the living options available to and chosen by individuals. The same problems and attempts at control can be widely perceived in working life as the process of precariatisation touches several groups of people. Still, the precariat is yet a class-in-the-making (Standing 2011, 7), sharing some characteristics of other classes and not yet a distinctive socio-economic group. Exactly this lack of group identity is an obstacle for controlled change on a wider scale because only a larger group of people, the crowd, could generate a change away from the Fordist society's practices and vocabulary (which no longer reflect the working life) (Jakonen, Peltokoski, and Virtanen 2006; Peltokoski 2012; Standing 2011). As an indication of the lacking group identity, the former cobbler does not bring her uncertain work situation into the political agenda. She does not have a forum in her life where she could see the experience of precarious work to be a shared one – instead the suffering is construed as an individual problem (Skeggs 2004, 59). The solutions are to be found individually.

As a result of the entrepreneurial mindset demonstrated both in employment and in entrepreneurship, the respondent has also experienced the negative consequences of excessive dedication: the time pressures and the stress. As young employees who work in glamorous fields that require specialised skills are the ones who can benefit the most from the entreployee attitude, this former cobbler is mainly a part of the less-successful but ever-growing group of people for whose work there is mainly short-term use without guarantees of the future (Pongratz and Voss 2003, 12–14; also Atkinson 2010). Because incomes are low – or, correspondingly, there is too much work to do – in this sense she reminds us of the working poor (Ehrenreich 2001; McDowell 2009; Standing 2011). These people do not make a sufficient living, even though they are active and have skills and education, because they cannot get the jobs that pay well enough or because there are long gaps between their contracts. They live mainly in large cities where the cost of living is high, but even in remote areas, when the jobs from the industry, farming and the public sector are cut, the amount of income generated from practising a business, part-time jobs or social benefits remains so low that it provides a limited existence. The cost of living can be low in remote areas, but moving about is expensive because it takes time and money to travel in search of the disappearing services and jobs. Many choose to move away, even though in expensive cities they can only access living conditions that they feel are inferior. The respondent, however, is one of those who, even rebelliously, want to retain one constant in her life when work or family are no longer a guarantee of permanence: her place of residence. Staying put feels like a voluntary choice, thus bringing a sense of well-being and faith in the future, which helps tolerate the scarcity and uncertainty caused by working conditions.

Funding

The writing of this article has been financially supported by funding from the Academy of Finland (decision number 232213). I am grateful to the referee for the comments on the earlier version of this article.

Notes

1. In Finland, entrepreneurship education is even incorporated into the school system from primary schools to universities (Komulainen et al. 2011). Still, the advocates of entrepreneurialism are criticising schools for poor results of entrepreneurial education. At any rate, both the supporters and the critics of entrepreneurialism understand that even by educating people to have an entrepreneurial attitude, it is impossible to control the operations of an economy that has broken loose from the old management logic. Critics conclude that citizens are meant to learn that they cannot rely on public systems, which means that they also learn to manage themselves and to rely only on themselves.
2. Even official statistics treat entrepreneurs' social statuses as too homogenous. Statistics Finland only divides workers into employees and entrepreneurs, even though the group of entrepreneurs is highly heterogeneous and people can alternate between the two statuses or even hold both simultaneously. Almost half of all entrepreneurs are self-employed, meaning that they do not employ others. Their number has increased dramatically and many have a low level of income and high level of poverty (Palkkatyöläinen 2011). In the contemporary world of work, entrepreneurs also include disadvantaged people, particularly women.
3. Rural policy starts with farms having to be able to reform themselves, thus linking entrepreneurship to them, and developing entrepreneurship completely independent of farming. One-third of farms do in fact practise business outside farming, usually machine contracting. New business and income opportunities are seen, for example, in care and other service industries and alternative energy generation. Adding value to foodstuffs and tourism are also potential industries. Women who live in rural areas generally find employment in the same industries as they do in towns and cities (Rural Development Programme 2007). The number of women entrepreneurs is high in the entire country: farming excluded, one-third of all entrepreneurs are women (in total 79,400 female entrepreneurs, the highest figure in the EU) (TEM 2010, 18). Despite the high number of women entrepreneurs, the Finnish Government has set the objective of increasing this share to 40% (Ibid, 26). Increasing the share is seen to be important for national competitiveness amidst global capitalism, tapping into women's workforce resources, and retaining a balanced demographic structure. The Government believes that promoting entrepreneurship among women improves the employment rate and equality between genders and regions and thus helps remote places become attractive locations for economic activity.
4. Staying is an objective and a desired state of affairs as seen throughout the data collected for this article (see Ikonen 2008, 2012). An indicator of the will to stay is the fact that of the 16 interviewees (with the exception of one), all lived in the same rural municipality at the time of the follow-up interviews. The only respondent who had moved to the nearby town had done so because she had to and did not feel at home in her new place of residence.

References

Adkins, L. 2008. "From Retroactivation to Futurity: The End of the Sexual Contract?" *NORA* 16 (3): 182–201.

Adkins, L., and E. Jokinen. 2008. "Introduction: Gender, Living and Labour in the Fourth Shift." *NORA* 16 (3): 138–149.

Atkinson, W. 2010. "The Myth of the Reflexive Worker: Class and Work Histories in Neo-Liberal Times." *Work, Employment & Society* 24 (3): 413–429.
Boltanski, L., and E. Chiapello. 2007. *The New Spirit of Capitalism*. London: Verso.
Chhetri, P., R. Stimson, and J. Western. 2009. "Understanding the Downshifting Phenomenon: A Case of South East Queensland, Australia." *Australian Journal of Social Issues* 44 (4): 345–362.
du Gay, P. 1996. *Consumption and Identity at Work*. London: Sage.
du Gay, P., and G. Morgan. 2013. "Understanding Capitalism: Crises, Legitimacy, and Change through the Prism of the New Spirit of Capitalism." In *New Spirits of Capitalism? Crisis, Justifications, and Dynamics*, edited by P. du Gay and G. Morgan, 1–42. Oxford: Oxford University Press.
Ehrenreich, B. 2001. *Nickel and Dimed: On (Not) Getting by in America*. New York: Metropolitan Books.
Eyles, J. 1985. *Senses of Place*. Wellingborough: Silverbook Press.
Gherardi, S., and A. Murgia. 2013. "By Hook or by Crook: Flexible Workers between Exploration and Exploitation." *Research in the Sociology of Organizations* 37: 75–103.
Heikkilä, K. 2011. "Jäädä vai lähteä?" In *"Yrittäkää edes!" Prekarisaatio Pohjois-Karjalassa*, edited by E. Jokinen, J. Könönen, J. Venäläinen, and J. Vähämäki, 37–50. Helsinki: Tutkijaliitto.
Herman, D. 2009. *Basic Elements of Narrative*. Malden: Wiley-Blackwell.
Ikonen, H.-M. 2008. *Maaseudun naiset yrittäjinä. Elettyjä käytäntöjä ja jaettuja merkityksiä yrittävässä yhteiskunnassa*. Tampere: Tampere University Press.
Ikonen, H.-M. 2010. "Muutu ihmiseksi, joka olet. *Maalla*-lehti jälkimodernin työntekijän ja paikan kuvaajana." *Alue ja ympäristö* 39 (2): 39–52.
Ikonen, H.-M. 2012. "Maaseudun naisyrittäjäksi tuleminen – esimerkki yrittäjäidentiteetin rakentumisesta." *Maaseudun Uusi Aika* 20 (1): 5–19.
Jakonen, M., J. Peltokoski, and A. Virtanen. 2006. *Uuden työn sanakirja*. Helsinki: Tutkijaliitto.
Jokinen, E. 2010. "Kodin, työn ja talouden uusi järjestys." *Janus* 18 (1): 48–60.
Jokinen, E., J. Könönen, J. Venäläinen, and J. Vähämäki, eds. 2011. *"Yrittäkää edes!" Prekarisaatio Pohjois-Karjalassa*. Helsinki: Tutkijaliitto.
Keith, M., and S. Pile. 1993. *Place and the Politics of Identity*. London: Routledge.
Komulainen, K., P. Naskali, M. Korhonen, and S. Keskitalo-Foley. 2011. "Internal Entrepreneurship – A Trojan Horse of the Neoliberal Governance of Education? Finnish Pre- and in-Service Teachers' Implementation of and Resistance Towards Entrepreneurship Education." *Journal for Critical Education Policy Studies* 9 (1): 342–374.
Lahikainen, L., and K. Mäkinen. 2012. "Luokka erona ja antagonismina." *Kulttuurintutkimus* 29 (1): 3–18.
Mäkinen, K. 2012. *Becoming Valuable Selves. Self-Promotion, Gender and Individuality in Late Capitalism*. Tampere: Tampere University Press.
Massey, D. 1994. *Space, Place and Gender*. Cambridge: Polity Press.
McDowell, L. 1999. *Gender, Identity and Place*. Cambridge: Polity Press.
McDowell, L. 2009. *Working Bodies*. Malden: Wiley-Blackwell.
Meriläinen, H. 2011. "Palkkatyöyhteiskunnan vaihtoehdot." In *"Yrittäkää edes!" Prekarisaatio Pohjois-Karjalassa*, edited by E. Jokinen, J. Könönen, J. Venäläinen, and J. Vähämäki, 143–162. Helsinki: Tutkijaliitto.
Miller, P., and N. Rose. 2008. *Governing the Present*. Cambridge: Polity Press.
Morris, J. 2012. "Unruly Entrepreneurs: Russian Worker Responses to Insecure Formal Employment." *Global Labour Journal* 3 (2): 217–236.
NíLaoire, C. 2001. "A Matter of Life and Death? Men, Masculinities and Staying 'Behind' in Rural Ireland." *Sociologia Ruralis* 41 (2): 220–236.
Obgor, J. 2000. "Mythicizing and Reification in Entrepreneurial Discourse: Ideology-Critique of Entrepreneurial Studies." *Journal of Management Studies* 37 (5): 605–635.
Palkkatyöläinen. 2011."Teema: itsensä työllistäjät." Accessed November 25, 2013. http://www.palkkatyolainen.fi/pt2011/pt-01-2011/pt-150211-t9.html
Peltokoski, J. 2012. "Luokka luokkaa vastaan." *Niin & näin* 19 (1): 98–101.
Pongratz, H. J., and G. Voss. 2003. "From Employee to 'Entreployee': Towards a 'Self-Entrepreneurial' Work Force?" *Concepts and Transformation* 8 (3): 239–254.
Relph, E. 1986. *Place and Placelessness*. London: Pion.

Ricoeur, P. 1991. "Narrative Identity." In *On Paul Ricoeur: Narrative and Interpretation*, edited by D. Wood, 188–200. New York: Routledge.
Riessman, C. K. 2001. "Analysis of Personal Narratives." In *Handbook of Interview Research: Context and Method*, edited by J. Gubrium and J. Holstein, 695–710. Thousand Oaks, CA: Sage.
Rose, N. 1992. "Governing the Enterprising Self." In *The Values of the Enterprise Culture: The Moral Debate*, edited by P. Heelas, and P. Morris, 141–163. London: Routledge.
Ross, A. 2009. *Nice Work if You Can Get It: Life and Labor in Precarious Times*. New York New York University Press.
Rural Development Programme. 2007. "Rural Development Programme for Mainland Finland 2007–2013." Accessed November 25, 2013. http://www.maaseutu.fi/attachments/6BQQITgHU/Rural_Development_for_Mainland_Finland_051012_EN.pdf
Sennett, R. 2006. *The Culture of the New Capitalism*. New Haven, CT: Yale University Press.
Skeggs, B. 1997. *Formations of Class and Gender: Becoming Respectable*. London: Sage.
Skeggs, B. 2004. *Class, Self, Culture*. London: Routledge.
Standing, G. 2011. *The Precariat: The New Dangerous Class*. London: BloomsburyAcademic.
TEM (Työ- ja elinkeinoministeriö). 2010. "MoniNainen Ja uudistuva naisyrittäjyys." Accessed November 25, 2013. http://www.tem.fi/files/25810/TEM_4_2010.pdf
Tolonen, T. 2005. "Locality and Gendered Capital of Working-Class Youth." *Young* 13 (4): 343–361.
Tuan, Y. 1977. *Space and Place: The Perspective of Experience*. Minneapolis, MN: University of Minnesota Press.
Uimonen, M. 2008. "Monikulttuurinen parisuhde ja suomalaisen julkisuuden sukupuolittuneet luokkakuvat." In *Yhteiskuntaluokka ja sukupuoli*, edited by T. Tolonen, 122–145. Tampere: Vastapaino.
Vähämäki, J. 2009. *Itsen alistus. Työ, tuotanto ja valta tietokykykapitalismissa*. Helsinki: Like.
Varis, S. 2005. *Pitkäaikaistyöttömänä maaseudulla*. Joensuu: Joensuun yliopisto.
Veijola, S., and E. Jokinen. 2008. "Towards a Hostessing Society? Mobile Arrangements of Gender and Labour." *NORA* 16 (3): 166–181.
Watson, T. 2009. "Entrepreneurial Action, Identity Work and the Use of Multiple Discursive Resources: The Case of Rapidly Changing Family Business." *International Small Business Journal* 27 (3): 251–274.

REPLY

Precarious work, entrepreneurial mindset and sense of place: female strategies in insecure labour markets: a response to Hanna-Mari Ikonen

Jeremy Morris

Department of Modern Languages, University of Birmingham, Birmingham, UK

This is a reply to:

Ikonen, Hanna-Mari. 2013. "Precarious work, entrepreneurial mindset and sense of place: female strategies in insecure labour markets." *Global Discourse.* 3 (3–4): 467–481 http://dx.doi.org/10.1080/23269995.2013.864085.

Hanna-Mari Ikonen's article offers an interesting case study from the 'margins' of the global north on how entrepreneurship and employment are entwined in debates on the meaning of precarity today among the working poor. She shows how individuals consider both strategies as available, but agonise over the merits of these labour resources. Entrepreneurialism is linked to self-employment and a sense of empowered placeness and rootedness – an interesting reversal of the usual association of self-governmentality with ultra-flexibility and becoming the active, self-responsible, self-reflexive constructor of one's own work capacities (du Gay 1996). Ikonen does not romanticise this strategy – for her informant it ultimately entails a level of self-exploitation that is incompatible with her gendered role as mother. Overall though, the article indicates that more reflection is needed on the overused metaphor of the 'rootlessness' of the working poor, not only in the global south, but in affluent countries like Finland also. The precariat are subject to insecurity as much in static community contexts as elsewhere.

It is very interesting that regional development in Finland rest largely on the hope of entrepreneurship, and yet the avenues for work in the huge rural hinterland of Karelia (and presumably elsewhere) are either agricultural, or gendered migration to the south. This would appear to be the reason why the number of women entrepreneurs is so high in the country: one-third of all entrepreneurs are women, the highest figure in the EU. This surely reflects the default position of self-employment in rural and small communities, whereas migration for men means employment elsewhere. Ikonen offers an empirical unpicking of the individual consequences of neoliberal reforms: the case study of a divorced mother of two children, living in a remote rural area of Finland and who balances entrepreneurial cobbler work and part-time employment selling shoes, except that the former has proved too much to bear physically and mentally; now she merely subsists through sales work. The study takes its cue from Atkinson (2010, 415) who questions the individualisation of risk as a wholesale undifferentiated process and points to the salience of classed responses to precarity, arguing that '*qualitative* evidence from narratives of occupational histories and job transitions is needed, something which has, to date, been rather less conspicuous in engagements with individualization'. He goes on to argue that a Bourdieusian understanding of class is required to really capture of the processes of pracaritisation and avoid one-dimensional (i.e. methodologically individualist) analysis of adaptation and management of uncertainty.

However, the article, in my view is only partially successful in discussing entrepreneurialism from a habitus and dispositions perspective. And this is due to the difficulty in marrying any discussions of the household reproduction of the working poor and the existing concept of the entrepreneur. Ikonen draws attention to local articulations of the individualist hypothesis around risk, showing how entrepreneurship education is even incorporated into the school system from primary schools to universities in Finland and pointing to the emphasis on lifelong learning. This is in some respects just what is needed in terms of qualifying the Beckian 'risk' hypothesis, rightly criticised for glossing over place-based and culturally differentiated responses to risk, and also for focusing on conditions in a narrow version of the global north (Bulkeley 2001; Waite 2009, 420). Similarly, in Standing's description of the precariat, apart from an acknowledgement of partial overlap with 'independent contractors' – i.e. the self-employed and trades people, these workers, who in many respects fulfil most of his seven criteria of insecurity that qualify the term, are only given passing mention.

Ikonen really gets to the nub of the problem with the word 'entrepreneur' when she says 'entrepreneurship as a socially stratified category […] has to be deconstructed, in contrast to its automatic social construction as middle-class'. But how to do this? Perhaps the answer is to get rid of the word altogether as another classed and classifying euphemism for self-exploitation and ends-directed speculative activity. I disagree with her when she argues that entrepreneurial status does not dictate the entrepreneur's social class. The word in English continues to have clear connotations of class. Similarly, in my own study cited by Ikonen, while I use the term as a kind of 'holding category', I preface it with 'unruly' to indicate my ironic use (Morris 2012). Similarly, my (non-tax-paying) self-employed plumbers and welders avoid the Russian-language equivalent term (which legally denotes the self-employed). They are just 'people who work' (as opposed to employees or others in white-collar work).

What then is 'entrepreneurial' about what the craft working of the Finnish poor of Ikonen's piece? Surely the term is to do violence to the notion of craft, of the socially dwelt-in meanings of work that still exist for such people. In a sense this classifying of craft labour is at the opposite end of the spectrum of academic misrecognition as the 'making do' and 'survival' literature on post-socialism in my own area. The latter similarly fails to capture the meaningful and in some cases highly dignified and autonomous, not to mention lucrative and hardly precarious, trades like plumbing and welding that at least some former factory workers of socialism are now engaged in.

Self-employment whether on a legally registered basis or not facilitates some kind of habitability within neoliberal regimes for those with the least economic capital. This is something Ikonen's fieldwork bears out when her informant expresses the spatially specific meaning of 'entrepreneurialism' with its embeddedness in the valuing of home, community and origin: 'Today, and in the near future, she wants her children to have a place to which they always feel they can return. In the future, the children may be able to use the house as their home or as a summer cottage, and it may also be possible to work from there again as an entrepreneur'. While the key informant describes herself as 'being on that road still' – meaning that temporary employment is the unsatisfactory reality of her insecure work and therefore precarious existence, the 'road' is not one away from family and home; the 'will to stay' in so-called marginal communities is strong. However, this is tempered by the dilemma in the article for the informant in terms of her understanding of the 'easiness' of temporary insecure work (which gives more of a life balance) versus the 'difficulty' of self-employment. Ikonen calls this a paradox, but perhaps it would be better to call it the double-bind of precarious entrepreneurialism: holding on to her craftsperson identity gives a feeling of control and achievement but is a position increasingly 'achieved' only through ruthless self-exploitation that is for many women (and men) not sustainable.

The point is not only that entrepreneurialism is naturalised as a white-collar, middle-class regime of self-regulation. By acquiescing to the term we presuppose choice and a stock of capital that the working poor often do not have. Perhaps, following on from de Certeau, we should stick to the less problematic 'tactics', prefaced by labour- to describe the limited ways in which the working poor access self-directed activities such as those described (cobbling). So instead of entrepreneurialism we would echo the diverse economies school and posit 'diverse tactics of labour'. This raises another question though. Entrepreneurialism, via du Gay and others in the classic form of governmentality it describes, remains an individualistic conception of action and self. Where is the community and sociality in this vision? Much of the current work in economic anthropology that encompasses informal and insecure work seeks to highlight how dependent even global chains of goods are on complex and affective (if informal) trust relations (Morris and Polese 2013). Beck suggests that 'individualization' is rife and assumes that his 'so-called "diy" biographies are more prevalent than traditional ties of, for example, class, gender and ethnicity' (Waite 2009, 420). Ikonen's work on Finland, like that of the post-socialist informal economies grouping, shows that precarity has to be approached in terms of intersectional meanings of place, work and personhood.

Ikonen cites my own case study of blue-collar workers in Russia who access class-based social networks in order to interrogate narratives of reflexive individualism (Morris 2012). My approach sought to problematise what I view as Standing's reification of class in his work on defining precarity (2011) that simultaneously denies any hope for collective action. Despite his intentions, the 'precariat', by the nature of employing a term tagging a group, brings to mind 'class characteristics' typified, according to Standing by 'minimal trust relationships' towards state and capital. But while trust relationships between people and state are lacking, social networks, especially horizontal and residual (including classed networks of the ex-industrial working class) might lead to something of a self-recognition as precariat among the insecure. While Standing's argument is about the precariat as process, 'the way in which people are "precariatised" [...] is analogous to "proletarianised", describing the forces leading to proletarianisation of workers in the nineteenth century. To be precariatised is to be subject to pressures and experiences that lead to a precariat existence, of living in the present, without a secure identity or sense of development achieved through work and lifestyle' (Standing 2011, 16). In that sense, precarity urgently requires engagement by working-class studies, if only to avoid an undifferentiated analysis that would characterise the precariat as passive and unable to reflect on their structured positioning and therefore unable to articulate self-understanding or dissent.

Notes on contributor

Jeremy Morris is Senior Lecturer in Russian at the University of Birmingham, UK. His research interests include informal economy, class, precarity and post socialism more generally. His current research is focused on ethnographic approaches to understanding actually lived experience in the former Soviet Union.

References

Atkinson, W. 2010. "The Myth of the Reflexive Worker: Class and Work Histories in Neo-Liberal Times." *Work, Employment & Society* 24 (3): 413–429.

Bulkeley, H. 2001. "Governing Climate Change: The Politics of Risk Society?." *Transactions, Institute of British Geographers* 26: 430–447.

du Gay, P. 1996. *Consumption and Identity at Work*. London: Sage.

Morris, J. 2012. "Unruly Entrepreneurs: Russian Worker Responses to Insecure Formal Employment." *Global Labour Journal* 3 (2): 217–236.

Morris, J. and Polese, A. eds. 2013. *The Informal Post-Socialist Economy: Embedded Practices and Livelihoods*. London and New York: Routledge.

Standing, G. 2011. *The Precariat: The New Dangerous Class*. London: BloomsburyAcademic.

Waite, L. 2009. "A Place and Space for a Critical Geography of Precarity?." *Geography Compass* 3/1: 412–433.

RESEARCH ARTICLE

The precariousnesses of young knowledge workers: a subject-oriented approach

Emiliana Armano[a] and Annalisa Murgia[b]

[a]*Department of Social and Political Sciences, University of Milan, Milano, Italy;* [b]*Department of Sociology and Social Research, University of Trento, Trento, Italy*

Over the past decades, a number of EU member states have recorded large rises in the use of temporary employment. Young people are far more likely than other groups to be employed in precarious jobs, independently of their education and skills. In the midst of the global economic-financial crisis, in fact, the assault on the conditions of knowledge workers goes on, according to the different lines of the neoliberalistic logics, which juxtapose with the current precarisation processes like underpayment and misalignment between subjects' educations and their working activities. How do young precarious knowledge workers recount their experiences? What relation holds between a high education level and the possibility of effectively deploying the competences and skills acquired? How do knowledge workers represent and deal with their precarious conditions? To answer these questions, this article proposes a definition of the concepts of 'precarity', 'precariousness' and 'precariat' and then focuses specifically on the precariousness experienced by young knowledge workers in Italy and the importance of investigating precarisation processes in light of their experiences. Hence, the present article discusses the invisible face of the conditions of young knowledge workers, which collides with the official face. The latter superficially presents them as 'independent professionals', although they increasingly experience conditions similar to those of dependent workers and at the same time suffer the effects of the further precarisation brought about by the crisis, but missing trade-unions support or political representation.

How many graduates are hired for jobs which do not match their qualifications
("to make photocopies," as the saying goes)?
How many fixed-term contracts pay 500, 800 euros a month?
And for how many hours? Have we forgotten that when talking of a wage
it is also necessary to state the working hours?
A freelance contract for three months, then a wait of six months,
and then another freelance contract for another three months.
Is this work, is this employment?
Sergio Bologna

1. Introduction

In recent years, numerous quantitative studies on the conditions of knowledge workers have emphasised the objective nature of their inquiry, the researcher's non-judgemental stance and the measurability of the phenomena investigated. By contrast, this article takes the opposite approach by recognising that narrators and listeners – the interviewees and the researchers – develop their representations and narratives within situated systems of power and knowledge. Our analysis therefore assumes the point of view of the subjects, and it assumes that this 'bias' is heuristically important. It therefore adopts a subject-oriented approach, which is less interested in verification of the 'facts' of lives. These it considers to be less significant than the manifold experiences and life stories that every individual can elaborate (Personal Narrative Group 1989).

At the centre of our narrative is the precariousness experienced by knowledge workers and, in particular, by precarious highly educated and highly skilled young people in Italy. The analysis centres on the intersubjective constructions of meaning by which young graduates represent their lives and, in particular, their work. The principal models and methodological references are Bourdieu's *Practical Reason* (1985), the tradition of social inquiry and 'co-research' (Alasia and Montaldi 1960; Alquati 1993) and narrative studies (Schutze 1987; Riessman 1993).

We therefore asked ourselves: how do knowledge workers represent their condition? And how do they cope with precariousness? To answer these questions, we shall conduct critical reflection on the trajectories and subjectivities of young knowledge workers. The discussion is based on the results from two qualitative research projects conducted in northern Italy between 2006 and 2011 (Armano 2010; Murgia, Poggio, and Torchio 2012).

2. Knowledge workers' subjectivities hanging in the balance: the experience of precariousness between job precarity and precariat

Having outlined the approach and the research questions, we now briefly state the theoretical perspective, which guided our inquiry. Investigating the conditions and subjectivities of young highly skilled people in Italy primarily concerns the formation of a young precariat. Before addressing the concept of precariat, however, we think it important to try to resignify and circumscribe some key terms often interchangeably used to describe precariousness although they refer to very different situations.

We first define the concepts of 'job precarity', 'precariousness' and 'precariat'. We then specify what we mean by the expression 'knowledge work', a social world that graduates endeavour to enter.

One of the standing points of our analysis is that for understanding how the process of precarisation is one of the essential features of current forms of subjectivisation, the definition of a precarious condition is required to be extended beyond the narrow confines of the labour market (Murgia 2010; Arienzo and Borrelli 2011).

Investigation must therefore not be restricted to temporary, discontinuous, uncertain and largely unprotected employment – in which, nevertheless, precarity is particularly evident. It is necessary to go beyond the term 'precarity' in its restricted sense of 'job precarity' so widely used in continental Europe (Booth, Francesconi, and Frank 2002; Clark and Postel-Vinay 2009) and in Italy (Berton, Richiardi, and Sacchi 2009), but little developed in the *English-speaking* countries and northern Europe.

We believe that the experiences of precarious young knowledge workers can be denoted (albeit with numerous nuances) by the term 'precariousness', which numerous authors employ to indicate the transformation of social relations amid uncertainty (Bourdieu 1998), especially at a time of the large-scale deregulation of the capitalist system (Castel 1995; Sennett 1998). This is not so much the effect of job precarity as the product of the liquefaction of the modern institutions (Bauman 2000) and of the insecurity and vulnerability of the entire corpus of social relationships now destructured by the diffusion of risk (Beck 2000). In this scenario, individuals are required to take charge of their destinies as entrepreneurs of their selves (Foucault 2008), their lives and their social protection (Ross 2009; Chicchi and Leonardi 2012). This condition transforms people into entrepreneurs of their own 'human capital', and it therefore entails processes of self-construction centred on individualisation. Above all for young knowledge workers, in fact, the experience of precariousness is inextricably bound up with job self-identification, which generates self-exploitation and conveys subsumption of skills, personal qualities and emotions that are put into value. Because the concept of precariousness – or perhaps it would be better to say *precariousnesses* – concerns the experiences of persons in their partiality and situatedness, it induces us to consider different, manifold, but simultaneously dynamic, positions that not only differ among individuals who define themselves as precarious but also change for the same individual over time. In a certain sense, therefore, we may use the term 'precarity' to denote a structural condition tied in particular to work and the contract. Instead, 'precariousness' denotes an experiential condition to do with the person's life as a quality inherent to that person and his/her specific positioning. The aim of this article is to make an original contribution to the debate that recognises precariousness as a condition so extensive that it permeates the entire life of individuals and transmutes into *existential precarity* (Fumagalli 2007) and *social precarity* (Murgia 2010).

A third concept, different from both those of 'precarity' and 'precariousness', situated in the critical Anglo-Saxon thinking, has been proposed by Guy Standing (2011), who identifies in the 'precariat' an emergent social actor potentially able to become a new political class with universal rights and legitimated to express an innovative politics marked by equity and social solidarity. Standing defines this emergent *class-in-the-making* broadly as those who face a number of related and often overlapping insecurities: labour market insecurity, employment insecurity, job insecurity, work insecurity, skill reproduction insecurity, income insecurity and representation insecurity. The precariat therefore consists of a wide array of self-employed autonomous or dependent workers, freelances, migrants, students, women and young people, increasingly less protected by an inadequate welfare system. It also comprises temporary workers and permanent employees whose jobs are threatened and who are subject to blackmail. To be stressed is that the growth of the precariat does not derive entirely from changes in the labour market and the increase in temporary contracts; it is also driven by the transformation of production processes, the rights connected with them and, above all, the deliberate governance strategies of capitalist society. In this complex scenario, it thus becomes difficult to understand the delimitations of the definition of 'precariat' (Bailey 2013). Standing himself, for that matter, stresses that the precariat does not consist of people with identical backgrounds. This means that there co-exist varieties of precariats, with different degrees of insecurity and attitudes to having a precariat existence. It therefore seems that this concept fully demonstrates its importance, not so much in defining a distinctive socio-economic group as in identifying the potential to construct an identity, an imagery and a collective experience of precarious subjectivities. 'Moving from symbols to a political program' (Standing 2011, 3) is, in our view, the shift, which constitutes Standing's main contribution. And among the main protagonists of this shift from a condition of precariousness to one of precariat are the precarious young knowledge workers at the centre of our following discussion.

Having theoretically defined the concepts of the precarity–precariousness–precariat, we now turn to the concept of knowledge work, which was of specific concern to our research on young highly educated and highly skilled workers. First, who are knowledge workers? Much time has passed since the first definition of knowledge work formulated by Peter Drucker. According to Drucker, knowledge workers are persons who use, entirely or predominantly, their intellectual, cognitive, relational, communicative faculties, in collaboration with others, to perform their work (Drucker 1994). This very broad and inclusive definition gave rise to systematic reflection: Florida (2003) described knowledge workers with a certain celebr*ative emphasis* as a new creative and innovative elite; conversely, Lessard and Baldwin (2000) described them as the victims of flexible technology.

A large body of literature then developed, from the analyses of Manuel Castells on the network society (1996), to the debate in Italy among authors arguing from sometimes very different theoretical positions – among them were Federico Butera (2008), Sergio Bellucci and Marcello Cini (2010) and then Sergio Bologna and Dario Banfi (2011). A broad definition of knowledge work comprised a wide range of occupational categories, from managers to call centre workers, with marked differences in pay and employment conditions. Thus identified was a form of work, which in recent decades has burgeoned numerically in all the tertiarised societies. Here we would specify that, from the analytical point of view, by 'knowledge work' we mean '(meta)knowledge work', that is not a concrete type of activity but a generalisation from a composite set of activities.

A distinctive feature of knowledge workers is that the majority of them are self-employed (at least formally): collaborators, consultants and freelances (Armano 2010; Bologna and Banfi 2011). In this regard, the expression 'molecular capitalists' (Bonomi 1997) has been used, although it is a definition that empowers a form of work that we would instead term '*de facto* wage-earning'. One witnesses, in fact, the '*enterprisation*' of work and human activity (Alquati 1997) and a process whereby precarious workers become enterprise. Here the emphasis is not on becoming the entrepreneur of oneself, but rather on a work condition that has only the constraints of an enterprise, because it is the individual worker who must assume, subjectively and creatively, enterprise risk (Rullani 2005).

Already in the 1980s in the Western countries, the use of formally self-employed labour and less regulated contracts enabled firms to outsource functions, increase organisational flexibility and reduce costs (Harvey 1990; Standing 2011). However, the precarity of the 2000s went even further and off-loaded risk in all its forms – productive, financial and social – on to the individual. Above all, it subjected the latter to the logic of 'enterprisation'. The new pattern of proactive participation and promotion of personal resources entirely overturned the system of discipline and obedience typical of Fordist society. At work was a financialisation of people's lives (Formenti 2011), which in everyday life took the form of a set of practices that replaced those that structured the previous paradigm. The place of wages regulated by rights and collective bargaining – still formally persist in some cases – was taken by individualised pay scales based on performance, productivity and reliability accompanied by increments linked to market results, leasing, indebtedness and credit. The rhetoric of self-fulfilment, and the dominant principle of merit and skill rewards, positioned workers in a field of internalised intents and aspirations (Lazzarato 2012), different from the field of values and choices from the past. The aim of this article is to understand these changes through the use of a subject-oriented approach.

3. The Italian context: the precarity shared by young highly educated and highly skilled workers

In this section, we briefly describe some features useful for contextualising the condition of young highly educated and highly skilled knowledge workers in Italy. This is a particularly interesting category because it is the protagonist of what has been called the new spirit of capitalism (Sennett 2006). These are workers who have both wanted and experienced task-oriented project work connoted by wide margins of autonomy. The 'artistic critique' carried forward since the protest movements of the 1960s to claim the right to express creativity (Boltanski and Chiapello 1999) has in fact been skilfully incorporated into both business organisations, which soon realised that large part of profits depend on worker's inventiveness and imagination, and into the regulation of work and the reforms enacted in Europe in recent decades. These processes of structural transformation of work are more comprehensible if one observes the experiences of young people who, on the one hand, begin to work in a production system already profoundly transformed and, on the other hand, unwillingly circumscribe and resignify the new social contexts of becoming vulnerable and open to blackmail of desire and subjectivity.

In Italy, this process began later than in other European countries, but it then developed rapidly. The labour-market reforms of 1997, 2003 and 2012 substantially altered the types of employment contracts. They fostered the rapid and extensive spread of *formally* autonomous employment relationships, such as 'semi-dependent' or 'quasi-subordinate' jobs based on fixed-term, project or temporary contracts, and the 'self-employed/dependent' or 'fake-autonomous' jobs undertaken by self-employed freelances working mainly for one employer. The features shared by these diverse forms of employment are the high education levels of the workers concerned, job insecurity, frequently low pay levels and the absence of the rights and protections typical of dependent employment, which is still the main channel of access to the Italian welfare system (Ranci 2012; Samek Lodovici and Semenza 2012).

In Italy, as in other tertiarised countries, one therefore witnesses the emergence of 'hybrid' cases such as that of highly skilled self-employed workers nonetheless exposed to the risk of unemployment, a lack of income and social marginality (Murgia and Poggio 2012). The onset of the economic crisis has exacerbated this trend, producing further insecurity for this category of workers (Villa 2010; Samek Lodovici and Semenza 2012). Nor does possession of a tertiary-level qualification provide protection. Graduates are, in fact, most at risk of unemployment: in 2009, the number of unemployed upper-secondary diploma holders or graduates increased to a greater extent (20%) than did the number of persons with lower qualifications (9.2%). And those most affected were freelances and 'self-employed/dependent' workers (Istat 2010; ACTA 2012; Armano 2013). Also pay levels seem to be increasingly less proportional to the investment made in training. In Italy, graduates aged between 25 and 34, in fact, earn only 22% more than high-school diploma holders in the same age class, compared with an OECD average of 40% more. There are also marked differences between those graduates who remain in Italy and those who go abroad to work: 4 years after graduation, those who have gone abroad earn almost €1800 net a month, while those who have remained in Italy earn around €1300. There is, moreover, a wide gender gap in all occupational sectors (Barone 2013).

Finally, compared with the rest of Europe, Italy confirms its particularly problematic position in regard to the match between educational qualifications and jobs, even though the proportion of highly educated young Italians is decidedly lower than the average of the other countries (Terraneo 2010). For many graduates, the transition from university to a permanent job is not only more protracted but also more difficult in terms of occupational stability, employment conditions and professional content (Blasutig 2008; Ballarino and Bratti 2009). Instability rates are higher among higher-skilled workers: 33% among graduates under 35 compared to 25.5% for high-school diploma holders and 23.6% among workers with a lower-secondary education diplomas. Moreover, in regard to occupation types, the most unstable working lives are found mostly among young adult professionals (aged 25–34), which indicates that 'a greater investment in training and human capital development is not finding an appropriate response in the labour market, where work is predominantly non-stable, even for the over-35s with a high level of education' (Dota 2013, 29). The dynamics just described depict a widespread and enduring mismatch (both quantitative and qualitative) between the demand for and supply of skilled labour (Schomburg and Teichler 2006; Blasutig 2012). The phenomenon of *over-qualification*, already present in Italy, has indubitably been accentuated by the economic crisis: in 2009 it affected around a million more people than in 2004 (3.4 million workers, with a 15.6% incidence). Of these, around half (47.1%) were young people aged under 34 (Istat 2010). In the same period, the incidence of workers with jobs requiring skills inferior to their qualifications rose from 24.2% to 31% among 15-to-34 year-old workers (compared with an increase from 5.3% to 8.5% among workers aged over 55). This applies all the more to young graduates, almost half of whom have jobs which do not match their qualifications (44.9% compared with 34.1% of the total labour force). Those most penalised are women, even though they outnumber men in almost all the disciplinary fields (Istat 2010).

Job precarity, which inevitably impacts on all the other spheres of a person's life, has thus expanded to become an existential precariousness. It characterises the lives of all young people, but with specific features for those with high qualifications, who are over-represented among self-employed workers and freelances. In the next sections, we shall discuss – through presentation of the main results of research conducted in various cities of northern Italy – the precarious and invisible circumstances of young knowledge workers that contradict the official account that superficially considers them 'independent and professional', though they more frequently have working conditions similar to those of dependent workers and experience the effect of the further precarisation brought about by the crisis, but without a trade-union or political representation. Starting from job precarity, we shall investigate the *precariousnesses* that extend beyond the confines of the labour market. Finally, we shall consider the difficulty of constructing collective experiences and practices against precariousness, which might enable identification of an emergent actor, that is to say, the precariat.

4. Research context and methodology

The discussion that follows is based on two different research projects conducted in northern Italy between 2006 and 2011. The first was carried out in Turin between the summers of 2006 and 2009, and it concerned events during the period which followed the Turin Winter Olympics of 2006. The study was based on 39 in-depth interviews conducted with young and adult knowledge workers employed in diverse sectors: information technology, digital production, the Web, the new media, multimedia arts, publishing, training and research (Armano 2010, 2011). Most of the interviews were carried out during various events held in Turin – Virtuality, Linux Day, Film Festival and Artissima.

The second research project was conducted in the cities of Milan, Bologna and Trento. During 2011, 30 narrative interviews (Schutze 1987; Riessman 2001) were conducted with precarious highly skilled young people. All the interviewees had at least 5 years of work experience and high educational qualifications (degree, master or doctorate), of which 8 were in sciences and 22 were in socio-humanistic subjects.

In both research projects, the large majority of the interviewees worked as semi-subordinate employees or freelances, both in jobs consistent with their training and in ones very distant from it.

The next section discusses some of the main results of the analysis of the interview texts. It will show two dimensions that characterise the lives of knowledge workers: (1) an ambivalent search for independence and freedom to express creativity; (2) the experience of misalignment, an experiential state of rescission, a sort of incongruity of status with respect to both training and previous work experience (which gives rise to the phenomena of deskilling, devaluation and impoverishment of knowledge) and the future, which appears uncertain, as well as distant from desires and expectations.

5. Discussion of the research results: stories of precariousness of young knowledge workers

The research results evidence a very broad array of specific situations. While the concept of homogeneity was applicable in the Fordist world, the condition of young knowledge workers is today characterised by heterogeneity and variety.

Notwithstanding the different concrete circumstances of the interviewees, some common and recurrent features emerge. In what follows, we shall describe a phenomenology of subjectivity, which expresses precariousness in knowledge work. We shall examine, on the one hand, the identification/self-exploitation nexus and, on the other hand, the experience of growing misalignment between the desires and aspirations of young knowledge workers and their everyday lives.

5.1. Precarious knowledge workers: between self-identification and self-exploitation

One of the main features apparent in the interviews was the self-identification of the respondents with the object of their work – to the point that they were willing to do their jobs for free, or almost. This is an aspect which defines subjectivity in the new forms of work: indeed, according to some authors, it is an attitude typical of the new *esprit du capitalisme* (Boltanski and Chiappello 1999). Because of these 'passions', jobs no longer have fixed time schedules and contractual provisions apply only in formal terms.

> It's great because – I'm lucky enough to work at the Polytechnic of Turin with organisations of a certain prestige. I have the good fortune of being in contact with people who can impart a great deal from both the cultural and personal point of view. [...] The positive aspects of my job [...] are certainly lifeblood for me. [...] I think that *if you do something with pleasure, that's the most important thing* [...] you're happy and stimulated. You can easily put in an extra two to five hours. But doing two hours more, or even a minute more, in work that you don't like certainly grinds you down. [29-year-old_Turin_Research Fellow]
>
> I like my job because it's very stimulating, because I switch from dealing with a review of the *** Festival to following a cultural event, which I usually find interesting and *that I also share as values... because obviously I've catered to my interests*, so that when planning the festival I select a review that interests me, and I therefore attend the planning meetings... deciding what films to discard or not... I watch the films at home... Then, of course, I'd like to earn a bit more. Now I don't get even one thousand euros, and there's always the issue of the six-month contract, and you never know if they'll renew it... There are two roads according to me: the job of your life and the job that pays, and *I'm trying in every way possible to do a job*

that impassions me, even if I don't earn very much. [32-year-old, Milan, Freelancer in a cultural association]

The key to understanding the phenomenon of work self-identification is the fact that a large proportion of knowledge work is immaterial and relational, with the consequence that behaviour, motivation and social and emotional skills play a significant role in its qualification and enhancement (Chicchi and Roggero 2009; Fumagalli and Morini 2009). And because human capital is inextricably bound up with its possessor (Cohen 2004), it transforms the person into a sort of enterprise based on the identity socially granted to it and on remuneration which is primarily motivational, not economic. This motivational and identitarian remuneration makes it possible to withstand what we have called job precarity and which, in the stories of the interviewees, often translated into dreadful working and contractual conditions:

> I wake up at half past six... I leave home in the car at a quarter past seven, lessons from eight to one o'clock... lunch at around a quarter to two... a quick stop-off here [*the interviewee's home*] to pick up my things, perhaps a last look at my lesson notes... by three o'clock at the very latest I must catch the train to be in time for the lesson, which begins at half four. Lessons end at six or a quarter past... By half past seven I'm at home, supper and then preparing lessons or correct exercises or looking up something for the school or writing an article... And then... okay, so I'm stupid... I became the contact person of the school/work transition project at my school, so I had to organise all the visits by the students... the work experience placements, contacts with firms, and so on... And I wasn't paid for it either... which is right because they didn't let us lack for anything! But I was wrong, wasn't I?. I was certainly wrong. But it seemed a really sensible thing to do... *I believed in that project*.... [31-year-old_Bologna_Teacher at an upper-secondary school]
>
> ... It's in the past two years that I've gone into economic …meltdown... I'm drawing on my funds, previous savings.. and... scraping away at them as long as it lasts... or until I'm fed up with it all. Because there are moments when I'm so discouraged that I say... *these are all jobs that I like, so much passion, but* ... Advanced training is all very well, and so are jobs which I won't say are prestigious but are of a certain level, right? However, teaching at university... I'm proud of what I've achieved. However, if this is the situation... it sometimes seems to me that I've done everything wrong. That's for sure. I want so much to emigrate.... [33-year-old_Milan_Spanish Teacher]

Moreover, in project work, self-identification with the job combines with the phenomenon – a spillover from 'second-generation self-employment' (Bologna and Fumagalli 1997) – called 'domestication', the end of the distinction between the person and his/her work role, between home and work, the voluntary and free contribution of time, knowledge, resources, relationships and constant availability (Marazzi 2005), in which the worker is voluntarily and wholeheartedly committed to fulfilment of the goal, despite the expansion of working time.

The interviewees stressed the growth in the amount of free work that is 'normally' required upstream, downstream, alongside and beyond the formal employment contract. This phenomenon assumes the characteristics of an extremely ambiguous process, which involves the creation of a potentially new kind of freedom and a more invisible type of subordination, which pushes people to work constantly and which blurs the distinction between work and private spaces.

> It's a shambles, as I see it. I have enormous difficulties in combining our schedules, because I love my job but I don't want to neglect my family. Because there's my schedule, my wife's schedule, and then there are the schedules of my children, although they're obviously not

> aware of them. I have often to travel for my job... it becomes really... In fact, I've invented a small code for the taking and fetching... every week we draw up a plan in my diary... my wife has her shifts, I have my shifts, plus the children to be taken to school, so I've invented... who'll take the boy? One code for me, one for my wife, one for the boy – who'll take him, who'll pick him up. I mark us like this, so I can see all the various tie-ups during the week. It's a mess…. extraordinarily difficult. [34-year-old_Trento_Architect]
>
> I'd say there's a very blurred boundary between work and, let's say, private life. This is generally so, by now it's a generally recognised feature of precarious work... you get on top of it whenever you can, so that there isn't time for private life and time for work. Things are mixed together. I reckon I belong in this new category because, among private lessons, more institutional work, collaborations... perhaps work for other people, for other employers... it's obvious that I must fit my work time into any space available during the day […] Also because you always need to look for new projects to have continuity of income, but also to keep on working. And this is time that's not counted as working time, even though it's the constant feature of my days. [34-year-old_Milan_Freelance researcher in History]

Finally, it is necessary to emphasise that partly underlying the identification/self-exploitation nexus is the implicit ambivalence of free work. On the one hand, in fact, the work of young knowledge workers is strongly based on informality, the free management of time and the expression of creativity. On the other hand, it is poorly paid, as well as pervading all the spaces of private and family life (Beverungen et al. 2013; Chicchi et al. Forthcoming). Empathic identification with one's work may therefore lead to devoting much more time to it than is actually paid, to the detriment of the private sphere and, moreover, without this corresponding to guarantees of continued employment (Zambelli, Murgia, and Teli Forthcoming).

Identification mixed with the constant blackmail (both material and emotional) to which precarious young knowledge workers are subject to is, we believe, one of the main obstacles to the construction of spaces for collective action in which to construct practices of resistance against precariousness.

5.2. The other side of the coin: the experience of misalignment

In the previous section, we described the experiences of highly educated and highly skilled young people who, although they had jobs that they regarded as rich with meaning, were at the same time liable to precarious subjectivisation because of the passion, involvement and creativity of their work. In a certain sense, this particular category of workers is caught in what we may call a 'passion trap' (Murgia, Poggio, and Torchio 2012). On the one hand, they have jobs that are a source of passion and pleasure; but on the other hand, they experience passion – in all spheres of their lives – in the most literal sense of the term: pain, suffering and fatigue caused by unstable contracts and working conditions. This is the paradox that typifies contemporary flexible capitalism, which puts cognitive and emotional skills into production (Chicchi 2011) but constructs deceptive spaces of freedom (Magatti 2009).

However, even more problematic – in that they add strong dissatisfaction and a lack of recognition of the work performed to the experience of precariousness – are the experiences of the interviewees who, because they could not afford long periods of inactivity after the end of a job consistent with their skills, had to accept another one far from their qualifications and previous experience. The high incidence of young people in jobs for which they are over-qualified testifies that the distress caused by a precarious job combines with that due to its poorer quality and its misalignment with abilities and expectations.

> You can't afford to have any gaps. I'd like to have loads of gaps, because it would mean that I'm living on a private income. But I don't have a private income. So the fact I've accepted a job for two years in a call centre has obviously been for purely economic reasons. Like the year I spent in a bookshop. They were jobs that I found through a temporary employment agency because I needed to work. [33-year-old_Bologna_Expert in gender policies]
>
> Being a graduate and qualified, and having a curriculum with five hundred courses on it, rather than... is an aggravating circumstance. You're worse off. You're worse off than anyone else. Because any job that they can offer you is anyway a lower-grade one. [34-year-old_Trento_Administrative worker]

Most exposed to situations of this kind are workers most liable to blackmail, with scant resources – particularly family support and income – on which to rely. Not to be forgotten, in fact, is the total absence in Italy of both a guaranteed minimum income and unemployment benefits for workers with quasi-subordinate or freelance contracts (Vercellone 2013).

The lives of young precarious knowledge workers therefore seem to oscillate between two situations of extreme difficulty: working precariously (or for free) in a job consistent with their training, or – as in the cases just described – working for low pay in a job which does not match their skills. This is the principal 'precarity trap' (Standing 2011, 73) in which young people with years of investment in training and upskilling are at risk of falling. The difficulty of finding jobs that match their qualifications and aspirations, that forces them to accept temporary as well as under-skilled works, is the result of their need for an income. What happens is a mechanism whereby 'if they turn down the temporary dead-end job, they may be branded as lazy and a scrounger. If they take it, they may be on a losing track. [...] In the end, the precarity traps reflect a discordance between young people's aspirations and the 'human capital' preparation system that sells credentialist qualifications on a false prospectus' (Standing 2011, 74–75).

To be stressed is that the mismatch between education and aspirations concerns an experience, which involves not only income and work but, in broader terms, also a sort of renunciation of one's *expected*, as well as desired, identity. The precariousness trap, in fact, leads – often inexorably – young knowledge workers towards underskilled careers, so that they are caught in what has been called a status incongruence (Dogan 2011; Raffini 2013). This constantly growing phenomenon is not explainable – at least not solely – in terms of the temporariness of employment relationship. Rather, it should be considered in light of its implications for subjectivities and, above all, the way in which it contributes to the creation of fertile ground for individualistic tendencies and the erosion of collective identifications.

Misalignment, moreover, was experienced by the interviewees because of both the mismatch between their everyday lives and the investments made in the past – which caused deskilling and the impoverishment of knowledge – and, especially, the discrepancy between their present lives and those imagined in the future as increasingly uncertain and distant from desires and expectations.

> I imagine myself as an ordinary person who does an ordinary job. If you live in a situation where a set of factors independent of you can decide that – in one day's, one month's, or six months' time –. you may find yourself not only out of work but also having to change your lifestyle, this means that in every area of your life you don't have the strength, the courage, the lucidity to be able to make choices – not epic choices or ones that affect the next twenty years, but life choices like buying a car, buying a house. deciding to study Kant, or anything else extraneous to your most immediate worries. However, as I see it, life has quality only if choices of this kind can be made. But also the social utility of any individual, whether

> functional to or critical of the system, develops only if he or she has stability. [29-year-old_Turin_Research Fellow]

For young knowledge workers on temporary contracts, as they shuttle from one job to another, between work and non-work, between unemployment and training and the multiple contexts of social life, the greatest suffering caused by precariousness seems to be their difficulty in shaping a coherent narrative, defining a story, recognising a 'plot' in their activities, identifying a goal to be achieved and, consequently, the means to do so. They suffer because their lack of credible long-term goals may make them extremely vulnerable to the urgency of the moment. The metaphor of the jigsaw puzzle, which must be assembled without the final picture being known and without the certainty of having all the pieces necessary to complete it, effectively conveys the uncertainty of life-courses (Bauman 2003).

What becomes important in this scenario is knowing how to manage the transition between one contract and the next, the interruption, the new hiring, the transfer from one city to another. These moments of transition assume central importance in biographies (Murgia 2010), those phases of bargaining and/or informal negotiation, conflict, dialogue, growth and learning, social promotion, exclusion and flight. One gains the impression from the narratives that the subjectively key elements are condensed in those particular moments of transition.

The young knowledge workers considered here were therefore in transition between a *no longer* and a *not yet* that redefines not only the world of work and its meanings but also the subjectivities of those who experience precariousness in their everyday lives. In fact, identity itself is configured as a short-term identity tied to the variable duration of employment. As Standing (2011) emphasises, subjects who live in precarious conditions do not have the sense of having an occupational identity and that they are developing themselves through work and the labour market. Yet, if on the one hand, occupational instability is not the pivot around which to build one's identity, then on the other hand, it nevertheless influences how one relates with others and with one's social world.

> According to me, our generation has absorbed it like a mindset, we're trained into believing that everything comes to an end, that we must live for the moment, and that what will happen later is unknown [...] you can't go beyond a certain limit. Also thought is short-term. [26-year-old_Turin_Teacher working as a freelancer]
>
> They're always friendships that come and go... because my job is a bit here and then somewhere else, so I keep in contact with only a few people [...] I spend time in one city and then in another, so that friends usually become colleagues. Periods pass in which I don't have any real company to go out with... because those that I used to go out with have gone away, and I have make myself a group, and this is certainly a negative aspect. [36-year-old_Turin_Programmer]

The difficulty of planning in the long term, however, does not seem interpretable as a lack of projectuality and self-confidence. Rather, it seems due to a widespread practice of 'playing it by ear', a self-projection into the future, which is entirely restricted to the opportunities that arise from day to day. The remote future therefore becomes merely the sum of numerous proximate futures, and the space of experience and the horizon of expectations become detached until they lose every reciprocal reference.

The experience of misalignment thus acquires the features of a 'precariousness trap'. As the present detaches itself from past investment, as well as from desires and expectations concerning the future, this experience of misalignment also becomes the device constituting the precariousness experienced. Moreover, young knowledge workers not only must decide their lives from time to time, constantly changing their expectations, but they must also do so individually. This *precarious generation* (Bourdieu 1998), in fact, is grounded on the well-known processes of individualisation and atomisation that make construction of solid collective identities and imageries difficult. It is a generation that has not yet developed forms of mobilisation and representation with which to turn a shared experience of marginality into political strategies for change, and it struggles to merge manifold precariousnesses into a collective experience that extends beyond individual subjectivities to construct a collective political actor. In other words, the difficulty is in constructing possibilities for individual precarious subjectivities to coalesce into a precariat expressing what Standing (2011, 3) has termed 'the agency of a politics of paradise'.

6. Discussion and conclusions

This concluding section discusses the two faces of precariousness experienced by young knowledge workers in the Italian labour market.

The foregoing analysis has shown that young knowledge workers suffer a precariousness increasingly dissimilar from the contractual and occupational precarity because of the temporary contracts much discussed in recent years. The different precariousness of knowledge workers with respect to that of other temporary workers is characterised by the precariousness of trajectories: that is to say, the need to be part of a network and to reconcile aspirations (and self-identification) with work opportunities, especially in the long period.

The precariousness of trajectories is specific to knowledge workers because they must know how to make choices. And knowing how to make choices is more important than it was in the Fordist system, where once workers had been hired, their careers consisted of a series of predefined advancements.

The main findings of the comparison between the two research projects can be summarised as follows. The categories that emerged from the interviewees' accounts centred on the following:

- H*igh informality and the network as an ambivalent environment* midway between a resource and a drawback, between the sharing of knowledge and its expropriation
- *Job self-identification as a trap for self-exploitation* as an attempt to give meaning to one's work, and at systemic level with the free production of a commodity made possible by the subjectivation processes described
- *Impoverishment of skills and invisibilisation*, that is, the 'choice' between two equally unacceptable options: precarious work in a job consistent with one's training or underpaid work in a job that does not match one's skills;
- *Precariousness of trajectories* as a Darwinian mechanism of long-term social selection between workers with sufficient resources to handle the transition between one contract/project and the next and those who do not possess those resources.

While the first two categories are mainly of help in disentangling the self-identification/self-exploitation knot, the last two more effectively illustrate the experience of misalignment, which we have described as an experiential state of rescission with respect to both one's skills and one's future and desires. All four of them, however, interweave to produce various combinations of the relationship between precariousness and knowledge work.

We believe that these are the main representations with which the respondents created a counter-intuitive self-image. They enable fruitful exploration of the concepts of precariousness and knowledge work. The latter thus emerges from invisibility and takes shape, contradicting the dominant discourse of the mythical e-topia enjoyed by the creative class (Florida 2003) and the facile rhetoric of professionalism (Prandstreller 2003).

Finally, to frame the most important findings of this specific empirical study within the more general debate, we may describe knowledge workers as forming a category with marked internal stratification, contractual differences and diverse experiences of social and private life. They do not constitute a homogeneous group in terms of either material conditions or self-recognition as a class. Nevertheless, they share a number of subjective features, which embryonically depict the physiognomy of a new and numerically growing occupational group.

Although partial and localised, the results of the research fieldwork have allowed us to delineate some exemplary subjective characteristics of knowledge work. The results have shown a condition based on contingent project works, so that in digital capitalism, the world of industrial production – centred on what the English historian of industry, Edward Thompson (1967), termed 'clock-work', regulated by the criterion of time as measured by the clock – has been replaced by a task-oriented world measured by the criterion of the result obtained. However, in that knowledge work is typically project-based (objective-result), it comprises new forms of subordination and precariousness, which depend more directly on internalisation of market constraints and assuredly less on the external disciplinary power exercised by the clocking-in machine of industrial society.

To bring the issue of subordination to capital into focus, we may say – recalling Deleuze (1990) – that we have shifted from a form of external disciplinary control to a control interiorised in the social factors of the work. Precariousness, therefore, is not solely contractual, and hence does not consist solely in job precarity. Rather, it is connected to the job self-identification, which generates self-exploitation and conveys a subsumption of skills and emotions that are put into value. Immersion in a task-oriented logic (demanding, temporary and revocable) and in contingency (of employment relationships, work contacts and knowledge at risk of obsolescence) distinctly reconfigures experiences centred on autonomy, identification and the informality of relations, and it prompts broader reflection on precarisation processes.

Thus, emerging from this transition is a new occupational category with an artisanal mentality embedded in the person (who dangerously does not perceive alienation) able to use/combine various forms of knowledge, including technical-scientific ones (Sennett 2008; Ross 2009). This requires reconsideration and enrichment of the notion of the *precariat* (Standing 2011) in light of the subjectivity of a young precarious and thinking generation, which embraces values and desires of self-fulfilment that do not necessarily correspond to either dependent employment or entrepreneurship. The key theme underlying these reflections concerns the implications of such processes for forms of representation and new models of welfare.

In this regard, we would stress two features that seem particularly significant: the economic and social impoverishment of cognitive work and the lack of a public voice, which characterise an entire generation, well-educated and highly skilled, but primarily engaged in precarious knowledge work with freelance, consultancy or project contracts. The precariat, therefore, consists of a generation whose public existence is based on blackmail: either accept an extremely precarious job (of which free labour is emblematic) in order to have work consistent with one's training, or – in order to be paid and at least minimally protected – suffer downskilling and under-employment, and in this case entirely forgo expression of one's knowledge in work and society. Thus apparent is an impoverishment of resources in the sense of a growing mismatch between training and the job. This risk is exacerbated by increased subordination and decreased autonomy, even though contracts define these employment relationships as freelance.

In general, all the features described above entail a redefinition of the knowledge precariat in light of the subjectivity evidenced by the empirical research. Evident from the foregoing discussion is the advent of an increasingly clearly defined, new precariat. However, the transition from the multiple precariousnesses experienced by individuals to the construction of a collective actor able to develop shared strategies to resist precarisation is still obstructed by the anomic condition of separatedness between the individual and social sides of subjective action (Chicchi 2005) and by the progressive erosion of all that is *common* because of the extreme competitive rivalry widespread in the world of work (Ehrenberg 2010). In this frame, even more evident is the historical cleavage of representation that coincides with transition to a post-Fordist society, which requires the reconsideration and redesign of forms of collective action and coalition able to respond to the challenges of the present. From this point of view, the proposal of co-working schemes, forms of income continuity (citizenship income) and the growing mobilisation of the cognitive precariat (Allegri and Ciccarelli 2011; Caruso et al. 2010; Rete dei Redattori Precari 2011; Rete San Precario and Intelligence Precaria 2011) suggest numerous ways to elaborate new forms of action undertaken, not by individual subjectivities, but by a collective actor – the precariat – which only through political action can develop new practices of resistance and aspire to becoming *the new dangerous class*.

References

Acta. 2012. *Indagine sul lavoro autonomo di seconda generazione*. http://www.actainrete.it/2013/01/indagine-acta-come-incide-la-crisi/

Alasia, F., and D. Montaldi. 1960. *Milano, Corea. Inchiesta sugli immigrati*. Milano: Feltrinelli.

Allegri, G., and R. Ciccarelli. 2011. *La furia dei cervelli*. Roma: manifesto libri.

Alquati, R. 1993. *Per fare conricerca*. Milano: Calusca Edizioni.

Alquati, R. 1997. *Lavoro e attività*. Roma: Il manifesto.

Arienzo, A., and G. Borrelli. 2011. *Emergenze democratiche. Ragion di stato, governance, gouvernementalité*. Napoli: Giannini.

Armano, E. 2010. *Precarietà e innovazione nel postfordismo. Una ricerca qualitativa sui lavoratori della conoscenza a Torino*. Odoya: Bologna.

Armano, E. 2011. "Notes on Some Features of Knowledge Work." *Sozial Geschichte Online* 6: 63–97.

Armano, E. 2013. "Freelance Professionals at Time of Crisis." ISA RC52 blog. Accessed August 16. http://researchcommittee52.wordpress.com/2013/02/13/freelance-professionals-at-time-of-crisis/

Bailey, G. 2013. "Precarious or Precariat?" *International Socialist Review* 85: Reviews. Accessed November 26. http://isreview.org/issue/85/precarious-or-precariat

Ballarino, G., and M. Bratti. 2009. "Field of Study and University Graduates' Early Employment Outcomes in Italy During 1995–2004." *Labour* 3: 421–457. doi:10.1111/j.1467-9914.2009.00459.x.

Barone, C. 2013. *L'inserimento professionale dei laureati*. Roma: Istat.

Bauman, Z. 2000. *Liquid Modernity*. Oxford: Polity Press.

Bauman, Z. 2003. *Intervista sull'identità*. Roma-Bari: Laterza.

Beck, U. 2000. *The Brave New World of Work*. Cambridge, MA: Polity Press.

Bellucci, S., and M. Cini. 2010. *Lo spettro del capitale. Per una critica dell'economia della conoscenza*. Torino: Codice Edizioni.

Berton, F., M. Richiardi, and S. Sacchi. 2009. *Flex-insecurity. Perché in Italia la flessibilità del lavoro diventa precarietà*. Bologna: Il Mulino.

Beverungen, A., B. Otto, S. Spoelstra, and K. Kenny, eds. 2013. "Special Issue on 'Free Work'." *Ephemera, Theory & Politics in Organization* 13 (1): 1–176.

Blasutig, G. 2008. "Dalla Laurea Al Lavoro. Le Rotte E Gli Approdi." In *Mobilità e transizioni nei mercati del lavoro locali*, edited by M. Colasanto and E. Zucchetti. Milano: Angeli.

Blasutig, G. 2012. "La condizione occupazionale dei laureati e le nuove sfide per le politiche del lavoro." DiSPeS working paper, Edizioni Università, Trieste.

Bologna, S., and D. Banfi. 2011. *Vite da freelance. I lavoratori della conoscenza e il loro Futuro.* Milano: Feltrinelli.

Bologna, S., and A. Fumagalli. 1997. *Il lavoro autonomo di seconda generazione.* Milano: Feltrinelli.

Boltanski, L., and E. Chiappello. 1999. *Le nouvel esprit du capitalisme.* Paris: Gallimard.

Bonomi, A. 1997. *Il capitalismo molecolare. La società al lavoro nel Nord Italia.* Torino: Einaudi.

Booth, A. L., M. Francesconi, and J. Frank. 2002. "Temporary Jobs: Stepping Stones or Dead Ends?" *Economic Journal* 112 (480): 189–213

Bourdieu, P. 1985. *Ragioni Pratiche.* Bologna: Il Mulino.

Bourdieu, P. 1998. "La précarité est aujourd'hui partout." In *Contre-feux.* Paris: Liber-Raison d'agir.

Butera, F., S. Bagnara, R. Cesaria, and S. Di Guardo. 2008. *Knowledge Working.* Milano: Mondadori.

Caruso, L., A. Giorgi, A. Mattoni, and G. Piazza. 2010. *Alla ricerca dell'Onda. I nuovi conflitti nell'istruzione superiore.* Milano: Angeli.

Castel, R. 1995. *La métamorphose de la question sociale.* Paris: Fayard.

Castells, M. 1996. *The Information Age: Economy, Society and Culture.* Oxford: Blackwell.

Chicchi, F. 2005. "Capitalismo lavoro e forme di soggettivitˆà." In *Reinventare il lavoro*, edited by J. L. Laville, C. Marazzi, M. La Rosa, and F. Chicchi. Roma: Sapere 2000.

Chicchi, F. 2011. *Soggettività smarrita. Sulle retoriche del capitalismo contemporaneo.* Milano: Mondadori.

Chicchi, F., and E. Leonardi. 2012. *Lavoro in frantumi. Condizione precaria, nuovi conflitti, regime neoliberista.* Verona: Ombre corte.

Chicchi, F., E. Risi, E. Fisher, and E. Armano, eds. Forthcoming. "Special Issue on 'Confini e misure del lavoro emergente. Gratuità, precarietà e processi di sogettivazione nell'era della produzione digitale'." *Sociologia del lavoro.*

Chicchi, F., and G. Roggero. 2009. *Lavoro e produzione del valore nell'economia della conoscenza. Criticità e ambivalenze della network culture.* Milano: Angeli.

Clark, A., and F. Postel-Vinay. 2009. "Job Security and Job Protection." *Oxford Economic Papers* 61 (2): 207–239.

Cohen, D. 2004. *Our Modern Times. The Nature of Capitalism in the Information Age.* Cambridge, MA: MIT Press.

Deleuze, G. 1990. "Post-scriptum sur les sociétés de contrôle." In *Pourparlers 1972–1990.* Paris: Editions de Minuit.

Dogan, M. 2011. "Status Incongruence in Advanced Societies." *Società, Mutamento, Politica* 2: 285–294.

Dota, F. 2013. "Young People's Work Difficulties." In *Young People at Risk: How Changes in Work Are Affecting Young Italians' Health and Safety*, edited by D. Di Nunzio. Brussels: European Trade Union Institute.

Drucker, P. 1994. "Knowledge Work and Knowledge Society. The Social Transformations of this Century." Paper presented at conference John F. Kennedy School of Government, Harvard University, Cambridge, MA, April 4.

Ehrenberg, A. 2010. *La società del disagio.* Torino: Einaudi.

Florida, R. 2003. *L'ascesa della nuova classe creativa. Stile di vita, valori e professioni.* Milano: Mondadori.

Formenti, C. 2011. *Felici e sfruttati, Capitalismo digitale ed eclissi del lavoro.* Milano: EGEA.

Foucault, M. 2008. *The Birth of Biopolitics: Lectures at the Collège de France 1978–1979.* Translated by Graham Burchell. Basingstoke: Palgrave Macmillan.

Fumagalli, A. 2007. "Precarietà." In *Parole di una nuova politica, Transform! Italia,* edited by VV. AA. Roma: XL Edizioni.

Fumagalli, A., and C. Morini. 2009. "La vita messa al lavoro: verso una teoria del valore-vita. Il caso del valore affetto." *Sociologia del lavoro* 115: 94–115.

Harvey, D. 1990. *The Condition of Postmodernity. An Enquiry of the Origin of the Cultural Change*. Cambridge, MA: Blackwell.

Istat. 2010. *Rapporto annuale*. Roma: la situazione del paese nel 2009.

Lazzarato, M. 2012. *L'uomo indebitato*. Roma: Derive Approdi.

Lessard, B., and S. Baldwin. 2000. *Net Slaves: True Tales of Working the Web*. New York: McGraw-Hill.

Magatti, M. 2009. *Libertà immaginaria. Le illusioni del capitalismo tecno-nichilista*. Milano: Feltrinelli.

Marazzi, C. 2005. "Il modello antropogenetico di produzione." In *Reinventare Il lavoro*, edited by J. L. Laville, C. Marazzi, M. La Rosa, and F. Chicchi. Roma: Sapere 2000.

Murgia, A. 2010. *Dalla precarietà lavorativa alla precarietà sociale. Biografie in transito tra lavoro e non lavoro*. Bologna: Odoya.

Murgia, A., and B. Poggio. 2012. "La trappola della passione. Esperienze di precarietà dei giovani highly skilled in Italia, Spagna e Regno Unito." In *Condizione giovanile e nuovi rischi sociali. Quali politiche?*, edited by G. Cordella and S. E. Masi. Roma: Carocci.

Murgia, A., B. Poggio, and N. Torchio. 2012. "Italy: Precariousness and Skill Mismatch." In *Precarious Work and High-Skilled Youth in Europe*, edited by M. Samek Lodovici and R. Semenza. Milano: Angeli.

Personal Narrative Group. 1989. *Interpreting Women's Lives: Feminist Theory and Personal Narratives*. Bloomington, IN: University Press.

Prandstreller, G. P. 2003. *Il lavoro professionale e la civilizzazione del capitalismo. Il capitalismo cognitivo americano e la sfida economica cinese*. Milano: Angeli.

Raffini, L. 2013. "Moratoria di classe, eclissi del ceto medio o Incongruenza di status? Il posto dei giovani nella società della precarietà." *Società, Mutamento, Politica* 4 (7): 207–230.

Ranci, C. 2012. *Partite Iva. Il lavoro autonomo nella crisi italiana*. Bologna: Il Mulino.

Rete dei redattori precari. 2011. "Voltiamo Pagina. Indagine Sul lavoro Atipico Nel Settore Editoriale." *Quaderni di San Precario* 2: 91–104.

Rete san Precario and Intelligence precaria. 2011. "Manifesto dei lavoratori della conoscenza." *Quaderni di San Precario* 2: 189–212.

Riessman, C. K. 1993. *Narrative Analysis*. Newbury Park, CA: Sage.

Riessman, C. K. 2001. "Analysis of Personal Narratives." In *Handbook of Interviewing*, edited by J. F. Gubrium and J. A. Holstein. Newbury Park, CA: Sage.

Ross, A. 2009. *Nice Work if You Can Get It: Life and Labor in Precarious Times*. New York: New York University Press.

Rullani, E. 2005. "Economia del rischio e seconda modernità." In *Il rischio e l'anima dell'Occidente*, edited by S. Maso. Venezia: Cafoscarina.

Samek Lodovici, M., and R. Semenza. 2012. *Precarious Work and High-Skilled Youth in Europe*. Milano: Angeli.

Schomburg, H., and U. Teichler. 2006. *Higher Education and Graduate Employment in Europe: Results from Graduate Surveys from Twelve Countries*. Dordrecht: Springer.

Schütze, F. 1987. *Das Narrative Interview in Interaktionsstudien*. Hagen: Fernuniversität-Gesamthochschule.

Sennett, R. 1998. *The Corrosion of Character. The Personal Consequences of Work in the New Capitalism*. New York: Norton.

Sennett, R. 2006. *The Culture of the New Capitalism*. London: New Heaven.

Sennett, R. 2008. *The Craftsman*. New Haven, CT: Yale University Press.

Standing, G. 2011. *The Precariat. The New Dangerous Class*. New York: Bloomsbury Academic.

Terraneo, M. 2010. "Istruzione e lavoro: la condizione dei neolaureati italiani." *Stato e mercato* 90: 425–470. doi:10.1425/33149.

Thompson, E. P. 1967. "Time. Work-Discipline and Industrial Capitalism." *Past and Present* 38 (1): 56–97. doi:10.1093/past/38.1.56.

Vercellone, P. 2013. "Il reddito sociale garantito come reddito primario." *I Quaderni di San Precario* 5: 41–49.

Villa, P. 2010. "La crescita dell'occupazione femminile: la polarizzazione tra stabilità e precarietà." *Lavoro E Diritto* 24 (3): 343–358. doi:10.1441/32521.

Zambelli, L., A. Murgia, and M. Teli. Forthcoming. "Ai confini dei libri, tra passione e lavoro. Mettersi in rete per resistere alla precarietà." *Sociologia del lavoro*.

REPLY

The production of precariousness and implications for collective action: a reply to Emiliana Armano and Annalisa Murgia

Nancy Ettlinger

Department of Geography, Ohio State University, Columbus, OH, USA

This is a reply to:

Armano, Emiliana, and Annalisa Murgia. 2013. "The precariousnesses of young knowledge workers: a subject-oriented approach." *Global Discourse*. 3 (3–4): 486–501. http://dx.doi.org/10.1080/23269995.2013.865313.

Emiliana Armano and Annalisa Murgia provide a welcome extension to Guy Standing's *The Precariat* by developing a subject-oriented approach based on interviews with young knowledge workers in Italy. They also suggest that 'precariousness' is preferable to 'precarity' because it offers a distinct term that captures the unstable and deleterious circumstances that people experience beyond a job and conditions of employment, notably an erosion of identity in light of work insecurity and misalignment between skills and goals with the deskilled, low-paid, ephemeral and careerless work to which increasing numbers of young knowledge workers are tied. Further, the authors explain that the experience of precariousness is dynamic; hence, 'precariousness*es*' is most appropriate. The interviews clarify how people find themselves drawn into work that entails material and emotional blackmail as passions give way to self-exploitation, beyond exploitation by employers. People work for low or even no wages, often below their skill capacity, well beyond the time for which they are paid, and in the process blur former distinctions between work and private space and time. The interviews also clarify the desperation produced by gaps between short-term work contracts, prompting highly educated, skilled workers to take jobs requiring few skills. One interview in particular helps clarify how the crisis of overqualification experienced by young knowledge workers produces crises of identity in light of internalized societal norms, which anchor identity in an apparently unattainable stable job that permits the exercise and development of one's capabilities.

In one provocative sentence, the authors indicate that precariousness derives not just from changes in the labour market but also from the transformation of production processes, although this point remains undeveloped in their article as well as in the literature on precarity/precariousness. All the authors' interviewees were in some way associated with educational and/or research institutions, reflecting a narrow slice of precariousness from the vantage point of production processes. More generally, novel corporate strategies facilitated by information and communication technologies (ICTs) have emerged and are growing worldwide that engender new regimes of work practices. Crowdsourcing – open electronic calls for contributed work – is one such strategy that can entail remuneration ranging from nothing or next to nothing to a considerable but one-time payment. What mode of production, then, has produced corporate strategies such as crowdsourcing? Answering this question is crucial for explaining new, objectified circumstances and subjectivities and, moreover, holds clues regarding prospects for, and problems of, collective action. Flexible production, the second industrial divide, helps to explain precariousness,[1] but it does not explain stunning developments such as working for *nothing* – something quite new.

I suggest that work without remuneration, by which people live on hope – often accepting nothing for their work with the hope of ultimately earning the privilege of a 'salariat'[2] or 'profician' job – is one of a number of effects of a new mode of production that emerged around the turn of the twenty-first century.[3] Broadly, a central feature of the new system is *openness* regarding two main dimensions: networks and innovation. Whereas networks under flexible production are either closed or partially open as actors from different networks strategically connect to ensure flows of new information (Burt 1992, 2005), networks as a means to access expertise are now fundamentally open, indeed global, as illustrated by crowdsourcing. An especially novel feature of crowdsourcing is both the effort and ability of firms to access expertise not only from people in other firms, but also from people 'on the street' who may be disassociated with firms and conceivably may not even be employed.

Open networks are, in part, a new vehicle by which firms develop innovations. In 2003, former corporate manager and Berkeley scholar Henry Chesbrough coined the term 'open innovation' in reference to the new system in which firms open their borders to externalize not just production (as in flexible production), but innovation either via linkage with other firms or through issuing open electronic calls globally that reach firms as well as individuals who have expertise or inventions to sell (Chesbrough 2006a, 2006b; Chesbrough et al. 2006). For example, in 2002 Proctor and Gamble issued an electronic brief calling for an invention to permit the printing of edible pictures on each potato chip in a Pringle's container; the call was answered by the owner of a small bakery in Bologna, Italy who had developed a means to print edible pictures on cakes and cookies (Huston and Sakaab 2006). Crowdsourcing also takes the form of online competitions. For example, in 2007 Cisco Systems orchestrated an online competition with a prize of $250,000 for an invention related to Cisco's core competency in internet technology. The result: entries from 2500 innovators from 104 countries. The one-time cash prize was considerable, although the rules stipulated that the commercial rights of the winning invention would go to Cisco, which would then use the invention to launch a billion-dollar business (Jouret 2009). Other types of online competitions offer virtually no remuneration. For example, Threadless, a company founded in 2000 that produces t-shirts, orchestrates online competition for t-shirt designs, offering a small cash prize to the winner. The competitions permit Threadless to remove the labour costs of the innovative, high-end, design part of production, while also crowdsourcing the evaluation of designs, offering a $25 gift code for a Threadless t-shirt to a single evaluator picked at random. This system extends well beyond the idea of 'prosumers'[4] – consumers who participate in production by, for example, checking themselves in at airports and out at stores equipped with self-service cash/credit registers. The innovation of innovation is to use people's talents without or with relatively little remuneration, all the while that such individuals very likely under-consume or consume in the self-torture of infinite debt in the absence of a living wage (Lazzarato 2011).

The strategies developed by Proctor and Gamble, Cisco and Threadless exemplify new avenues by which firms reduce the costs of innovation and increase profitability for themselves as well as their shareholders, while offering little to nothing in remuneration to workers in tasks or competitions or considerable to nothing in one-time events that lack any semblance of security. These corporate strategies represent the initial stages of an emergent mode of production. The first survey of open innovation, published in 2013, showed that over ¾ of firms in the United States and Europe with sales over $250 million reported practicing open innovation; further, most reported that support for open innovation by top management is increasing and, moreover, no firms already practicing open innovation have abandoned it (Chesbrough and Brunswicker 2013). Although the survey covered only large firms, small- to medium-sized firms (SMEs) also are important players because large firms often rely on them in the externalized system of innovation.[5]

Beyond crowdsourcing high-level expertise or inventions for little to no remuneration or for one-time prizes, another type of crowdsourcing accesses skilled labour for tasks that are low-level but non-routine and therefore unamenable to computer-driven processes. One exemplar is Amazon.com's Mechanical Turk[6] subsidiary, which lists 'human intelligence tasks', HITs, for companies that pay Amazon.com 10% of the fee for completed tasks. On 28 December 2013, rewards for HITs ranged from 0 for a task that would require 30 minutes to $25.72 for a task that would require 7 days (that is, about $3.67 a day). A survey conducted in 2010 showed that 46.8% of Turkers come from the United States, 34% come from India and the rest are dispersed around the world (Ipeirotis 2010). Although most Turkers generally use their income from Mechanical Turk to supplement other income, over 10% of US Turkers and almost 30% of Indian Turkers rely on their Mechanical Turk earnings. Significantly, Mechanical Turk exemplifies a new expression of industrial piece work (work by the job, not by a unit of time), which traditionally has characterized sweat shop labour. Mechanical Turk and other operations like it represent a new frontier of virtual sweatshops of the digital economy that have not replaced, but rather complement, on-the-ground sweatshops organized for production and distribution.[7]

Open networks as a means to tap skilled labour for repetitive, mundane tasks as well as for innovative activity explain the crises of misalignment and overqualification as well as the problem of short-term contracts and gaps between jobs that Armano and Murgia discuss, including but extending beyond educational and research organizations. More generally, such networks call attention to an emergent, worldwide mode of production that complements a global reserve army of unskilled with skilled labour. Constant transitions between what Armano and Murgia cite as 'a no longer and a not yet' normalize liminality as a mode of existence even while specific experiences change.

Framing the new desperations by a system of production and innovation that are in their initial stage suggests that problems for people trying to earn a living are likely to deepen. The focus specifically on young adults in Italy and Europe more generally (Lodovici and Semenza 2012) implies a somewhat more stable existence for older adults, but may reflect vestiges of more stable systems that cover older adults; as young adults age, it is unlikely that their circumstances will change. Circumstances in the United States, where the dismantling of the (mild) welfare state via Keynesianism occurred much longer ago, are instructive: job instability and declining opportunities for earning a living wage increasingly characterize work across the demographic spectrum. The youth issue in Europe at this point is but the tip of the iceberg.

Armano and Mugia as well as Standing, while embracing the prospect for collective action, nonetheless provide robust arguments regarding obstructions to the formation of a political class. New regimes of work that individualize and render people vulnerable to the immediate present by means of the ephemeral nature of specific jobs implicitly dissolve connections and organizational capacity. As Standing has pointed out, the explosion of each individual's problems alongside increasing debt results in alienation, erodes even community and family support, and further, fosters tensions among those who are subjugated by the same system.

If there is to be a political response to the new regime, what, then, are to be the mechanisms or tactics of resistance? If the new vulnerabilities are produced by an emergent mode of production, then effective 'counter-conduct' (Foucault 2007, 201) must be directed to oppressive techniques of governance, such as crowdsourcing and short-term employment without a living wage and benefits. In light of the increasingly global scope of production and innovation strategies, it seems unlikely that localized protest can be effective. Networked refusal to participate in crowdsourced and short-run work is a possibility, although a tough sell to the large numbers of people who individually experience immediate material and subjective pressures. Another possibility is that states can develop incentives for long-run hiring practices and the provision of living wages (and penalties such as higher corporate taxes for short-run employment without benefits), although the governance of governments via corporate financing and political pressure suggests that this avenue also may be an improbable possibility. Perhaps the design of a system that subverts existing strategies to work for people in addition to firms may be fruitful; that is, replace revolutionary strategies that are unlikely to be sustainable with a strategy to work with the system but reconfigure the goals. Consider, for example, the possibility of using open network dynamics through non-profit organizations with the financial support of governments at local and national scales to crowdsource problems in a system that *continually* employs a heterogeneous domain of people with expertise to sell, providing a living wage and benefits. The construction of such a system recognizes the short-term project nature of work and accordingly develops a federation of ephemeral networks that accesses requisite expertise and then continually reconfigures networks relative to context-specific demands of projects. Governments might respond positively to such a strategy because their administrations are territorial even if their reach extends beyond national and local boundaries; they can ill afford dramatically increasing localized socio-economic polarization accompanied by economic, social, cultural and, indeed, political disenfranchisement of their constituencies. Effective organization, however, is unlikely to be top–down. It is through grass-roots developments and oversight of non-profit organizations that such a system, with financial support of government, may be possible.

Notes

1. Flexible production, which constructs precarious regimes of work, emerged in the United States in the 1980s concurrently with dismantling of Keynesian welfare and 'roll-back neoliberalism' (Peck and Tickell 2002) associated with Reagan–Thatcherism. As Armano and Murgia indicate, precariousness in Italy did not occur until the end of the 1990s. A central point of this essay is that at least some of the problems that Armano and Murgia and others observe may pertain to a new mode of production (i.e. not necessarily flexible production).
2. The 'salariat' and 'proficians' are relatively privileged jobs in Guy Standing's (2011) hierarchical classification of jobs.
3. Considering the much longer duration of the welfare state in many countries in continental Europe compared with the United States, precariousness occurred later in Italy and elsewhere (endnote 1), and thus the rate of change across industrial divides in countries such as Italy is accelerated. More generally, the point here is that change occurs at different rates in different contexts and is contingent, contrary to conventional unilinear periodization conceptualizations. Also departing from the usual periodization schema, modes of production may emerge at different times across space, but they do not necessarily replace modes of production that

emerged earlier; this perspective recognizes diverse organizational strategies in any one time/space context relative to contingent pressures, demands and the like (Grabher and Stark 1997).

4. The term 'prosumer' was coined in 1980 by Alvin Toffler (1980) to capture the participation of consumers in the production of the goods and services they consume.
5. Large firms often use the innovations developed by suppliers (formerly considered 'peripheral' in the previous system of production). In addition, while the availability of venture capital has declined from the traditional source – venture capital firms – venture capital for start-ups is increasingly available through large firms, which have developed internal venture capital programmes (corporate venture capital, CVC) to invest in new firms that develop innovations of interest to the large firms (Battistini, Hacklin, and Baschera 2013).
6. The name 'mechanical turk' derives from an eighteenth century wooden manequin, represented as an expert chess player and dressed as a Turk in a robe and turban. Presented as an invention of artificial intelligence, it was, however, a hoax. The Turk was kept in a wooden cabinet with gears and springs inside, and its owner worked the chess game from behind the mannequin. Digital workers for Amazon.com's Mechanical Turk subsidiary are called 'Turkers' because they perform tasks for which robotics currently are unsuited.
7. Although on-the-ground sweatshops tend to be associated with the production of goods, the increase in online shopping has generated sweatshop labour in distribution centres, where workers pack, lift and prepare items for shipping under horrible work conditions. Amazon.com's distribution centres are a case in point (Streitfeld 2011).

References

Battistini, B., F. Hacklin, and P. Baschera. 2013. "The State of Corporate Venturing: Insights from a Global Study." *Research-Technology Management* 56: 31–39. doi:10.5437/08956308X5601077.

Burt, R. S. 1992. *Structural Holes: The Social Structure of Competition*. Cambridge, MA: Harvard University Press.

Burt, R. S. 2005. *Brokerage and Closure: An Introduction to Social Capital*. New York: Oxford University Press.

Chesbrough, H. 2006a. *Open Business Models: How to Thrive in the New Innovation Landscape*. Boston, MA: Harvard Business School Press.

Chesbrough, H. 2006b. *Open Innovation: The New Imperative for Creating and Profiting from Technology*. Boston, MA: Harvard Business School Press.

Chesbrough, H., and S. Brunswicker. 2013. *Managing Open Innovation in Large Firms: Survey Report, Executive Survey on Open Innovation*. Berkeley, CA: Fraunhofer Verlag.

Chesbrough, H., W. Vanhaverbeke, and J. West, eds. 2006. *Open Innovation: Researching a New Paradigm*. Oxford: Oxford University Press.

Foucault, M. 2007. *Security, Territory, Population: Lectures at the Collège de France, 1977–1978*. Translated by G. Burchell and edited by M. Senellart. New York: Palgrave.

Grabher, G., and D. Stark. 1997. "Organizing Diversity: Evolutionary Theory, Network Analysis and Postsocialism." *Regional Studies* 31: 533–544. doi:10.1080/00343409750132315.

Huston, L., and N. Sakkab. 2006. "Connect and Develop: Inside Proctor & Gambles's New Model for Innovation." *Harvard Business Review*, March, 58–66.

Ipeirotis, P. 2010. *Demographics of Mechanical Turk*. New York: archive@NYU.

Jouret, G. 2009. "Inside Cisco's Search for the Next Big Idea." *Harvard Business Review*, September, 43–45.

Lazzarato, M. 2011. *The Making of the Indebted Man: An Essay on the Neoliberal Condition*. Translated by. J. D. Jordan. Los Angeles, CA: Semiotext(e).

Lodovici, M. S., and R. Semenza, eds. 2012. *Precarious Work and High-Skilled Youth in Europe*. Milan: FrancoAngeli for European Commission.

Peck, J., and A. Tickell. 2002. "Neoliberalizing Space." *Antipode* 34: 380–404. doi:10.1111/1467-8330.00247.

Standing, G. 2011. *The Precariat: The New Dangerous Class*. New York: Bloomsbury Academic.

Streitfeld, D. 2011. "Inside Amazon's Very Hot Warehouse." *New York Times*, September 19. Accessed November 29, 2013. http://bits.blogs.nytimes.com/2011/09/19/inside-amazons-very-hot-warehouse/?_r=0.

Toffler, A. 1980. *The Third Wave*. New York: Bantam Books.

RESEARCH ARTICLE

Precarious subjectivities are not for sale: the loss of the measurability of labour for performing arts workers

Mauro Turrini[a] and Federico Chicchi[b]

[a]*Department of Philosophy (Cetcopra), University of Paris 1 'Panthéon Sorbonne', Paris, France;*
[b]*Department of Sociology and Business Law, University of Bologna, Bologna, Italy*

Contemporary work increasingly presents itself as an immeasurable endeavour. The social and subjective spaces in which it is practiced are no longer easily circumscribed, and the conceptual categories that traditionally described its relationship with value now appear practically unusable. In particular, workers in the 'creative industries' are paradigmatic subjects of the 'work fragmentation' process of the post-Fordist era. Cutting across divisions between life and work, employment and unemployment, the performing arts are in many ways a laboratory of job flexibility, where innovative contractual arrangements and professional trajectories have been developed.

In this article, we have mapped the multiple forms that work has taken in the last two decades in Italy. The empirical data is derived from a combined method that utilizes both quantitative surveys and in-depth interviews with artists, technicians and organizers working in the fields of theatre, music, dance and video making. A central feature of the new regulative conditions, and therefore the experiences of these professionals, is the new relationship with time and, more specifically, the 'loss of measurability' of hired labour. The aim is to provide a multilayered analysis of the interactions between the socio-economic conditions, career pathways and cultural aspects, i.e. the expectations, reputation, self-perception and social recognition of these jobs. Accordingly, these work patterns are studied as self-employment strategies based on the diversification of activities and expertise, and at the same time, attempts to devise new spatial and temporal configurations of labour, epitomized by the hybrid condition of the 'salaried employer'.

In these cases, precariousness emerges as a generative terrain of ambivalent subjectivities. On the one hand, the workforce is spontaneously mobilized and autonomously organized by the realization of desires, expression and self-fulfilment, beyond mere economic rewards. On the other, the labour itself becomes increasingly intertwined with ones life, as well as becoming immeasurable. Time loses its function as a unit of measure for compensation (i.e. as in work for a flat rate). This situation frequently leads to the spread of labour into other spheres of life and the risk of self-exploitation. To conclude, the new experiences of union organization and social movements, manifesting in the occupations of theatres, are examined as spaces where differing, and even opposing, solidarity and 'class composition' practices within the new creative labour(s) are experimented.

1. The sacrifice of work. The new paradigm of production of value

Throughout the twentieth century, the history of the work has been inextricably intertwined with the production of specific forms of subjectivity. The recognition of ones social worth was, in fact, largely determined by the quality of the position that the person occupied within national production forces. The specific way work was conducted allowed one to specify a social *measure* of subjectivity. Work consisted, in other words, in the primary criterion for individual social inclusion in the capitalist and industrial society (Castel 2002).

The economists of the Regulation School demonstrate that (Aglietta 1997) the *wage society* was based on a fundamental institutional compromise between the owning-class (of the means of production) and the non-owners. This compromise organized and stabilized relations between capital and labour, in the sense that labour wage consistency conversely corresponded to company-mandated work organization, which also implies a strict subordination of labour. In that context, the value of labour (salaried) was primarily measured through the time that an individual spent on any given productive task. In the industrial society, work-time also had precise characteristics. It had a sequential and repetitive pattern. It was, in fact, a type of time marked by production machines and their scientifically preordained and automated procedures. It was a chronographically ordered type of time, punctuated by commanded labour. 'The rules of the value of work-time thus presents themselves as an expression of bio-power that insinuates the clock into all the spheres of life, synchronizing and subordinating sets of social time to the discipline and rhythm of the factory' (Vercellone 2009, 37). In this manner, it was fairly easy to divide work into homogeneous units of time and impose a determined measure of its value. In addition, the hegemony of labour subordination made it possible to discern, with some certainty, that which was actually related to individual productive action, and that which was unrelated and therefore not to be compensated. This division was based on the fact that work was an activity with rather precise specific confines, both formal and substantive, established legally for the most part through the device of the contract (see Chicchi 2012; Perulli 2012).

In this paper we wish to argue that with the disappearance of such a scenario, through the crumbling of the wage society, work blurs the traditional boundaries and becomes an activity without measure, a socially *immeasurable activity.*[1] In the first place, the criteria and categories with which labour's relationship with value was calculated, its accountability, now appear totally inadequate. Second, work increasingly expresses itself as an activity of *general intellect* that is generated in informal spaces of social cooperation outside the traditional property frame of the capitalist factory. 'Value in the current situation must refer to life activity as a whole, and therefore the immeasurability and overflowing of productive labour is a process that traverses the entire biopolitical fabric of society' (Hardt and Negri 2009, 317).

The knowledge, skills and self-organization create an increasingly important value resource, which unlike work in general 'is not reducible to a quantity of abstract labour [...]. It covers – and refers to – a wide diversity of *heterogeneous* capacities, including judgement, intuition, aesthetic sense, level of education and information, ability to learn and to adapt to unforeseen situations, which are capacities themselves brought into play by heterogeneous activities ranging from mathematical calculation to rhetoric and the art of persuasion, from techno-scientific research to the invention of aesthetic norms' (Gorz 2010, 35–36). Therefore, work re-inserts itself into the social relations of value with such unprecedented features that traditional *social representations* are rendered completely inadequate in the attempt to describe its emergent properties (see Chicchi and Roggero 2009). Robert Castel (2009) recently showed in an exemplary manner, how work today is situated completely outside of the typical form of wage employment. The latter, in fact, was characterized by a precise and explicit social discipline, inscribed in the legal corpus of labour law. In case of difficult situations for the worker, this also provided institutional care and protection. The post-Fordist rupture and the following contemporary extinction of employment structures, according to the French sociologist, foreshadow the problematic horizon of a society characterized by social insecurity and widespread individual economic precariousness. If we consider this hypothesis as correct, we must ask ourselves, *first and foremost*, in what manner the labour *statute* is changing in this post-wage socio-economic scenario.

In this regard, it is increasingly difficulty to clarify the empirical and conceptual boundaries of contemporary work. The link between production and subjectivity seems, in fact, to be to opposite of the past. The second has become an indispensable condition that generates wealth, and no longer a factor to contain, eliminate or otherwise inscribe within *abstract*, standardized and objectified mechanistic tasks. The explosion of subjectivity in production practices is also the result of the rise of a genuine *passion* that animates contemporary work biographies. The growing desire for autonomy, education and knowledge of self-production that animates contemporary subjectivity seems, then, to write the social history of an unprecedented escape route from the bounds of the *wage society.*

Work, that was understood in industrial society as an essential component of the development of Capital through both formal and material radical transformations, is increasingly intertwined and confused with the social exercise of other activities (carework, leisure, consumption, training). It is increasing difficult to delineate a precise social space for the power of valourization which bio-political capitalism needs to extract surplus value. This is not simply an analytical exercise, but an immediate political issue, which highlights the burning problem of the exploitation of life *tout court* without any social and/or institutional mediation, under the guise of generalized insecurity and the financialization of all human activity (Marazzi 2008). This is one of the most disturbing aspects of the rise of the bio-economic accumulation paradigm (Amendola et al. 2008). The distance between life and economic rational becomes less and less substantial.

Not only the subjective experience of work, but social life as a whole, is infected with deep uncertainty and unpredictability. The rules and disciplines that in the past guaranteed, for better or for worse, a certain social and legal consistency of work, today seem hopelessly *incomplete.*[2] The labour contract becomes an increasingly opaque and shadowy regulatory framework (Perulli 2012), which recognizes, in terms of income, only a fraction of the types of *work alive today* that are mobilized and required in the manufacture of digital capitalism and the increasingly important *creative industries* (Raunig 2013).

Rather than a uniform and synthetic image that represents all the features of contemporary labour, as we were used to in Fordism, we must search for an image that can describe its intrinsic and irreversible *fragmentation* (Chicchi and Leonardi 2011). Fragmentation can also be seen as a deterritorialization of the social ties that work brought, certainly not without profound ambivalences, to the core of social inclusion processes and citizenship devices. But, *fragmentation* is also a rupture and profound revision of the disciplinary powers of panoptical bio-power (Foucault 2004) that the wage society had inscribed in its *DNA* in the process of social direction (according to the vertical hierarchy model of the Fordist factory and the mythical narrative of economic growth without limits). A prospective of contemporary work, therefore, which must be read starting from overturning and/or overcoming of a series of variously complex axioms and operating codes that were understood as hegemonic and given in the 'industrial' process of value production. This horizon must be questioned in the light of the imperatives of creativity, surplus and flexibility that are now continually being placed within networked supply chains of capitalist organization. It is a horizon that utilizes subjectivity in new ways: it does no longer compress it; rather, it stimulates and channels its independent and projective abilities. These subjectivities are a new indispensable source for sustaining development processes, that at the same time *cast* the workforce into a general and structural condition of precariousness (Standing 2011). It is in fact a subjectivity that is not free of constraint, exploitation and subjection, largely embedded within a control device that produces and stimulates desires, ambitions, frustrations and new inequalities at the same time. It is, in fact, these exaggerated characteristics of uncertainty and unpredictability that led us to investigate the labour phenomenology that were first (and most extremely) subject to the cutting edge of the ambivalent contemporary production scenario, which Raunig (2013) calls the cultural industries.[3]

2. Sedimentation and intensification of instability in the performing arts

While in the Keynesian welfare state the performing arts workers' landscape was a relatively stable environment, in recent decades, the field has exploded both in quantitative and qualitative terms. Restricting our attention to the Italian context, the numbers of this phenomenon are particularly eloquent. In Italy in 2011, there were 250,000 live performance employees out of the approximately 23 million national workers (INPS 2012). This means not only that nowadays this field is a remarkable portion of the working population, but also that there has been a renewal of languages, places and performance audiences. A diversified and innovative demand by non-elite social groups traditionally alien to this type of consumption found room to develop in a constellation of spaces and moments not traditionally assigned to performance, such as town halls, provincial towns, festivals, exhibitions, community centres, clubs and schools. The new kind of audience matched with support from new institutional entities, *primarily* local agencies. Performance, as well as culture in general, represents a strategic sector for urban development, generating wealth through urban and territorial renewal processes[4] (Harvey 2001).

From our point of view, in this context the formation of new working subjectivities in performance is particularly interesting, especially those related to the execution, preparation and organization of live performance. Intercepting without mediation an increasingly segmented and fluctuating demand for culture, these new job positions are, intentionally or due to necessity, located outside or on the margins of traditional and institutionalized circuits, such as permanent companies, opera companies, and the more established television, radio, film and recording circuits. Working in the entertainment industry also means, more and more, managing projects, being flexible, taking the risk in the first person, in other words, marrying self-employment culture. Performing arts' overflow out of *mainstream* and *big corporate* channels (public and private) can therefore also be interpreted as a break in the organization of labour based on the standard relationships of dependence, and at the same time of the acceptance of the competitive conditions of the market. In this manner, entertainment workers have become an integral part of the new wave of *independent workers* that particularly characterizes Italy (Bologna and Fumagalli 1997), as well as other western economic societies (see, for an US example, Pink 2001). Displacing the priority to curb the intermittency of working relationships, show business labour has instead emphasized a predisposition to independence, improvization, the unexpected and the informal, as seen in most new jobs in the knowledge and creative industry (Virno 2004).

As an 'inherently precarious' industry (as performing art workers like to repeat without exception), this process can be defined as already regimented with an increase in the intermittent condition of the profession. Regarding the distinction between old and new precariousness, our investigation relies on the in-depth interviews conducted with more than twenty professionals, the answers to the online questionnaire (which was distributed through both festivals and the associations we had contact with), found on a specially created website (www.inchiesta-loisir.it) which includes original articles about the work conditions of freelance performing art workers.[5] It should be noted that 'precariousness' does not refer here to the negative effects of flexibility in terms of the difficulty of creating ongoing income and access to social safety nets as intended in socio-economic debates (Berton, Richiardi, and Sacchi 2012). Not that this labour sector is unfamiliar with these elements of discomfort. Confirming the results of another recent major investigation focused on the theatre world, the quantitative data of our investigation indicates income levels that average just above the poverty line,[6] as well as uncertain access to the most basic measures of social protection.[7] In any case, in the common sense prevalent in this professional field, 'precariousness' is seen as an essential, inevitable, and already part of the reality in which they practice their occupation.

Other empirical studies have shown how the desire for a self-employed fulfilling job atones for uncertain work situations and the failure of the work-contract. The desire for recognition is often accompanied by exacerbation mechanisms regarding the work-rate and self-exploitation (Huws 2006; Reidl, Schiffbanker, and Eichmann 2006). In this sense, as some have argued (see, in particular, Menger 2002), the artist's craft and more generally that of show business is paradigmatic of the reorganization of contemporary work, described by some as the next great transformation of 'cognitive capitalism' (Moulier-Boutang 2012). A specific aspect that is particularly worth investigating is the loss of the value of time as a measurement of labour, characteristic of this labour sector. In the following section we intend to discuss this issue, and investigate it in the light of its impact on the legal system, work experience and the composition of work.

3. Salvador Dali's soft watches: work without timing

One way to describe the end of Fordist organization of labour is as the breakdown of the severe and invisible division between production and reproduction, as well as between work and leisure.[8] In the former context, time spent in 'productive activities' was recognized as labour and strictly regulated. Nowadays, these restrictions are increasingly fading away as many aspects of life can be put to work. As a result, time loses its capacity to order and classify labour, and working time becomes dispersed, especially in fields regarding knowledge and creativity. In their investigation on the French *intermittents du spectacle* (casual workers in the performing arts), Antonella Corsani and Maurizio Lazzarato (2008) show in detail how the performative professional vocation easily translates into strict mandatory discipline marked by flexibility, diversification of activities and sources of income, arriving at an uncritical acceptance of unpaid work and an exhausting search for self-employment. Gerald Raunig analyses a similar phenomenon in the context of the 'creative industries'. The dissolution of the traditional dichotomies between work and leisure, between production and reproduction, between employment and unemployment, is read in terms of a smoothing of Fordist labour discipline, defined by the dual organization of temporality. While expressing a liberating potential, this movement away from the dual-time division often ends up fragmenting, dividing and multiplying work time, sometimes colonizing one's entire life (Raunig 2013). Compared to subordinate relationships, self-employment in the field of entertainment has lost its stable relationship with time, which, as already mentioned, loses its ability to act as a unit of measurement of labour and wages.

> Our work is by nature atypical. I, when I chose this field, did it also for that. However, we would like it recognized that our jobs are made up of multiple actions, many of which are not paid nor recognized. All training and self-training, all the workshops in which these skills are used, all the rehearsals, which are often paid as a lump sum at best, are all part of a whole set of tasks that mean you do not work just those 80, 100 working days per year that you declare to ENPALS.[9] (Gianni, director and organizer of cultural events)

The above passage presents several insights. Precariousness, rather than being an exception to be remedied, is paradoxically accepted as a structural aspect that is grounded in their professional experience. The critical element invoked instead refers to the remuneration and recognition of their activities. The lump sum payment is then mentioned as a favoured form of payment, as if indicating a new paradigm of remuneration (which is defined, in French, as *la forfaitisation du salaire*; the flat-rate salary), where time loses its key position in favour of a service, a performance or the resolution of a problem. The self-employment imperative in the conduction of activities that were once traditionally subordinate (artistic, technical, administrative), generates, as we shall see in more detail in the next section, a *hybridization* of the worker's legal status. In addition, it seems to result in the multiplication of duties, from accounting to project design, from management to event organization, from teaching to promotion. The same individual is often found covering more than one task at the same time.

The proliferation of activity does not necessarily correspond to a growth of work understood as economically and socially recognized activities. Work, by losing its unit of measure, becomes at the same time all-encompassing and impalpable. A second dimension of overwork comes into play, implicated by self-perception, self-fulfilment and satisfaction. In his tips for independent workers, Pink (2001, 321) connects this type of remuneration to a form of valourization of work: 'When possible charge by the project, not by the hour. [...] Why? You're talent. Do Julia Robert, Tiger Woods or Itzhack Perlman charge by the hour? No way. They charge by the performance'. Although didactic, the quote clearly shows the link between economic value and socio-cultural recognition manifest in performing arts. However, it is interesting to note that *la forfatisation du salaire* often means an impoverishment and regression of working conditions. As Corsani and Lazzarato note, there is a less visible element that is equally important: 'the flat-fee turns the salary into fees, and basically, turns the wage labourer into the self-employed' (Corsani and Lazzarato 2008, 64). In essence, the classical categories of labour regulation are being strained.

4. Neither employees nor independent. The hybridization of working arrangements

The immeasurability of labour has established a hybridized terrain in-between the classical dichotomy of juridical categories of labour. Jurist Alain Supiot (2000) has highlighted how a growing need for autonomy has laid the groundwork conditions for a 'grey area', an area without precise formal positioning, inhabited by employees that are forced to manage projects, act on their own initiative, be flexible and autonomous, take responsibility and yet subject themselves to precise work hours and locations. In other French research, conducted in light of the struggle to reform the role of the casual entertainment worker (*intermittent du spectacle*) at the beginning of the twenty-first century (Menger 2002; Corsani and Lazzarato 2008), other hybrid employment schemes were discovered that are not attributable to either the role of entrepreneur nor that of the employee.

In our investigation a similar phenomenon appeared, in the moment when the composite job profiles clash with the existing regulatory framework. Job diversification is often tackled by using multiple contractual regimes, which change based on the task, location or employer. Behind this difficulty often lurk disadvantageous conditions, a proliferation of bureaucracy, an inability to negotiate, a low awareness of ones actual rights and a systematic abasement of jobs that, even in the most elevated sectors, struggle to build solid social security or assistance coverage.[10]

The answer to this difficult situation in many cases is a propensity to deregulation. The second Berlusconi government tried to capture this spirit by instituting, within the 2004 budget, a wholly innovative, anomalous legal role, 'il lavoratore autonomo esercente attività musicale' – a rather weird expression that might be translated as 'the self-employed musical operator'.[11] Intended to absolve the employer from any bureaucratic work, and render the worker self-sufficient, in this legal framework all liability falls on the shoulders of the individual operator, as well as all of the complex bureaucratic procedures involved in the working relationship.

The development of practices aimed at forcing the legal instruments to meet both the various and flexible requirements of multiple and heterogeneous employers, and the desire for professional recognition and autonomy, is particularly interesting. The complex phenomenology of individual tax IDs (Partita IVA) is particularly illuminating in this regard. Certain tax IDs are linked to non-profit cultural organizations (especially common for theatre companies, musical ensembles and other formations[12]) because this allows members to invoice a performance, and simultaneously sign an employment contract with the association of which they are president or vice-president. This apparent stretching of legal instruments, which falls in what the French have defined as the 'monstrous' institute of the 'salaried employer' (Corsani and Lazzarato 2008), actually ties the project autonomy to the recognition of working days and, therefore, relates to an unclear measure of work.

Take the case of a small theatre company made up of two people who 'sell' a performance to an institution. Their remuneration will not depend in any way on the hours they actually work. It is rare in these situations they will even take the trouble of reporting their total working hours. Anyway, it would be rather difficult to define the wide range of tasks performed, and therefore the time that was not work. In contrast, the work hours that the company is able to pay itself will be dependent on the fee, which varies greatly from case to case. If the figure is low, the work that is recognized as a paid activity will be limited to a minimum corresponding to the single performance; this limit can be lowered even more through the use of expense reimbursements. A higher fee will be spread over more work hours. Considering that these workers often play a wide range of roles that include, in the case of this example, assembly, transport, rehearsal and even promotion, all of their activities are recognized as work. Within the same tasks, according to the fee, the time recognized as work will change substantially from a single day to up to one month.

The subversion of the dichotomies on which labour law has classically structured is the result of a revised strategy that addresses autonomy and recognition. The juridical monster of the salaried employer tries to reintroduce the measure of time in a context where not only has it lost its value, but has also become something difficult to isolate and identify.

5. The disturbing loss of work boundaries

Several studies on cognitive work have indicated that work satisfaction often makes up for other considerable losses. Increased flexibility in working hours and pay are often bartered for artistic recognition; and employment uncertainty, unpaid work and self-exploitation are occasionally exchanged for autonomy (Ross 2003; Huws 2006; Reidl, Schiffbanker, and Eichmann 2006). In our inquiry we found similar mechanisms. In particular, the salary that is transformed into a set-fee implies a loss of work measurements, not only in terms of economic value, but also socio-cultural recognition.

> [If] we believe that culture and entertainment are elements that enhance social life and the appeal of a country like Italy, then we must find solutions [*for protection and support*] not simply for those who decide to become an artist, but for those who somehow manage to show that they get a *certain level of attention* for their work. (Luke, actor, drama teacher, organizer of cultural events and association activist; Italics are mine)

In this passage, professionalism is not interpretable in economic or formal terms, but, in a more subtle way, as the ability to arouse 'a certain level of attention'. These words indicate that the work is not identified as much with the activities themselves, as with the reputation, influence and resonance that one is able to acquire. These are the qualities that, by classifying their activities as social resources and 'immaterial' qualifications of the territory, compensate for the lack of legitimacy that emanates from these words.

The need for professional recognition is personal and social, cultural and economic, and leads to an *extraordinary diligence* based on the *intensification* of work hours and *labour diversification* both inside and outside the principle profession. As Maria, a musician as well as music and foreign language teacher, states: 'The amount of time worked is endless, phone calls, contacts, travelling'. In other words, the loss of typically Fordist compartmentalization between life and work risks misplacing the confines of one's job. The loss of measurement, then, means that the work that cannot be measured, is also boundless, not circumscribed, not containable.

In a situation where work has been increasingly distributed from production sites to the realm of consumption and social networking, work opportunities for artist, sound engineers, designers and cultural organizers have multiplied in areas of corporate communication, event planning at different levels, healthcare and education. In the words of the interviewed dancer, this means *hybridizing*, using ones skills by adapting them to unrelated situations. Similarly, entertainment industry workers respond to a fluctuating demand by reinvent their professions, running the risk of distorting them, crossing different *genres, skills and contexts*. In the words of a drama teacher, musician and sound engineer, 'professionalism is hard to find, everyone lives by one's wits, hybrid situations arise in which I *can do this, that, and yet another thing and even another more and more'*.

Paradoxically, a profession chosen for passion and self-expression leads to extraordinary and unpredictable diversification, a hybridization of artistic languages and methods. In addition, the encounter with the productive fabric outside of the spaces of material production does not extend exclusively to the immaterial production level, but also seeks alternative sources of income through highly precarious work in the service industry.

> On one hand, it wouldn't even be a problem, if there was virtuosity, a creative eclecticism. The activity is the problem. If one says, 'I am a *lighting designer*, director, teacher and then I go to work at the bar of my friend because it is very trendy and I find inspiration there …' Damn, you're eclectic, you have fun, live. But often you do it because you have to get by …

> it's different! Of all the ones I listed, if you skip the bar, maybe it becomes a problem, because the others [are barely useful as a source of income] ... (Marino, theatre and convention director, theatre and public speaking teacher, director of a small theatre)

The chronic contingency of employment conditions creates proximity between these highly skilled workers and the fringes of lower skilled workers, particularly migrants. Furthermore, the shift to a post-industrial economy has expanded women's employment options, in particular in the creative industries of the affluent countries where there had been a strong feminist tradition. For certain aspects, the rise of post-Fordist production is, in this manner, associated with an increased participation of women, particularly young women in the urban-based new culture industries. Accordingly, they bring typically feminist issues into the realms of labour, such like the relationship between work and reproduction, the excessive demands of multi-tasking careers, the priority of self-realization, and the new kinds of pain and injury that result from the stress and uncertainty (McRobbie 2010). The need to engage in different tasks, or different activities, for different employers, at the same time is experienced both as a limitation of ones expressive ability, and as an opportunity to create value for oneself in different situations. In a paper that elaborates our qualitative data, we show how professional fulfilment, just like other conditions such as gender, income and age, is proportional to the number of work contracts and relationships one is able to handle (Chicchi, Savioli, and Turrini 2014). At the same time, however, the fear of career loss is particularly strong. In this regard, it is interesting to note that in all these professions, despite their distance, the term 'a hustle' (*marchetta*) is used negatively to indicate a performance devoid of any aesthetic value and carried out exclusively for economic purposes. The profession is not what one does to make a living. Instead, often in order to continue one's profession, one is forced to live by ones wits and take other jobs. Work is instead a self-realization journey based on an *investment in oneself and self-expression*. In the wake of the unruliness of the traditional subordination of ones activities, these subjectivities exemplify what Christian Marazzi calls the 'anthropogenetic model of production', in which the living being, the human, becomes the end and means, the final product and capital (Marazzi 2008). The *affects* of the work experience[13] that are at stake are not so much remedying precariousness, creating continuity to intermittent wage employment, but rather the affirmation of total (*i.e. all-consuming) professions*. In this sense, we see a psychological significance tied to professional affirmation. The majority of the answers to an open question in our survey converged remarkably in the rather recent condition of occupational medicine, psychological distress, in the form of anxiety, depression and panic. The *immeasurable* workload takes intermittency as a starting point for disrupting the divisions of traditional labour organization, dangerously exposing oneself to intense mechanisms of exploitation and self-exploitation.

6. Emergencies: autonomous subjectivities and composition

Andrew Ross (2008) in a recent paper discusses the premises but also the problems with the Italian post-operaist thesis on temporary workers. Described as a multitude of professional profiles, they join together the interests and demands of all of the jobs that are most affected by flexibility, from the knowledge and culture industries to the service industries. Disputing the too often taken for granted assumption, the American sociologist shows how often the search for autonomy does not preclude solidarity and labour social structures that include heterogeneous kinds of workers. In the case of the entertainment industry, jobs with very different professional statuses, qualifications and fees, blend within a very small economic area. It is therefore interesting to explore some of the organizational work paths that were exceptionally common in Italy in recent years, particularly in theatre, outside of the spaces that the more established unions have devoted to music, theatre, film and so forth.[14] Once again, the loss of measurability of work provides us with a good analytical tool with which to read this discontinuity in the work organization processes.

The season of theatre occupations, a new tactic for Italian social movements, was read by many commentators as coming from out of the blue. In reality, the unrest in the entertainment industry was already present in the professional associations. Of these associations, the Trade Union of Musician Entertainment Workers (Sindacato Operatori dello Spettacolo Musicisti – SOS), the Zeropointthree Association and the Coordination of the Contemporary Scene (Coordinamento delle Realtà della Scena Contemporanea – CReSCo) differ in several respects from classical trade unions. Their direction is more inclusive of the emerging realities than the traditional forms of labour representations in the trade union. The labour protections, therefore, do not make a distinction between professionals and semi-professionals, or between employees and employers. In this manner, certain issues we have previously addressed are recognized. In the first place, professional boundaries are no longer defined through a qualification, employment contract or income source, in a situation where second jobs (teaching, sound engineer, etc) are common even for famous artists. In addition, amateurism, rather than a phenomenon to curtail, is seen as part of an important source of income and recognition of the professionalism of show business in a culture that increasingly escapes from its traditional channels. Second, in a situation where performance workers and companies are very close, if not overlapping, protest forms must be rethought, such as traditional ones like strikes (which are widely used in orchestras and choruses). These efforts converge on one hand in the creation of self-regulatory codes that clearly indicate the minimum requirements for a performance, and on the second hand, actions such as lobbying political institutions (including surveys).

Far more interesting, however, are the socio-political movements that have emerged from the creative industries in recent years. We have already mentioned the important *Intermittents et Précaires* French movement, which continues to operate, even if it has lost its momentum. More recently, a Canadian militant group named *Cultural Workers Organize* is researching the creative economy in order to add to the creation of flexworkers labour movement. In Italy, there has been a remarkable season of theatre occupation that started with the occupation of the eighteenth-century Teatro Valle in Rome. Conducted in the aftermath of the victory of the referendum against the privatization of water, this event inspired many other similar experience of cultural space appropriation in many medium-sized and large cities (Milan, Palermo, Catania, Naples, Pisa) throughout the peninsula. These various occupied spaces also organized special events that stressed similarities between performing arts workers and other precarious employees. Teatro Valle Occupato also devised an interesting experimental institutionalization process called 'private foundations for the common goods'. These are, once again, hybrid forms. A legal institution of a private nature, used for a public purpose; private capital to run the theatre was formed through small membership fees, in which both an autonomous and participative management was experimented (VV.AA. 2012). What is at stake here is the desire for professional recognition that often leads to self-exploitation to a collective reorganization of both work and the relationship with the audience in performing arts. Independent career paths create new ground of value creation out of social and affective relationships, which potentially act as an adhesive that could bandage the immeasurability of work.

7. Final remarks

The reflections that we have presented regarding labour in the world of the entertainment industry, or rather on the labour imaginary and phenomenology as they appear in these *widespread cultural factories*, indicates how the relationship between product and service is confused to the point of becoming nuanced and subtle. Social interaction and its commodification can be found at the centre of the entertainment industry's production process. The context in which the labourers we investigated work is therefore one where the *aesthetic* issue is the beating heart of value production for their economy – fictional economics (of *fiction* production). In this context, the work itself is atypically structured from the beginning (in its substance, even before addressing the formal level), with respect to its activities, its molecular (or evasive) self-employment, liberty of task definition and the dense emotionality of the productive action. The work is therefore hidden in a shadow zone in which neo-servile levels of exploitation can be found, or in other cases, a complicity is created between labour supply and demand that, in Italy, forms the dense substrate of *submerged* local *economies*. We cannot grasp anything regarding the contemporary anthropology of precarious and cognitive labour, if we do not first address it in terms of the relationship structure between economics and the imaginary of goods, between economics and subjectification processes, and between desire and the commodification of cultural activity.

The experiments that the subjects at work produce here (experiments because *no one knows in advance the feelings of which he is capable*) act in a fabric of production and employment relations that are increasingly opaque and random. These relationships refer to conventional practices more than legislative bodies, whose geographic and regulatory boundaries are continually crossed, violated and rewritten by the social pragmatics of entertainment workers' production. In this sense, entertainment industry workers seem to describe inherently *nomadic* forms of existence. Experimenters of contingent solutions, continuously running out of time and out of place. Carriers of knowledge without proprietary vocation. Subjectivities continuously in the making, not easily recognizable or placed with the 'traditional' identities and representations of socially constituted and culturally stratified labour. In other words, the workers are absorbed into a social temporality that is characterized by their intrinsic *excess* respect to criteria and traditional economic roles, and by their inherent slipperiness, impermanence and improvization. They are inserted in a discourse that insists on the imperative of the self-organization of their professional activity, which immediately appears ambivalent and highly exposed to precarious employment traps. What appears is the possibility to create a subjective definition of a new mode of professional agency, which we could perhaps say is constructed in opposition to the typical salaried form, placing *the culte de la perfomance* at its fundamental core (Eherenberg 2010).

Terms such as implication, motivation, flexibility, responsibility, project, communication, informality, which become the liturgy of the post-Fordist management manuals as well as code words for entertainment workers (see Boltanski and Chiappello 2005). In the space of this nomadic work (in the Deleuzian sense) there are, in fact, the territories (or the socius) at stake produced by identification lines that intersect and isolate the subjective experiences. In other words, new and complex processes of de-territorialization and re-territorialization are at stake. Multiple lines that intersect and/or move away on the same *plane of consistency*. Lines that produce new forms of subjectivity beyond the shrinking channels of salaried sociality. The problem is that these escape routes are not yet able to plough the terrain they encounter. Often they are routes that remain phenomenologically dependant on enthusiastic and ephemeral outbursts of professional autonomy, which are then ruined and diverted into 'reparative' destinations, not expected and not desired, but necessary for material needs. The subjectivity at stake is, in fact, held, captured in a double bind: instability and self-exploitation that on one side assumes the aspect of blackmail and harassment, but on the other represents the only way out of the grips of external management and passive labour.

The dynamics that describe the actions of the people at work in *world* of entertainment organize themselves according to the configurations of social relations they encounter. But these processes follow subjectivation *lines* and supply chains that no longer have a pre-ordered *geography*. They are contingent in a certain sense. They create *cartographies* that contain streaks as well as invasive and segmental power apparatus. The resulting differential inclusion devices can be felt (that hold) on bodies, or as enhancing devices (bio-power), through the distributive application of a part (often insufficient and unlikely) of a financial measure of value to the creative paths of artistic enterprise.

They can be defined as a true and proper *governance of social desires and emerging passions*. A pleasure district where value is produced through the commodification of knowledge and pleasures that these workers know how to infiltrate and distribute in the recreational activities of the widespread and *molecular factory* of tourism and cultural consumption. Art, care, surprise, invention, relationships, but also discipline and resistance to the unusual and agonizing working rhythms. This is what ends up constituting the worth (Boltanski and Thévenot 2006) of the performing arts worker.

It is then important to emphasize how, according to Raunig (2013), the smoothing of Fordist social temporality is accompanied by a striation process of hierarchical time, fragmented at multiple levels. It is insufficient to describe this process as an economization of culture or as industrialization of creativity. It is something more: a growing modulation of creativity, the inscription of creative time in evaluation processes based on modularization and modulations. This modulation is established in the interstices between individuals and collectives, in subjectivation modes and forms of life.

The production of an increasingly thick *aesthetic soul* within contemporary work (evaporating it, changing its 'social nature' (Chicchi 2012), still does not define a clear and predictable political and social outcome. In other words, the escape from the wage society is not immediately one of emancipation from work, but produces ambivalent effects that need to be continuously politically addressed. As Guy Standing (2011, 168) clearly states 'Although the precariat is not yet a class-for-itself, it is a class-in-the-making, increasingly able to identify what it wishes to combat and what it wants to construct. It needs to revive an ethos of social solidarity and universalism, values rejected by the utilitarians'. In the end, what entertainment workers present us with today, through their emancipatory practices and collective expropriation of metropolitan areas that have been assaulted and humiliated by real estate speculation, is exactly this possibility to become.

And yet precariousness, as we have seen, is developed and realized in ambivalent terms, in attempts to corrupt subjectivity, it spills over elsewhere without any planning. In the sense that, when activating the 'free' and docile disposition of market subjects, it cannot help but disrupt the balance inside this same power and its super-structural consummatory trap (financially saturated and caricatured). This subtle but profound rupture lets us glimpse, even if only for a few moments, a passage, a luminous trail that leads towards a collective and shared elsewhere, if properly placed in focus. It is therefore necessary to construct the imaginary and the symbolic horizon of the less tangible side of this ambivalence, build the political and social possibility for a *radical change of the signs of precariousness*. We need to start from here, from this ambivalence that the entertainment worker carries in order to create, inside the crisis, a new great project of constitutional democracy.

Despite the fact that the general situation is anything but rosy, it still seems possible to inspire new subjectivities. There are firefly that swarm across our night with the bold claim of wanting to imagine the beginning of a new democratic phase, there are fireflies that do not seem willing to disappear under the blinding media spotlight of the *capitalist* post-modern and post-industrial *discourse* (Chicchi 2012), nor under the hard blows of the administrative apparatus that manage and protect the privileges of the financial megamachine. As Georges Didi-Huberman (2009, 35. Our translation) states: 'it is necessary to respond to this "enlightened" despair with the fact that the lively dance of the fireflies takes place right in the heart of darkness. And that this is nothing more than a dance of desire that gives life to a community.'

Notes

1. In introducing the theoretical figure of *excess* labour here as the preferred interpretive key of our empirical data, we inherently refer to the theoretical contributions of Antonio Negri on this subject. Among other work, see Negri (1999), Hardt and Negri (2000, 2009). Keep in mind, in addition, that the way in which the issue of value *inequality* in Antonio Negri's recent work is directly related to the concept of 'common' and its social production.
2. Regarding the concept of the incompleteness of the contract, we refer primarily to the work of Oliver D. Hart. In extreme synthesis, a contract is incomplete when its terms are observable by the parties, but not verifiable or enforceable, that is executable with certainty and capable of being enforced by a third party (arbitrator or judicial authority) in the event of a dispute.
3. Overturning, as Gerald Raunig (2013) correctly indicates, Horkheimer and Adorno's hypothesis that the cultural industry would have been the last bastion of resistance to the processes of the progressive industrialization of production activities. Instead, he emphasizes how labour in this area of advanced services anticipates and then highlights the new paradigmatic features of contemporary post-Fordist work. Therefore, our specific intention was to investigate contemporary labour situating the subjective ambivalence that is produced in the so-called passion trap (Murgia and Poggio 2012) at the heart of our analysis. In other words, we tried to show the other side of labour uncertainty starting from the need to maintain this ambivalence, rejecting the limitations of considerations based on the hypothesis of the industrialization of the cognitive, as well as other theories that are too 'optimistic', focused on the total cognitivization of production hypothesis.
4. In Italy, these interests have led to the foundation of entertainment observatories (Osservatori dello Spettacolo) by different regions (Emilia–Romagna, Piedmont and Tuscany). These entities have the highest profile of the local authorities and are the only one with fiscal autonomy within the national administrative system.
5. The data was collected from June to December 2012. Three hundred and fifty seven practitioners of the performing arts replied to the questionnaire. Through this process the average age of the selection was relatively young: for the average age, 34 years old; regarding the length of service, an average of 9 and a half years; regarding professional insertion, which occurred on average at 24 years old, a few years younger than the national average. There were more women (53.2%), with high level of education (57.7% held university degrees) and vocational training. Totally, 61.3% had a high school diploma, a university degree or had taken a specialist course before entering the labour market.
6. In the sample that we analysed, 53.3% said a pre-tax annual income just below 10,000 euros derived from performance activities. In the other mentioned investigation, *Rispondi al Futuro*

(*Answer to the Future*) (Bacchella, Bollo, and Carnelli 2011), the average annual income earned by these professional is between 9,150,000 and 11,400,000 Euros.

7. A total of 77.3% of those who fell ill in the past five years had no access to sick pay, having to work or forfeit income. Only 16.7% were instead able to enjoy a continuity of income.
8. In a similar way, Cristina Morini (2010) describes the passage towards the post-Fordist organization of labour as 'the feminisation of labour', in the sense that productive work assumes the style of reproductive work.
9. In Italy, ENPALS (Ente Nazionale di Previdenza e Assistenza per i Lavoratori dello Spettacolo) is the social security fund for entertainment and sports workers. Since its absorption into the general social security fund (INPS – Istituto Nazionale per la Previdenza Sociale), in 2012, its correct name is 'ex-ENPALS'. Not having changed the special arrangements for the collection and payment of subsidies, it is still commonly called by the old label.
10. The resigned attitude to a situation that forces one to pay into various social security funds is significant in this regard. More than 44% of the respondents pay into at least two different national social security funds.
11. Ex. art. 3, cc. 98, 99, 100, law n. 350 of December 24 2003.
12. Of the 171 companies that responded to a recent national survey, 132 (83%) are cultural associations (Bacchella, Bollo, and Carnelli 2011, p. 46).
13. Antonio Negri (1999) notes that affect has been traditionally a marginal aspect in the historical development of the theory of value of political economists, while it becomes crucial in contemporary re-organization of work.
14. The most important, with the longest history, is undoubtedly the Section of Italian Actors (Sezione Attori Italiani – Sai), part of the larger Italian trade union, the Italian General Confederation of Labour (Confederazione Generale Italiana del Lavoro – Cgil).

References

Aglietta, M. 1997. *Régulation et crisesd u capitalisme*. Paris: Odile Jacob.

Amendola, G., L. Bazzicalupo, F. Chicchi, and A. Tucci. 2008. *Biopolitica, bioeconomia e processi di soggettivazione*. Macerata: Quodlibet.

Bacchella, U., A. Bollo, and L. Carnelli. 2011. *Rispondi al futuro*. Accessed June 14, 2013. http://www.fitzcarraldo.it/ricerca/pdf/rispondialfuturo_report.pdf

Berton, F., M. Richiardi, and S. Sacchi. 2012. *The Political Economy of Work Security and Flexibility: Italy in a Comparative Prospective*. Bristol: The Policy Press.

Bologna, S., and A. Fumagalli. 1997. *Il lavoro autonomo di seconda generazione: scenari del postfordismo in italia*. Milano: Feltrinelli.

Boltanski, L., and E. Chiapello. 2005. *The New Spirit of Capitalism*. Translated by G. Elliot. New-York: Verso.

Boltanski, L., and L. Thévenot. 2006. *On Justification: Economies of Worth*. Translated by C. Porter. Princeton: Princeton University Press.

Castel, R. 2002. *From Manual Workers to Wage Laborers: Transformation of the Social Question*. New Brunswick, NJ: Transaction.

Castel, R. 2009. "Au-delà du salariat ou en deçà de l'emploi ? l'institutionnalisation du précariat." In *La montée des incertitudes*, edited by R. Castel, 159–183. Paris: Seuil.

Chicchi, F. 2012. *Soggettività smarrita. Sulle retoriche del capitalismo contemporaneo*. Milano: Bruno Mondadori.

Chicchi, F., and E. Leonardi. 2011. *Lavoro in frantumi: condizione precaria, nuovi conflitti e regime neoliberista*. Verona: Ombre corte.

Chicchi, F., and G. Roggero, eds. 2009. *Lavoro e produzione del valore nell'economia della conoscenza: criticità e ambivalenze della network culture, special issue of sociologia del Lavoro*. Milano: Franco Angeli.

Chicchi, F., M. Savioli, and M. Turrini. 2014. "Soggettività intermittenti. Un'inchiesta sulla scomposizione del lavoro nell'ambito del loisir." In *Boundaries and Measurements of Emerging Work*, edited by E. Armano, F. Chicchi, E. Fisher, and E. Risi, 43–58. Milano: Franco Angeli.

Corsani, A., and M. Lazzarato. 2008. *Intermittents et précaires*. Paris: Editions Amsterdam.

Didi-Huberman, G. 2009. *Survivance des lucioles*. Paris: Les Editions de Minuit.

Eherenberg, A. 2010. *La société du malaise*. Paris: Odile Jacob.

Foucault, M. 2004. *Naissance de la biopolitique cours au collège de france*. Paris: Gallimard-Seuil.
Gorz, A. 2010. *The Immaterial*. London: Seagull Books.
Hardt, M., and A. Negri. 2000. *Empire*. Cambridge, MA: Harvard University Press.
Hardt, M., and A. Negri. 2009. *Commonwealth*. Cambridge, MA: Harvard University Press.
Harvey, D. 2001. *Spaces of Capital: Towards a Critical Geography*. New York: Routledge.
Huws, U. 2006. "The Creative Spark in the Engine: Creative Workers in a Global Economy." *Work, Organization, Labour & Globalization* 1 (1): 1–12.
INPS (Istituto Nazionale Previdenza Sociale – Gestione ex-ENPALS) 2012. *Lavoratori e imprese dello spettacolo e dello sport professionistico: principali dati occupazionali e retributivi. Anno 2011*. Accessed June 14, 2013. http://www.inps.it/docallegati/Mig/Enpals/Trasparenza-valutazione-merito/Dati-e-bilanci/statistiche/occupazione-retribuzione-spettacolo-sport/occupazione_retribuzione_lavoratori_imprese_2011.pdf
Macherey, P. 2013. *Il soggetto produttivo. Da foucault a marx*. Verona: Ombre Corte.
Marazzi, C. 2008. *Capital and Language: From the New Economy to the War Economy*. Translated by G. Conti. Los Angeles, CA: Semiotext(e).
McRobbie, A. 2010. "Reflections on Feminism and Immaterial Labour." *New Formations* 70: 60–76. doi:10.3898/NEWF.70.04.2010
Menger, P.-M. 2002. *Portrait de l'artiste en travailleur*. Paris: Seuil.
Morini, C. 2010. *Per amore o per forza: femmilizzazione del lavoro e biopolitiche del corpo*. Verona: Ombrecorte.
Moulier-Boutang, Y. 2012. *Cognitive Capitalism*. Translated by E. Emery. Cambridge: Polity Press.
Murgia, A., and B. Poggio. 2012. "La trappola della passione. Esperienze di precarietà dei giovani highly skilled in italia, spagna e regno unito." In *Condizione giovanile e nuovi rischi sociali. Quali politiche*?, edited by G. Cordella, S. E. Masi, 105–123. Roma: Carocci.
Negri, A. 1999. "Value and Affect." *Boundary 2* 26 (2): 77–88.
Perulli, P. 2012. *Il Dio contratto*. Torino: Einaudi.
Pink, D. 2001. *Free Agent Nation: How America's New Independent Workers Are Transforming the Way We Live*. New York: Warner Books.
Raunig, G. 2013. *Factories of Knowledge, Industries of Creativity*. Translated by A. Derieg. Los Angeles, CA: Semiotext(e).
Reidl, S., H. Schiffbanker, and H. Eichmann. 2006. "Creating a Sustainable Future? The Working Life of Creative Workers in Vienna." *Work, Organization, Labour & Globalization* 1 (1): 48–58.
Ross, A. 2003. *No-Collar: The Humane Workplace and Its Hidden Costs*. Philadelphia, PA: Temple University Press.
Ross, A. 2008. "The New Geography of Work: Power to the Precarious?" *Theory, Culture & Society* 25 (7–8): 31–49. doi:10.1177/0263276408097795
Standing, G. 2011. *The Precariat: The New Dangerous Class*. London: Bloomsbury Academics. doi:10.5040/9781849664554
Supiot, A. 2000. "Les nouveaux visages de la subordination." *Droit social* 2: 131–145.
Vercellone, C. 2009. "Lavoro, distribuzione del reddito e valore nel capitalismo cognitivo. Una prospettiva storica e teorica." *Soicoloiga del lavoro* 115: 31–54. doi:10.3280/SL2009-115002
Virno, P. 2004. *Grammars of the Multitude: For an Analysis of Contemporary Forms of Life*. Translated by I. Bertoletti, J. Cascaito, and A. Casson. Los Angeles, CA: Semiotext(e).
VV.AA. 2012. *Teatro Valle Occupato: La rivolta culturale dei beni comuni*. Roma: DeriveApprodi.

REPLY

A reply to 'Precarious subjectivities are not for sale: the loss of the measurability of labour for performing arts workers' by Mauro Turrini and Federico Chicchi

Heather McLean

University of Toronto Scarborough, Toronto, ON, Canada

This is a reply to:

Turrini, Mauro, and Federico Chicchi. 2013. "Precarious subjectivities are not for sale: the loss of the measurability of labour for performing arts workers." *Global Discourse.* 3 (3–4): 507–521. http://dx.doi.org/10.1080/23269995.2014.885167.

Let me start by saying how much I enjoyed reading Turrini and Chicchi's (2013) essay. The authors discuss two main insights. First, the post-Fordist creative economy presents opportunities for cultural workers to pursue their desires and a sense of self-fulfillment. But, always-networking and always-innovating 'creative' laborers end up self-exploiting themselves in order to compete for jobs. These dynamics not only undermine a sense of worker solidarity, but can also provide convergence points for political mobilization, especially cross-occupation alliance building. To craft their analysis, the authors draw from quantitative surveys and in-depth interviews with workers who they consider to be 'paradigmatic subjects' of work fragmentation processes: artists, technicians, and organizers working in the fields of theatre, music, dance and video making.

Drawing from empirical work, the authors provide grounded accounts of the psychopathologies precarious subjectivities reinforce. Their thoughtful analysis contributes to a politically important body of work examining precarity, which can be understood as the experience of precariousness within lifeworlds characterized by uncertainty and instability (Waite 2009). Standing uses this hybrid term that combines precarious and proletariat to examine what he identifies as a 'class in the making'. (Standing 2011, 7) He situates the precariat in a fragmented class structure below the working class, and is careful to separate this socio-economic group from the underclass by highlighting their attractiveness to international capital. For Standing, the precariat lack seven kinds of labor security: income-earning opportunities; protection against arbitrary dismissal; opportunities for advancement; protection against accidents and illness; a chance to build skills; assurance of a stable wage; and a collective voice. As a result, the precariat are 'alienated, anomic, anxious and prone to anger' (Standing 2011, 12) and more like to think and act opportunistically. But, he also contends, precarious subjects 'in the making' are also enacting strategies to build solidarity and self-organized structures even as they autonomously work towards their goals.

The authors contribute to these lines of inquiry by contending that the ambivalent experience of living and work in this a state of precariousness has inspired new critical subjectivities and contestation practices. For example, referring to their research data, they claim that the breakdown of Fordist hierarchies and professional boundaries in the entertainment industry opens up new opportunities for flexworkers to organize. Here they refer to examples where workers have collaboratively lobbied industry organizations for better working conditions and pay. They then connect these examples with similar strategies in France and Canada, where cultural workers have sought ways to build alliances and fight for better pay and benefits.

These examples add nuance to burgeoning literature tracing the political possibilities of precarious work. In particular, they align with scholars who propose that there is political potential encapsulated in the production of new subjectivities and 'new forms of political struggle and solidarity' (Gill and Pratt 2008, 3), as 'the steady march of contingency into the lower and middle levels of the professional and high-wage service industries' continues (Ross 2008, 34). Further, they add to claims that the rise of immaterial labor ('labor that produces an immaterial good, such as a service, a cultural product, knowledge, or communication') (Hardt and Negri 2000, 290) potentially embodies immanent resistance to capitalism through its cooperative qualities and, as an alternative, to 'productivist values' (Gill and Pratt 2008, 6).

In general, I find myself in agreement with Turrini and Chicchi's analysis of the pitfalls and potential of precarious work. However, I take a different approach to this subject. My work, an intersectional feminist analysis of creative city policies in Canada, examines the lifeworlds of the precariat to think through contemporary gender, class and race inequalities. Critics claim that the 'imaginary subject' at the heart of the precariat is a man (Fantone 2007), but I and others contend that concepts such as precarity and immaterial/affective labor capture some of the conditions of women's paid and unpaid work, as well as the multiple social and economic practices that make up work (Gill and Pratt 2008). By focusing on Canadian public–private partnerships encouraging city officials to 'reinvent' neighborhoods with 'creative city' initiatives, I argue that neoliberal urban policies entrench inequalities (McLean 2014). These initiatives venerate precarious cultural labor while devaluing service work, a racialized and gendered work force. And these strategies rely on the gendered work of unpaid community to drive place-based capital accumulation strategies.

In line with the authors, I also argue that ambivalent 'creative' subjectivities present opportunities for contestation. However, I map feminist strategies, including self-organized structures, to contest this labor regime. The Creative Class Struggle (CCS) collective is one of the examples I analyze. This collective has brought together cultural workers, union activists, artists and service worker advocates to collectively critique public–private-led efforts to reinvent downtown neighborhoods with 'arts-led regeneration' (Creative Class Struggle 2014). Approaching their projects with an intersectional feminist lens that takes into consideration the range of factors that constitute subjectivities – gender, race, ethnicity, class and sexuality to no name a few – CCS illuminates the variegated terrain of oppression the post-Fordist accumulation regime reproduces. For example, the collective and the academics they work with (myself included) have made connections between cuts to municipal services, the rise of precarious cultural work, and private sector-friendly culture-led planning in town halls, workshops and activist interventions (McLean 2014). Importantly, CCS has also called attention to the rise of precarious work in the university sector. Taken together, CCS has found generative potential in what Turrini and Chicchi refer to as 'ambivalent' precarious subjectivities. Echoing feminist activists and scholars who claim that political conjunctures always present opportunities for vital decentering practices (Rankin and Delaney 2011), CCS draws found ways to generate critical dialogue and praxis from the uneven labor conditions that shape everyday life in Toronto.

To return to my opening point, Turrini and Chicchi are to be congratulated on their salient critique of labor conditions within the post-Fordist creativity regime. Although I make a slightly different connection between cultural economy work, gender and race, there is no question that precariousness presents a generative terrain of ambivalent subjectivities and work practices.

References

Creative Class Struggle. 2014. Accessed February 25, 2014. http://creativeclassstruggle.wordpress.com

Fantone, L. 2007. "Precarious Changes: Gender and Generational Politics in Contemporary Italy." *Feminist Review* 87: 5–20. doi:10.1057/palgrave.fr.9400357

Gill, R., and A. Pratt. 2008. "In the Social Factory?: Immaterial Labour, Precariousness and Cultural Work." *Theory, Culture, and Society* 25: 1–30. doi:10.1177/0263276408097794

Hardt, M., and A. Negri. 2000. *Empire*. Cambridge, MA: Harvard University Press.

McLean, H. 2014. "Digging into the Creative City: A Feminist Critique." *Antipode* 46: 3.

Rankin, K., and J. Delaney. 2011. "Community BIAs as Practices of Assemblage: Contingent Politics in the Neoliberal City." *Environment and Planning A* 43: 1363–1380. doi:10.1068/a43301

Ross, A. 2008. "The New Geography of Work: Power to the Precarious?" *Theory, Culture and Society* 25: 31–49. doi:10.1177/0263276408097795

Standing, G. 2011. *The Precariat: The New Dangerous Class*. Huntingdon: Bloomsbury Publishing.

Waite, L. 2009. "A Place and Space for a Critical Geography of Precarity?" *Geography Compass* 3: 412–433. doi:10.1111/j.1749-8198.2008.00184.x

BOOK REVIEW SYMPOSIUM: *THE DOWN-DEEP DELIGHT OF DEMOCRACY*, BY MARK PURCELL

The down-deep delight of democracy by Mark Purcell, Oxford, Wiley-Blackwell, 2013, 184 pp, £55.00/€67.80 (hardcover), £19.99/€24.70 (paperback), ISBN 978-1-4443-4997-9

Review

Mark Edward

In the following review I want to make two interconnected arguments which might appear to contradict one another. First, I want to argue that Purcell does not go far enough in his extension of democracy. In particular, I want to argue for the inclusion of non-human actors into the conceptualisation of democracy. Second, in some cases, an argument can be made for assemblages that have a 'top-down', rather than 'bottom-up', leaderless self-organising, decision-making process. Instead, I suggest that a type of Chomsky's inspired position should be adopted, where authority, unless justified, is inherently illegitimate and the burden of proof is on those desiring authority structures to explicitly justify the reasons for their existence. If this situation does not occur then a default 'bottom-up' assemblage should be the default position.

I should first state that Purcell's book is both an enjoyable and worthwhile read, especially for people interested in political theory and the conceptualisation and praxis of democracy. In addition, Purcell offers an excellent demonstration of how to use, develop and interlink often diverse theoretical thinkers.

The Down-Deep Delight of Democracy does not offer a coherent definition of democracy with defined parameters. Such an approach would go against the spirit and method of the book. Readers desiring this should look elsewhere. Rather, Purcell weaves together an account of democracy from the work of political thinkers such as Gramsci, Lefebvre, Deleuze and Guattari, Hardt and Negri, Laclau and Mouffe, and Ranciere. According to the author, it is possible to discover in their work a shared and deep desire for democracy (30). For Purcell, a contextual characteristic of all these thinkers is that they try to develop critical, revolutionary alternatives to capitalism beyond the oligarchies of neo-liberalism or Keynesianism, with a categorical rejection of state socialism (35). Although, as Purcell illustrates, some of the political thinkers are more optimistic about the potential for revolution, while others are more likely to regard revolution as a temporary transformation before returning to a status quo.

Overall, it is fair to claim that Purcell's democratic desire is one that aims and strives for an expansion of democracy and for there to materialise an ever more democratic society that exists without ever identifying a particular telos. In becoming democratic, there would be more forms of self-organisation and fewer, if any, forms of centralised control. As Purcell writes, 'becoming-democratic means to be continually fleeing oligarchy and pushing ourselves toward the horizon of democracy' (87). Becoming-democratic is then strongly correlated to becoming-active, which has the dual effect of including more people into the democratic process and, as Purcell notes, helping to explain why we desire our own servitude, as, for example, in the cases of people beholden to their consumer whims.

It is without doubt that Purcell's formation of becoming-democratic and becoming-active are clearly more inclusive than current forms of (representative) democracy. Indeed, as Hardt and Negri (2005) argue, representative democracy could in itself be a barrier to absolute democracy of the multitude. However, there remains the question of whether the democratic desire embodied in this book goes far enough. Could democratic theory not expand, ontologically, to include 'non-human' agents?[1]

Granting 'democracy' to non-human actors would move democratic thinking into a non-anthropocentric ontology and would offer a richer and more complex conceptualisation of agency. I would even make the claim that the failure of democratic thinking to consider non-human actors is undemocractic and exclusionary, practicing what Levi Bryant has termed the hegemonic fallacy, which is a form of reductionist thinking that 'consists in treating one difference as being the only difference that makes a difference or as treating one difference as over-determining all the other differences' (Bryant 2011, 277). In the case of democratic thought, this difference would be the human. This is not to make the claim that humans are not a crucial correlate in democracy. It is rather the point that humans are not the only actors in the world and other actors have the capacity to act upon the world. A simple but nevertheless illustrative example would be the introduction of social media into everyday life. Once this has penetrated into the everyday life of people, it also then impinges, or feeds back, into how those people behave, act and think. In other words, the very existence of this technology in our everyday life also changes, in some ways, our very existence.

Extending democratic thinking to include non-humans actors and allowing their capacity to alter and transform life has some important implications, which to a certain degree challenge some of the arguments Purcell puts forward. Arguably, the practice of democracy Purcell defends would be an absolute democracy that favours horizontal interactions, rather than vertical interactions. Horizontal interactions are self-organising bottom-up assemblages, whereas vertical ones are central top-down assemblages with commands flowing in a hierarchical order. I would suggest that Purcell's 'absolute democracy' is limited by what David Harvey has critiqued as the 'fetishism of organisational form'. The idea being that there should not be an automatic preference to have either centralist or self-organising forms of assemblages in all areas of life. Instead, there should be questions relating to scale and the type of components within a particular assemblage, which would include the non-human components. Harvey makes the point clear when differentiating between a nuclear energy station and a university:

> 'We live in a world where there are a lot of tightly coupled systems around, tightly coupled in such a way that you need command and control structures immediately to deal with them. For example, a nuclear power station is a tightly coupled system. When something goes wrong in it, you need to react immediately because otherwise it will go very fast through the whole thing and explode. The university is not a tightly coupled system. If something goes wrong in it, say somebody doesn't turn up for a lecture, it doesn't matter. The university survives perfectly well. But in tightly coupled systems you need very quick decision making.' (Harvey 2012)

In other words, the material components of a certain assemblage might make a bottom-up horizontal assemblage impractical and potentially dangerous. Another example from Harvey is illustrative. For Harvey, having a horizontal assemblage in an air traffic control tower would have a degree of absurdity. The idea being that it would be impractical and infeasible to apply the horizontal principle because those in the tower going into assembly mode when a pilot is requiring clear instructions is impractical. The point might seem trivial, but it awakens thought to the principle that the world contains a rich array of non-human actors, which clearly feed back into the everyday existence of human beings. To a certain, and inevitable, degree, they have determinacy in shaping the possible forms in which humans assemblage, be they more horizontal or vertical.

This does not mean that we have a false choice between vertical or horizontal assemblages. It is rather that life is more complex and will likely be a combination and mixture of both. As previously indicated, a potential way to overcome the impasse would be to propose a Chomskyian inspired categorical imperative when considering how components will interact in different assemblages (e.g. societies, hospitals, governments, businesses…). Overall, the position would be that those persons desiring 'top-down' assemblages, with a clear command structure and defined roles, are governed by the onus to explicitly demonstrate and justify why that particular assemblage requires this composition. In addition, I would also add, there is the potential to experiment between the extent to which an assemblage is vertical or horizontal.

Note

1. I should make it clear that Purcell is not making an ontological argument in his book. However, in the review I want to consider some of the ontological implications associated with Purcell's arguments.

References

Bryant, L. 2011. "The Ontic Principle: Outline of an Object-Oriented Ontology." In *The Speculative Turn: Continental Materialism and Realism*, edited by L. Bryant, N. Srnicek, and G. Harman, 261–279. Melbourne: Re. Press.

Hardt, M., and A. Negri. 2005. *Multitude*. London: Penguin.

Harvey, D. 2012. "Urban Revolution: An Interview with David Harvey." *New Left Project*. http://www.re-press.org/book-files/OA_Version_Speculative_Turn_9780980668346.pdf

Mark Edward
Independent scholar
m.d.edward22@gmail.com

http://dx.doi.org/10.1080/23269995.2013.836375

Review

Stuart Elden

This is an important and timely book. The recent events in Turkey have helped to highlight this – many of the protestors were told that, as Turkey was a democracy, they should simply try to vote Prime Minister Recep Tayyıp Erdoğan out of office. Popular protests were seen as a challenge to democracy, rather than one of the forms democracy could take. In other recent popular uprisings, such as those in Egypt, Western politicians and commentators said that with the immediate aim of toppling President

Hosni Mubarak achieved, they were waiting for "a transition to democracy" (26 n. 21), as if this was an end state. Criticisms of Occupy, of anti-EU protests in Greece and elsewhere, and anti-austerity and counter-globalisation demonstrations have worked in a similar register.

Purcell rejects both of those assumptions – that democracy is something to achieved; and that once achieved the people should only act within prescribed parameters. Instead, in the company of a range of political and social theorists, he argues for the idea of democracy as a process, continually enacted through actions, reactions, struggles and arguments. The book makes extensive use of a range of different thinkers, from Deleuze and Guattari to Nietzsche, Gramsci, Hardt and Negri and Rancière. If the differences between these thinkers are sometimes elided, the plural, contested nature of what they took democracy to be, with all its contradictions and tensions, speak to the very nature of the issues at stake. Purcell suggests that contemporary liberal democracies have become oligarchies, and that political-economic positions – from neo-liberalism to Keynesianism – are complicit within this wider structure. In that sense, Purcell returns the focus of political geographical and urban questions to the role of the state. One of the great tragedies of the post-1970 period is that the critique of the state has come most forcefully from the Right, with the supposed "rolling back of the frontiers of the state" proposed by neo-liberalism. And yet, that was only a limited state in a few areas, notably the regulation of the market and the provision of welfare. In other areas, such as military spending, the police and security apparatus, and the limitation of personal freedoms, the state is as dominant as ever. In the political-economic realm, Purcell suggests that "Neoliberalism and the Keynesian welfare state thus offer a choice between one kind of oligarchy and another" (12).

The use of Henri Lefebvre's work is particularly interesting. Purcell pays particular attention to Lefebvre's notion of *autogestion*. This term can only be narrowly translated as self-management, which was the sense it had in the context of workers taking control of factories from their bosses, such as the LIP watch factory in the mid-1970s (see 39–42). For Lefebvre, *autogestion* also has a sense of what we might call grassroots democracy, the localised, popular control of political decisions. Purcell returns the focus to Lefebvre's essential four-volume study of the state, *De l'État* (1976–1978; see Elden 2004, Ch. 6). As Purcell rightly notes, Lefebvre's "work on the state is designed to move us decisively beyond the state" (82). There, and in various other places, Lefebvre elaborates the two aspects of *autogestion* – the political-economic version of workers' control, and what he calls *territorial autogestion* (see, for example, 2009, 110, 147, 151, 163, 250–251). That latter sense is, in part, a development of Lefebvre's now widely invoked call for a "right to the city" (1996). Some of Lefebvre's arguments were translated into English in the *State, Space, World* collection (2009), which Purcell draws on extensively. In that collection, Neil Brenner and I suggested that the notion of *autogestion* should remain untranslated, as like the notion of *mondialisation* – a word related to globalisation, but with a stress on the world, *le monde*, rather than the globe (Brenner and Elden 2009, 3, 14–17) – there was no straightforward equivalent (Brenner and Elden 2009, 14). Purcell accepts the argument of no simple equivalent, and says "'self-management' is vague and appears bureaucratic and apolitical in English", but simply takes the word into English (40 n. 13). As Purcell elaborates, Lefebvre really understood the term to be the actualisation of the process of the "withering away of the state" in the way understood by Marxist thought.

Purcell also relates this work to what Lefebvre called a "new contract of citizenship" (2003), which outlined a series of rights – "the right to difference, the right to information, the right to autogestion, and the right to the city" (Purcell, 36). As Purcell rightly notes, these cannot simply be understood as liberal-democratic rights that can be enacted through state legislation, but as the rights necessary for the continual transformation of political-social relations, a way of becoming-active citizens, taking power and "managing their own affairs for themselves" (27). And of course, following Lefebvre this is not simply of affairs *in space* – in a locality, city, region, nation-state – but affairs *of space* as well. As Purcell argues, "Democracy and autogestion, for Lefebvre, are thus always spatial projects; they are always struggles by users and inhabitants of space to collectively manage their space in a way that meets their needs and satisfies their desires" (42).

Purcell suggests that "we live in a world that equates democracy with a liberal-democratic state, which is a form of oligarchy that sets severe limits on democracy and insists that anything beyond those limits is impossible" (26). This helps to understand the restrictions placed on what is supposedly allowed with a "democracy" such as Turkey or Brazil, or the expectations placed on a country in transition, such as Egypt or Tunisia. It helps provide a context within which we can understand the anti-austerity protests in the UK, reactions against the EU's measures for bailout countries, or the Occupy movements across the world. Purcell argues that "democracy must be understood not as a final end beyond politics, but as becoming-democratic, a process by which we move towards the horizon of democracy" (120). This book provides a powerful account of what this might mean in theory, with several indications of its relations to practice.

References

Brenner, N., and S. Elden. 2009. "Introduction – State, Space, World: Lefebvre and the Survival of Capitalism." In *State, Space, World: Selected Essays*, edited by Neil Brenner, Stuart Elden, and Henri Lefebvre, 1–48. Minneapolis: University of Minnesota Press.

Elden, S. 2004. *Understanding Henri Lefebvre: Theory and the Possible*. London: Continuum.

Lefebvre, H. 1976–1978. *De L'état*. 4 vols. Paris: UGE.

Lefebvre, H. 1996. *Writings on Cities*. Translated and edited by Eleonore Kofman and Elizabeth Lebas. Oxford: Blackwell.

Lefebvre, H. 2003. "From the Social Pact to the Contract of Citizenship." In *Key Writings*, edited by Stuart Elden, Elizabeth Lebas, and Eleonore Kofman, 238–254. London: Continuum.

Lefebvre, H. 2009. *State, Space, World: Selected Essays*, edited by Neil Brenner and Stuart Elden. Translated by Gerald Moore, Neil Brenner, and Stuart Elden. Minneapolis: University of Minnesota Press.

Stuart Elden
University of Warwick
stuart.elden@warwick.ac.uk

http://dx.doi.org/10.1080/23269995.2013.836376

Review

Ian Buchanan

The answer to the age-old question "What is to be done?" is democracy, according to Purcell, but only if by democracy we mean a form of self-rule in which all the standard institutions of power such as the state, the church, the judiciary, and so on, have been abolished. We must, in effect, reclaim democracy from itself, or at least from the version that obtains in most so-called democratic countries, wherein the election of political representatives amounts to a wholesale abrogation of one's rights. In a parliamentary democracy, our elected representatives do not speak for us, they speak instead of us, and most of the time they seem to speak in spite of us. The Occupy Wall Street movement's key slogan "We are the 99%" sought to make exactly this point. Indeed, the entire Occupy campaign focused on this basic fact of modern life: government might be of the people, but it hardly ever seems to be for the people.

The US government's response to the 2008 banking crisis brought this into stark relief. Billions of dollars were made available to save banks that were allegedly too big to be allowed to fail, with the obscene result that the bankers who brought about the crisis profited directly from the crisis while thousands of small-holder businesses and home-owners went to the wall. And rather than tax those who profited so handsomely from the catastrophe, and thereby restore the health of the economy, the government has instead pursued a policy of austerity, slashing and burning the already slender threads of the so-called safety net of the welfare system. No wonder so many of us today have difficulty in deciding which party we should support – it is hard to reconcile what many politicians say and do with any sense that we might have of what *we* would say in *their* place, given half the chance. The age of clear majorities in parliamentary democracies seems to be behind us. Today governments are formed from unholy alliances of interest groups rather than ideologically coherent political parties supported by a large membership base. The split between parties of the left and labour movements is perhaps the most pernicious instance of this trend.

Democracy for Purcell is not to be found in the meagre fare dished out by parliaments in any case. In fact, by its very nature, parliamentary democracy is actually undemocratic because it is built on a foundation of delegation, whereby the people as a whole give up their right to speak to an elected representative who is supposed to then speak on their behalf but in fact speaks in their place. His model of democracy then is much nearer to what most people would recognize as anarchism, which is a government of the people by the people in which no other institutions of power obtain. This model of democracy turns on the age-old dialectic enumerated by Hobbes in the distinction between constituent power – the power of the people, if you will (or what Hardt and Negri famously call "the multitude") – and constituted power – the power of institutions (or what Rancière simply calls "the Police"). The standard assumption in political theory is that constituent power will disintegrate into the proverbial nightmare of "all against all" (as Hobbes put it) without the restraint of constituted power. So in this sense, our freedom from persecution by others is bought at the price of our loss of freedom. Disturbingly, for many critics, including Purcell, most people seem to welcome this loss of freedom, almost as if subservience was desired.

There are then two problems to be overcome if absolute democracy (Purcell's useful phrase) is finally to reign. First, we have to overturn the assumption that constituent power is incapable of existing on its own. Second, we need to overcome the apparent need people have for subservience. Here I disagree with Purcell. The first problem is real enough and I will discuss that further in a moment. But the second problem is false – what is more it is false according to Deleuze and Guattari in whose name he invokes the problem in the first place. It is certainly the case that Deleuze and Guattari raise the question of why "man" seems to desire his own servitude (citing a long line of philosophers who have raised this question going back to Spinoza), but it is also the case that in the end they reject the question as badly formed. Yes desire can be made to desire its own servitude, but only once it has been captured and deformed. To equate this state with childhood and addiction as Purcell does is to blame the victims of a social machine for not being able to see better how that machine is constantly at work blinding them to the real conditions of existence. Purcell's model of "activation" here, growing up/recovering from addiction is not helpful in my view and certainly is not consistent with Deleuze and Guattari's thinking.

Concerning the assumption that constituent power cannot stand on its own, Purcell marshals an impressive array of theoretical allies in making his case that constituent power can function in its own right in the absence of constituted power. Hardt and Negri are centremost, but Purcell rightly points out their debt to Deleuze and Guattari, and he draws deeply from their work as well as I will discuss further. He is also rightly critical of Agamben and Rancière for their unwillingness to consider the possibility of radical change, that is, change that does not merely rearrange the political order of things, but seeks to transform that order itself. In Hobbes' terms, Agamben and Rancière effectively assume that constituent power cannot exist on its own, so the best we can hope for is a more ameliorative form of constituted power. Purcell is unwilling to accept this defeatist premise and turns instead to Deleuze and Guattari via Hardt and Negri. (87–91) We need to go further than Rancière, he says, we need to "press for a breakthrough, a generalized democratic explosion." (89) The Arab Spring is a signal example for Purcell of the way a single spark – the desire and demand for democracy – can turn into a wildfire sweeping through an entire region.

The real problem though, as he acknowledges, is not where will these revolutionary sparks come from, but how can one keep the flames going. He criticizes Lefebvre for failing to address this problem in any adequate way, but unfortunately his own attempts are no less unsatisfactory inasmuch as he ties it to problems of growing up/overcoming addiction. (98)

In many ways, the core of this book is to be found in a pair of quotes from Italo Calvino and David Foster Wallace, both of which seem to be written in answer to Paul Virilio's question in *L'insécutité du territoire*, cited by Deleuze and Guattari in the last section of the chapter on the refrain in *A Thousand Plateaus*: To dwell as a poet or an assassin? The assassin bombards the people with molecules (messages, memes, *mots d'ordre*) that close off all the assemblages (living arrangements might be a better translation) and hurl us into a black hole devoid of people. The poet unleashes molecules that open some or all of the assemblages in the hope that these will give rise to a new people capable of retrieving all the assemblages from the black hole they have been cast into. Only time will tell if the poets can save us from the assassins.

To dwell as a poet or an assassin? This question is important today because the world situation has changed such that we are constantly confronted with questions and problems for which there is no clear cut answer, no obvious right or wrong choice to make. It is no longer a question of deciding what is the right thing to do, but rather of finding a way to let the "right thing" thrive. As Purcell reports, Calvino instructs us to "seek and learn to recognize who and what, in the midst of inferno [black hole in Deleuze and Guattari's terms], are not inferno [i.e., not assassins], and help them endure, give them space [to become poets, in effect]." Similarly Wallace says in "dark times [when the whole world seems to be sucked into a black hole], the definition of good art [i.e., poetry] would seem to be art that locates and applies CPR to those elements of what's human and magic that still live and glow despites the times' darkness [i.e., in spite of the assassins that seem to pervade every level of society]." This is radical politics of the same order (though articulated in different terms) as John Holloway's model of changing the world without taking power (see John Holloway 2005). It banks on the fact that constituted power is only ever a derivative of constituent power and therefore really only exists because the latter allows it.

Purcell turns away from the potential here when blames the failure of political activation on a lack of maturity in today's political subjects and accuses them of being lost in the addictions of late capitalism. This is a very old school form of Marxism. While I am sceptical of Hardt and Negri's concept of the multitude, which has always seemed a little too easy to me – all we have to do is wake up because the multitude is already formed – I nevertheless think it has the virtue of forcing us to think more about the political potential of constituent power. Purcell is clearly motivated to do just that, but it seems to me he misses a real opportunity by focusing on why constituted power always seems to win rather than – as Hardt and Negri do – looking more closely at the composition of constituent power.

Reference

Holloway, J. 2005. *Change the World Without Taking Power: The Meaning of Revolution Today.* London: Pluto.

Ian Buchanan
University of Wollongong
ibuchana@uow.edu.au

http://dx.doi.org/10.1080/23269995.2013.836377

Managing ourselves

Mark Purcell

I want to thank *Global Discourse* for hosting this review symposium of my book, *The Down-Deep Delight of Democracy.* In the book, I try to make a compelling case that what we need today, politically, is to reinvigorate the concept and practice of democracy. Or rather, I argue that what we need to do is to pay attention to how democracy is already being reinvigorated, all around us, and we need to invent ways to help it grow. I understand democracy radically, not as a form of government with limited popular input, but as a perpetual struggle by everyone to increasingly govern themselves in common.

It really is an honor to engage in this symposium with such able and respected scholars. Their reviews are provocative in a productive way, and I want to thank them very much as well. In my response, I discuss each review in turn, and I try to briefly respond to (and perhaps even develop) the thoughtful points they raise.

In the book, I develop my idea of democracy by engaging with a range of thinkers for whom I have an affinity: Deleuze & Guattari, Hardt & Negri, Nietzsche, Rancière, Gramsci, Laclau & Mouffe, among others. This kind of work is Stuart Elden's metier, and so I appreciate the generosity of his comments. He is a much more accomplished scholar of Lefebvre's work than I, and so I am happy that he broadly approves of how I use Lefebvre in the book. As Elden says, I am particularly drawn to Lefebvre's idea of autogestion, because it emphasizes the act of people becoming active and managing their affairs for themselves. This idea was almost absent in Lefebvre's English-language corpus before Brenner and Elden's edited collection of Lefebvre's work (Lefebvre 2009), and so I very much hope that now autogestion can occupy a much more central place in our imagination of his work. I also want to reiterate Elden's point about Lefebvre's spatial imagination. Lefebvre insisted that autogestion must be spatial, that it must involve people producing and managing *space* for themselves.

Elden is widely respected for his careful and nuanced interpretations of the work of many different thinkers, and so I am piqued by his passing suggestion that in the book, I sometimes elide the differences among the various thinkers I use He is right, and I take his point very seriously because in the book I consciously adopt an approach that is a bit different from the more meticulous one Elden uses in his work. My approach is inspired by Nietzsche and Deleuze, and it treats each thinker, and his or her work, as intensely multiple, as a tangled mass of desires, wills, and affects. Each of these desires can resonate with a thinker's other desires, but it can also contradict them. Moreover, these desires can change over time, even over the course of one book. Faced with this complex mass, I wade into it, looking for something I can use. I look for desires that I can stream into the flow of desires I am collecting and holding together in my own work. I try to do this with great respect for the thinker and with a rigorous understanding of their larger body of work. At the same time, my purpose is not primarily to comprehend and describe each thinker's work for its own sake. Rather, I am pulling out strands and re-purposing them to operate in my project. For example, Lefebvre imagines autogestion in the context of the LIP watch factory, the Yugoslavian experience, and Paris 1968. For me though, autogestion also takes on the sensibilities and energies of 1977 in Italy, of the sequence Argentina-2001-and-then-Spain-2011, of the Arab Spring, and of Occupy. Moreover, the autogestion I present has been passed through my mind, which has been extensively refashioned by thinkers (e.g., Deleuze and Guattari, Rancière, Negri, Virno, Agamben), who had minimal or no influence on Lefebvre.

I recognize that this method of scholarship might seem a bit free to some, and that might put me at a disadvantage in my big disagreement with Ian Buchanan over Deleuze & Guattari. Though I think he and I broadly agree on the importance of people becoming active and managing their affairs for themselves, we differ perhaps on a technical theoretical question: do D&G think desire can desire its own repression? Buchanan suggests the answer is no, that D&G think desire is unable to desire its own repression, that it only *appears* to desire its own repression when it has been deformed by an apparatus of capture. We never really desire to be ruled by the State, or consume alienated products, or watch TV, or get high and give in. We only desire these things when our desire has been perverted or deformed by dark apparatuses. My position is, instead, that D&G *do* think that desire can desire its own repression. This conclusion follows logically from their argument that desire is the only productive force in the world. It produces everything. If repression exists, it must have been created by desire. When we desire to be ruled, or to consume, or to give in, we really *do* desire those things. Collectively, we desire what diminishes us, and so we construct apparatuses to satisfy that desire.[1] On the other hand, and my book is at great pains to emphasize this, we also desire what nourishes us. We desire to rule ourselves, to produce goods for ourselves, to take control of our own lives. We desire both oligarchy and democracy.

This is an important theoretical question, about what D&G think. But resolving it would require lots of textual exegesis,[2] and working through it properly is beyond the scope of this response.[3] But whatever we conclude about D&G's position, perhaps I could just say a word on which approach to desire is more useful, politically, today. I think there is much more political value in locating the source of all production within us, within our own desire, rather than thinking that we desire only liberation and that there is a dark force beyond us, that we do not produce or control, that corrupts our desires. I think we should think with Bakunin here. He is adamant that so many things we think exist outside ourselves (gods, the State, capital) are really our own power that we have agreed to let be alienated from us. This is true of desire too: all desires are our own creation. We desire both our own liberation and our own repression. This assumption is crucial politically because it means that the project to liberate ourselves depends not on the whim of a dark force but only on ourselves. We must look to ourselves to solve our own problems. We are the source of all production, of all desire, and of all power. The struggle we face, I think, is the struggle to augment our desires that nourish us and let atrophy our desires that diminish us. I think this is precisely the struggle that D&G propose schizoanalysis to be.

That is my approach to politics. And so, I think Buchanan is really underestimating my argument when he says I am 'blam[ing] the victims of a social machine for not being able to see better how that machine is constantly at work blinding them to the real conditions of existence' (531), and that I am 'focusing on why constituted power always seems to win rather than … looking more closely at the composition of constituent power' (532). My obsession throughout the book is to seek out constituent power, to redirect our attention toward ourselves, to rediscover our own power, to begin to put it to use, and to teach ourselves just how much we are capable of. For me, this must be the project. But it is not a simple project. Our power is virtually infinite, but it is not unproblematic. We must learn to use it well. We must not fall into the trap of thinking that our power (and our desire) is only a pure force for liberation and good. That would mean that once we are in control, everything will be fine. Our power can also repress and harm. As Bakunin insists, we are both gods and beasts. And we are, most of us, relatively inexperienced at using our power. We are raised in an oligarchical society (of our own making) that inhibits democracy. In general, we are not now all that capable of managing our own affairs, at least not yet. We are still too susceptible to succumbing to our desire to be ruled, and our desire to rule ourselves is not yet strong enough. We must therefore practice democracy. We must gain strength through the struggle to manage our own affairs for ourselves. We must grow up. This is why I am so drawn to David Foster Wallace's metaphors of addiction and maturation. Becoming democratic does not mean overcoming a dark force that is beyond us, it means overcoming ourselves: our desire for democracy must overcome our desire for oligarchy.[4]

Lastly, let me agree wholeheartedly with Mark Edward's argument that we should be thinking very seriously about what role nonhuman actors should (and do) play in democratic life. Bruce Braun and Sarah Whatmore (2010), for example, have recently explored this very issue, and of course there is a whole tradition of work on similar themes around Bruno Latour, among others. My book extends the democratic community radically to include all humans, but Edward is right that it implicitly excludes nonhuman actors. Clearly such actors play a vital role in these communities. So, what would it mean to think democracy not merely as the affairs of the polis, but as the affairs of enormously complex assemblages of human and nonhuman actors? Might nonhuman actors be considered full members of a democratic public? Should they be equal to humans? Are they different than humans? How so? Can they be held accountable? Can they speak? Such questions promise to deepen our empirical understanding of how democratic communities actually work. It is hard to deny that such communities go far beyond a group of citizens gathered in the agora. Such questions can also challenge and clarify our ethical values with respect to democracy. What is the nature of the good that democracy offers us? Is that good only a human one? How are such ethical questions fundamentally shifted off their axis when nonhuman actors are considered?

At the same time, I do want to object eagerly to the main implication Edward draws from this new line of thinking. He seems to think that when we better appreciate the complexity of the assemblages in which we live, we will realize the need for hierarchical, centralized organization. I really would hate to see us use the nonhuman to smuggle back in the old-school Marxism of people like David Harvey. I think it really is time we admit it: that well has run dry. Harvey's line of argument starts with an unsubstantiated, top-of-the-head claim: 'we live in a world where there are a lot of tightly coupled systems around….' It then draws an unsupported conclusion: therefore 'you need command and control structures immediately to deal with them.' No. We do not need command and control structures. We are perfectly capable of managing all systems ('tightly coupled' or not) through emergent organization, just as we are also perfectly capable of managing them through hierarchical organization. We are capable of anything. To be sure, we are not necessarily capable of anything today. It might not work well if we try tomorrow to run a nuclear power plant by committee. But obviously we should not conclude, with Harvey, that therefore we are inherently unable to do so, ever.[5]

That is the importance of thinking about democracy as a process of growing up, of becoming democratic. The current limit of our ability to manage our affairs for ourselves is never an absolute limit. We can always grow to be better democrats. We are the source of all power. That power does not have an absolute limit. It is not a 'fetishism' to prefer governing ourselves to being governed; it is an ethical commitment to democracy.

Notes

1. Calvino (1972) says it like this: 'the inferno of the living … is that which is already here, the inferno that we inhabit every day, that we create by being together….'
2. I would begin with the paragraph about Spinoza and Reich on p. 38 of *Anti-Oedipus*.
3. Though I hope he and I (and others) can do it together soon.
4. I recognize this all sounds very individualist, like it is a personal struggle. That is because on one level it is. But of course the struggle to become democratic is also necessarily a collective one, and in the book I spend a chapter, mostly in the company of D&G, thinking through what kind of collective relations we should be working to create.
5. Maybe we should also wonder if we need those tightly coupled systems (nuclear power plants, air traffic control towers, and armies) that seem to work better under hierarchical control.

References

Braun, B., and S. Whatmore, eds. 2010. *Political Matter: Technoscience, Democracy, and Public Life*. Minneapolis, MN: University of Minnesota Press.

Calvino, I. 1972. *Le Città Invisibili*. Turin: Einaudi.

Lefebvre, H. 2009. *State, Space, World: Selected Essays*. Edited by N. Brenner and S. Elden. Translated by G. Moore, N. Brenner, and S. Elden. Minneapolis: University of Minnesota Press.

Mark Purcell
Department of Urban Design & Planning,
University of Washington, Seattle, WA
98195, USA
mpurcell@uw.edu

http://dx.doi.org/10.1080/23269995.2013.840121

BOOK REVIEW SYMPOSIUM: *THE PRECARIAT: THE NEW DANGEROUS CLASS*, BY GUY STANDING

The precariat: the new dangerous class, Guy Standing, London, Bloomsbury, 2011, ix + 198pp., £19.99 (paperback), ISBN 978-1-8496-6351-9

Review

Catherine Lawlor

Broadly summarised, Guy Standing's *The Precariat* presents an account of those worst affected by the 'flexibility' characteristic of the globalised contemporary labour market – the ubiquity of which means that its conditions affect old and young, migrants and citizens, the West and the developing world and so on. Lacking the traditional industrial exchange of discipline for security, the precariat is not to be understood simply as a reconceptualised proletariat, nor is precarity confined to those in low-wage, menial or unstable employment. Rather, Standing, in what is at core an elaboration of the relationship between labourer and capital, details several different forms of labour security (employment, job, work, skill reproduction, income, representation and labour market [10]) that are largely out of the precariat's reach but enjoyed by the 'salariat' (the salaried, executive class), the 'proficians' (specialist freelancers who happily flit from project to project) and the élite. While Standing acknowledges the existence of 'varieties of precariat' (13) and cautions that '[i]t must not desert multiculturalism or the legitimation of multiple identities' (159), these concerns are bracketed in order to identify the precariat in essence (a) as sharing a particular relationship to the means of production and (b) in contradistinction to other classes.

It is not at all clear, however, that the relationship to capital experienced by different elements included in the precariat is of sufficient uniformity to warrant such identification. Standing presents, for instance, an account of the 'grinners', for whom a precarious labour market facilitates a liberating, flexible lifestyle, and the 'groaners', for whom it means grinding uncertainty and draining, unremunerated work-for-labour (59). Despite their polar experiences, we are to accept that the relationship to capital of a retired teacher supplementing a pension by giving summer-school lessons and that of a migrant worker cleaning houses below minimum wage for cash-in-hand are similarly precarious. If the precariat is elastic enough a concept to include these disparate groups, the distinction between it and the salariat seems somewhat arbitrary, especially given that, despite the latter's 'privileged' (37) relationship to capital, the élite reacted to the economic crisis by 'laying off some of the salariat and limiting career opportunities of others' (50). Standing acknowledges that the threat of falling into the precariat constantly hovers over the salariat (30); but what is the threat of losing labour security other than a lack of labour security? The precariat 'are us or could be at any time' (174). If, then, the salariat is subject to much the same uncertainty as the precariat and the precariat can accommodate significantly divergent and even clashing forms of labour insecurity, the distinction between the two cannot reasonably be defended.

Given the disparity between, for instance, an investment banker ordering champagne by the magnum and the double-jobbing, part-time bar worker serving him, the conclusion to be drawn is not that the precariat is insufficiently expansive but, on the contrary, that it is an untenably reductive category. Despite Standing's insistence that this highly differentiated plurality shares a 'common set of vulnerabilities' (25) and is divided only by each faction's perception thereof, it is not evident that diverging interests will not clash in real, material terms. When, for instance, manufacturing is 'off-shored' or temporary jobs for retirees supplant entry-level positions, one worker's labour market security ('adequate income-earning opportunities') is bought at the expense of another's job security ('ability and opportunity to retain a niche in employment') in a tangible way.

For Standing, however, such conflicts are illusory, fomented by the 'populist politicians and neo-fascist messages' (25) by which the 'infantilised' precariat is 'easily seduced' (153) and prevented from recognising itself as a class for itself. That such a depiction and dismissal of the precariat's concerns is itself infantilising does not seem to trouble Standing: a tone of well-intentioned paternalism, compounded by hints of conservatism that jar with the project's professed progressive sympathies, pervades *The Precariat.* Standing, for instance, laments the erosion of 'constructive attitudes to work' (23) and those 'work ethics ground out by strong occupational communities' (24) and, rather than embracing fully the radical utopian possibilities of the admittedly double-edged sword that is flexible labour, calls upon us instead to 'identify what would be needed to make [it] *tolerable*' (31, emphasis mine). His solution is a 'Politics of Paradise' that will 'draw [the precariat] in better directions' (153) than it would choose for itself. For instance, Standing – despite extensive denigration of state paternalism and 'nudging' (138 on) – enthuses that a universal basic income could prove 'an instrument for encouraging deliberative democracy' (181). Although, then, '[p]eople should be trusted ... to respect others [... and] should not be treated as lazy, potential criminals, law breakers or inherently selfish' (156), they nonetheless require appropriate 'encouragement'. If not somehow appeased, the precariat is 'dangerous' (1) and prone to 'lashing out' (153) mindlessly at scapegoat minorities in its midst. Framed like this, the proposed 'Politics of Paradise' seems to amount to little more than placatory crumbs from the table, when the table itself is not fit for purpose.

This last point is the central flaw in Standing's analysis. So intent is he on diagnosing the precariat and prognosticating its inevitable 'inferno' (the precariat, we are told, is 'bound to become explosive' [154]), he overlooks the real conclusion to which all evidence and even at times his own observations about 'systemic insecurity' (156) point: we are faced not with a 'new, dangerous class' but with a system characterised by crisis and uncertainty at all levels, wherein '[e]verything becomes contingent and open to renegotiation' (29) and has a plurality of effects. Standing remarks that '[h]uman society has not been built over the centuries on permanent incessant change; it has been based on the slow construction of stable identities and rather "rigid" spheres of security' (24). In contrast, the 2008 financial meltdown and its ongoing repercussions, wild swings in share prices, collapsing banks, pressure to cut costs, firms being 'traded, split up and repackaged' (29) are, along with labour insecurity, all aspects of a precarious system incompatible with any sort of end-of-history idealism or narrative of beneficent stasis.

That a preponderance of hardship falls on certain sectors of society due to this systemic precariousness is not in dispute here. Drawing on an abundance of diverse research and statistics that would perhaps otherwise have remained discrete, Standing provides a potentially valuable resource for refuting the arguments of those who claim that contemporary conditions of labour do not warrant a revised analysis. Unfortunately, although a not inconsiderable bibliography is included, *The Precariat* lacks so much as a single footnote linking assertions in the main body of the text with their source. Explicit in-text citations are rare and where these do not exist the reader is left to speculate. To select an example at random, we are told that '[i]t was no surprise that as the recession deepened many [NGO workers] left to work in supermarkets' (53). How many? Most? Some? A significant minority? And how exactly is Standing privy to this implied trend (which is certainly a surprise to this reader)? Ironically, he at one point decries governments' use of limited anecdotal evidence to extrapolate to broader trends ('Thus, a government can cite two examples to suggest that most of the unemployed suffer from "a habit of worklessness", and readers can be led to believe that these two cases represent millions' [146]), and is wary of 'what [we] are told are complex topics "best left to experts" ' (128). Perhaps, however, Standing would prefer that we apply his exhortation that we 'trust [our] professionals to be professional' (138) in his own particular case.

Catherine Lawlor
School of Philosophy, University College Dublin, Dublin, Ireland
Catherine.lawlor@ucdconnect.ie

http://dx.doi.org/10.1080/23269995.2014.880253

Review

Jörg Wiegratz

There are only a very few analytical terms that become known and used almost simultaneously in both the academic and public debates, suggesting that the term captures something important at the time of its coinage. The term 'the precariat' is one of these terms. It articulates the observation that a number of changes in the global political economy have altogether recalibrated both the balance of power in the relationship between capital and labour, and levels and forms of exploitation. In countries that have undergone neoliberal transformations in the past two decades, many workers are facing a labour market in which capital calls the shots ever more blatantly and employment practices are ever more rapidly and drastically modified to cater for profit imperatives, to the detriment of significant parts of the working population. The job world looks more shaky, risky and hostile to a lot of workers. The mentioned rise in the usage of the term precariat suggests that this observation, experience or feeling is apparently shared by many.

Guy Standing is the most well-known author in this debate about the rise of the precariat and related political-economic and socio-cultural issues. His book *The Precariat: The New Dangerous Class* (2011) has already been reviewed elsewhere, and I recommend reading the respective submissions and Standing's replies (Seymour 2012; Standing 2012a, 2012b). I am not going to repeat or discuss in detail the points that have been made by other reviewers. Suffice to say that these debates raised issues regarding whether (1) Standing's definition of the precariat is appropriate and useful; (2) there is anything new about the current plight of workers (or rather historical continuity), and the precariat is indeed a new 'class in the making', as Standing calls it; (3) empirical data support his arguments; and (4) his analysis of future scenarios of the respective politics plausible and his proposed policy suggestions useful. Finally, reviewers noted that (5) the style of writing, analysing and referencing was at times somewhat vague, unsubstantiated or sloppy. Standing's responses to these critiques help to put the book's genesis into context and better understand its purpose. For instance, Standing (2012a) tells us that it was an important aim for him to offer an accessible book for non-specialists and that the text's analytical narrative is the result of decades of research and publication by himself and his collaborators, thus some of the detailed data that is not in the book can be obtained from there.

That said, in my view Standing's book – despite some shortcomings – is a successful attempt to shed light, characterize and interpret an important phenomenon of contemporary capitalism. Standing focuses on the phenomenon of the rise of the so-called precariat, especially but not only in the global North. He analyses what the precariat is, where it comes from and what the societal repercussions of it are to date and might be in future. The conceptual core of Standing's definition of the term precariat is composed of several characteristics, the main one being the lack of seven labour-related security forms that made up the 'industrial citizenship' agenda in various Northern capitalist countries in the post-World War II welfare state era. Accordingly, people in the precariat have problems regarding income-earning opportunities, protection concerning arbitrary dismissal and regulations on hiring and firing, upward mobility, protection regarding accidents and illness at work (regulation of working hours, night shifts, compensation for mishaps), training and the use of skills, income stability and having a collective voice (i.e independent union, strikes). Put in more technical terms, they experience problems with regard to labour market security, employment security, job security, work security, skill reproduction security, income security and representation security.

Crucially, in this view, people that make up the precariat do not just face one or two forms of insecurities but a combination of several ones, i.e. all seven. It is the accumulative effect of this 'bundle of insecurities', this insecurity multiplicity that is the problem. These insecurities that characterize 'unstable labour' bring about subsequent problems in terms of workers' incomes, occupational identities, status insecurities and frustrations, and feelings of alienation and fear. They also contribute to a disrupted and shaky (i.e. 'minimal trust') relationship of the precariat with both the state and capital. Standing furthermore argues that the social contract relationship of past days – labour securities in return for workers' subordination and loyalty – does not apply to the precariat. Finally, the precariat is said to have a peculiar status, i.e. its status position is different from high-status professional or middle-status craft occupations (8–11). Due to this, there is a high level of shortism, opportunism and anger among the precariat. For instance, Standing writes that the precariatized existence is characterized by 'living in the present, without a secure identity, or sense of development achieved through work or lifestyle' (16).

In the remainder of the review, I draw out the significance of the subject matter of the book and then offer some further comments and questions. I will focus on aspects of the phenomenon itself and leave out the book part that discusses future politics. To start with, the merit of the book is to bring attention to the pace and magnitude of societal change that decades of neoliberal reforms and programmes have brought about. It is an investigation into some of the empirical micro-level realities of everyday life for the subaltern classes in neoliberalized societies which highlights general characteristics of the emerging social order of such market societies. It gives an insight into what it means these days to live as a member of the defeated classes and to engage with the victors, i.e. capital.

It focuses on one of the key arenas of neoliberal restructuring: societal practices and the political and moral economies – or political moral economies (PMEs) – that underpin practices (Harrison 2010; Wiegratz 2010, 2012). Standing shows that neoliberal transformations have resulted in a distinct practice repertoire regarding how the precariat is made to work for capital: flexible, on-off, temporary, low-paid, insecure, alienating and so on. In other words, there are neoliberal-specific adjustments or innovations regarding the social practices of exploiting labour in the North, despite historical continuities in character. Moreover, the rise and existence of the precariat symbolizes and manifests (1) shifts in power relationships, societal hierarchies and forms of domination and control as well as (2) the advanced commodification of labour power, a thinning out of pro-worker institutions, and a restructuring, i.e. hardening of a number of PMEs that underpinned labour markets in particular and society in general prior to the neoliberal attack. The latter meant, as Standing shows, that the precariatization process had to destabilize and transform relevant non-neoliberal PMEs and thus undermine institutions that underpinned collective life in the welfare state era, including respective securities for and actions of workers.

Next, Standing makes the important point that the precariat and the world of 'unstable labour' did not emerge overnight but is the outcome of a long (and ongoing) process that he calls 'precariatization'. This process that made people 'precariatized' was deliberately advanced and entrenched institutionally by specific social actors. The precariat then – much like other major features of our current social formation such as fraud, corruption, war and xenophobia – is to a significant extent a result of a sequence of actions of predominantly the state and capital, e.g. specific policy decisions (re-regulation, etc.) of subsequent governments. Thus, the precariat – just as the condition of precarity – is a child of the neoliberal capitalist political economy and its dominant power dynamics. It is therefore a multi-layered phenomenon that is at same time a political and economic, but also a cultural phenomenon. Furthermore, Standing tells us that precariatization of society benefits specific actors, i.e. capital. The precariat is good for profits, at least for some firms, for some time. The insecurities and welfare losses of the precariat are functionally linked to the security and welfare gains of capitalists and their allies; profit and precarity are twins in market societies. This highlights (new) inequalities that are produced by precariatization: maximized uncertainty for one party, to ensure the (profit-enhancing) minimized uncertainty of the other party. Precariatiztion in many instances is a zero-sum game. In sum then, the precariat is a political-economic creation that is in the interest of specific classes. This reality questions the liberal assumption and talk of capitalism being or becoming a win-win, positive-sum, (more) civilized and responsible social formation.

The shifts highlighted above – together with other relevant transformations – have contributed to changes in the way in which capitalist societies in the North integrate (i.e. include–exclude) significant sections of the population into the state market system. Thus, precariatization comes with changes in both the capital–labour relationship and the state–society relationship bringing about political-economic *and* socio-cultural repercussions. The term 'denizens' encapsulates this double shift; Standing uses it for precariat members with few entitlements or rights, fewer than 'citizens', i.e. the members of the 'salariat' (14). Standing's analysis helps us to see better; e.g. that yet again it is the combination of several factors – i.e. the combination of insecurities, the combination of changes in the way in which workers are connected with capital and the state – that make up social change and related phenomena. Finally, other reviewers have a point to say that there is in some important ways a historical continuity when it comes to the unstable position and lives of workers in capitalism. But in my view, analysts who attempt to sketch out and conceptualize the latest feature change in contemporary forms of capitalism do a vital analytical job. Not everything stays the same over a period of centuries; while, of course, phenomena such as the one under scrutiny here are a product of past and present.

That said, as requested by the editors, I have tried to come up with some further questions and comments for Standing.[1] First, given the discussions around the book since its publication, it would be interesting to hear from Standing what he considers to be the analytical core of the book and its central concepts such as 'the precariat', 'precariatization', 'precariatized mind' or the 'precariat phase of development' (107)?[2] Furthermore, what are other existing concepts that are in the analytical proximity of 'the precariat' and might be useful to theorize and study empirically the issues raised in the book? Perhaps, concepts such as adverse incorporation, advanced marginality, surplus population, social exclusion, structural violence, power, vulnerability, commodification, high-speed society, human waste, modern outcasts, state of exception, moral disengagement? Second, what does the precariat analysis mean for post-colonial capitalist countries (especially in Africa and also elsewhere) where phases of production arrangements that come with expansive labour securities and welfare state benefits have been (very) limited and patchy in the past decades. Third, what would be key issues and variables for comparison of precariat-related issues across countries, i.e. for comparative precariat studies, besides the obvious ones such as the speed, scope, forms and repercussions of precariatization, or the role of the specifics of state, capital and labour? Fourth, if a multidisciplinary team of researchers would have a lot of resource and time at hand, what would be the key questions that should be investigated regarding the precariat?

That said, in my view one important set of questions for future research might be related to exploring via empirical research not just the specific responses of members of the precariat to their precariatized existence but also the responses of various categories of actors that engage with the precariat? How do actors use their newly gained increase in power vis-à-vis the precariat? How do they respond to the vulnerability of precariatized people? Has the precariatization of society contributed to a hardening of some moral economies, towards a more targeted, explicit and heightened exploitation, including defrauding and abusing of precariat members. What is the role of the state and other institutions in these processes? What are the effects regarding the moral economies in which the precariat operates in when they do not labour for capital? What are the repercussions of precariatization for societal institutions that require a sense of long-termism, stability, commitment and predictability? What are the repercussions for various effected moral economies (e.g. family, neighbourhood) and the moral climate in society more generally. How are patterns of relevant inter-personal relations and interactions affected? How does the ruling elite perceive, manage and steer not just the political but also the socio-cultural and especially moral changes related to the precaritization? How do rulers organize norm transmissions and reproduction in such a social order? How do they deal with the repercussions of the phenomenon, e.g. regarding social reproduction (child-bearing, family life) (Streeck 2011)?

Next, because Standing indeed writes at times in a somewhat sweeping manner – perhaps to make the text accessible and give the key messages more weight – future research might want to pick up some of the grand points made in the book and explore in more analytical nuance some of the processes and trends that Standing's text highlights. Take, for instance, the statement that a precaritized system of 'an environment of infinite flexibility and insecurity must jeopardise any sense of cooperation and moral consensus… We do what we get away with, acting opportunistically, always on the edge of being amoral. This is easier to rationalise… when there is no shadow of future in our dealings' (22). Or consider this passage: 'actions and attitudes, derived from precariousness, drift towards opportunism' (12). As a reader I wonder what this statement is based on: the state of the art in the relevant literature, latest case studies, anecdotal evidence? I had similar questions when reading sentences such as these: 'The precariat knows … there is no future in what they are doing' (12); 'The precariatised mind is fed by fear and motivated by fear' (20); 'Those in the precariat lack self-esteem and social worth in their work' (21); the 'lack of occupation creates an ethical vacuum' (21).

These are interesting points that deserve further theorizing and follow-up studies, among others to explore causality, in-between stages, border cases and so on. For instance, what is the percentage of those in the precariat that show more opportunistic attitudes, apply a more short-term oriented thinking, etc.? What about different stages or categories of opportunistism? What shapes who turns opportunistic; how far-reaching, immediate and permanent is this opportunism turn? What about those who do not turn opportunistic? What are the moral dilemmas that the members of the precariat face and how do they respond to them?

Furthermore, Standing argues that the spread of precariatization leads to mental, emotional and behavioural change (19). Future research might investigate in what way, how and why there are respective changes in that direction, and, more generally, which phenomena are indeed causally related to precariatization and/or to other phenomenon (as well). Research is also needed to explore for different country contexts which PMEs were restructured and how in order to institutionalize and normalize precarity in these countries.

To conclude, Standing has helped to put on the agenda labour-related consequences of the institutionalization of market societies in our era. He has singled out the issue of the proliferation and normalization of multiple labour-related insecurities to be critical for our understanding of what is specific about the current form of capitalism. Such insecurities have arguably existed in abundance and for a long time for most workers in the most deprived areas of the global South that have faced 'naked' imperialism (Bracking and Harrison 2003) and not seen the welfare state or a capital–state duo that provides any or many of the labour-related securities. To date, the power structure and dynamics in such places never really forced the ruling classes into this form of 'class compromise'. Standing's book signals that matters of power in the so-called advanced capitalized countries of the North have now also been adjusted and the rise of the precariat is one of the consequences of that. Just as the making of the precariat and its very existence is a phenomenon of power in capitalist social formations, so will be its future development.

The final word then goes to the late Eric Hobsbawm who has formulated a question that simmers thorough the precariat debate as well:

> Marxists have rightly focused on changes in the mode of production and their social relations as the generators of historical change. However, if we think in terms of how 'men make their own history', the great question is this: historically, communities and social systems have aimed at stabilization and reproduction, creating mechanisms to keep at bay disturbing leaps into the unknown. Resistance to the imposition of change from outside is still a major factor in world politics today. How is it, then, that humans and societies structured to resist dynamic development come to terms with a mode of production whose essence is endless and unpredictable dynamic development? Marxist historians might profitably investigate the operations of this basic contradiction between the mechanisms bringing about change and those geared to resist it. (Hobsbawm 2010, 150)

Notes

1. I am raising some questions as a scholar that researches matters of political and moral economy especially in the context of capitalist development in the global South. I am aware that some of these issues might be addressed already in Standing's other publications or in the wider literature labour studies, etc., that I do not know about.
2. Perhaps, Standing could include a glossary of terms in the book's next edition.

References

Bracking, S., and G. Harrison. 2003. "Africa: Imperialism Goes Naked." *Monthly Review* 55 (6): 12. doi:10.14452/MR-055-06-2003-10_2.

Harrison, G. 2010. *Neoliberal Africa: The Impact of Global Social Engineering*. London: Zed.

Hobsbawm, E. 2010. "World Distempers – Interview." *New Left Review* 61, January–February. Accessed March 2011. http://newleftreview.org/II/61/eric-hobsbawm-world-distempers

Seymour, R. 2012. "We Are All Precarious – On the Concept of the 'Precariat' and its Misuses." *New Left Project*, February 10. Accessed August 20, 2013. http://www.newleftproject.org/index.php/site/article_comments/we_are_all_precarious_on_the_concept_of_the_precariat_and_its_misuses

Standing, G. 2012a. "Response to Book Review Symposium." *Work, Employment and Society* 26 (4): 690–692.

Standing, G. 2012b. "Response: Misunderstanding The Precariat." *New Left Project*, March 15. Accessed August 20, 2013. http://www.newleftproject.org/index.php/site/article_comments/response_misunderstanding_the_precariat

Streeck, W. 2011. "Flexible Employment, Flexible Families, and the Socialization of Reproduction." In *Imploding Populations in Japan and Germany*, edited by F. Coulmas, and R. Lützeler. Leiden: Brill.

Wiegratz, J. 2010. "Fake Capitalism? The Dynamics of Neoliberal Moral Restructuring and Pseudo-Development: The Case of Uganda." *Review of African Political Economy* 37 (124): 123–137. doi:10.1080/03056244.2010.484525.

Wiegratz, J. 2012. "The Neoliberal Harvest: The Proliferation and Normalisation of Economic Fraud in a Market Society." In *New Directions in Crime and Deviancy*, edited by S. Winlow, and R. Atkinson. London: Routledge.

Jörg Wiegratz
School of Politics and International Studies, University of Leeds
j.wiegratz@leeds.ac.uk

http://dx.doi.org/10.1080/23269995.2014.880257

Review

Jo Grady

The Precariat is a book that needs little introduction. Since its initial publication in 2011, it has received praise from the Left generally and from those in academia. Indeed, the book received an endorsement from Noam Chomsky, which it wears with pride on its front cover. It has, however, also prompted critique from the same circles that have praised it.

The main pull of Standing's contribution is that it draws attention to the growing problem of employment insecurity and high unemployment. It is thus prescient, given the revelation that even by modest calculations a minimum of 250,000 workers in the United Kingdom are on zero-hour contracts (ONS 2013). Standing also raises the important concern that in the vacuum of despair created by such circumstances, the political right often benefits. Thus, it is clear that the subject matter deserves taking seriously, and Standing deserves credit for bringing a debate that is central to work and social relations into open discussion.

The starting point of Standing's argument, that changes in capitalism have not only made workers more vulnerable to the vicissitudes of the market but that those changes have also made traditional Marxian class analysis more difficult too, is undoubtedly correct. This is because the various jobs that went along with industrial capitalism have largely disappeared in the West and have been outsourced elsewhere, along with the easily identifiable and strong class structures and working movements that underpinned them.

In trying to understand what these changes have meant for class analysis, Standing (2011a) argues that there are now essentially four classes. These are (1) a top 'elite' 'consisting of a tiny number of absurdly rich global citizens' (7); (2) the 'salariat' who are still in stable full time employment and who enjoy all that this type of employment has tended to deliver, such as holiday and sickness entitlements, pensions and other employment 'benefits'. Such workers tend to be concentrated in large corporations such as 'government agencies and public administration, including the civil service' (7); (3) alongside the 'salariat' sit the 'proficians' who Standing argues are a far smaller group and tend to consist of highly-paid consultants/contractors who rarely conform to the employment norm of 'a job for life' or '9–5 working hours'; (4) and finally the old working class, who are made up of 'shrinking core of manual workers, the essence of the old working class' (8). Standing argues that the 'battalions of industrial labourers who formed the labour movement have shrivelled and lost their sense of social solidarity'. Underneath these four classes, sits Standing's 'precariat'. It is with Standing's class analysis that this review first turns.

Defining class and gaining solidarity

Obviously Standing takes on a difficult task in sketching out new economic classes. He describes the precariat as a 'class in the making' and asserts that this newly emergent class is replacing the old working class/proletariat. The extent to which this can be demonstrated, however, is questionable given that in *The Precariat* Standing's claims tend to be mostly based on unsubstantiated generalizations, and there is a tendency to ignore examples of growing working class communities in industrializing nations. Indeed, Standing never really convincingly differentiates the precariat from the working class. This is particularly pertinent given the growing number of people that lack security, clear career progression or occupational identity, traits which Standing claims are central to being a member of the precariat but are also increasingly ubiquitous for the working class. In addition, dismissing labourism, as Standing does (and so too, he claims, does the precariat) ignore the fact that in recent years it has been trade unions that have been campaigning on the very issues that Standing claims are central to the precariat – living wages, abolition of zero-hour contracts and fit-for-purpose social security. Indeed, often it is organized agencies such as trade unions that have provided funding for campaigns and demonstrations, which beg the question as to why trade unions and other mobilizing institutions are so quickly dismissed by Standing.

This is a serious point because austerity measures – which are essentially being used as an excuse to systematically remove major components of the Welfare State (which *many* rely on) –are having a major impact on a good number of people, the working class included. Though Standing seems relevantly unconcerned about the working class, unless they slip into the 'precariat', and in trying to convince the reader that Standing's 'precariat' are new, distinct and thus need special attention, he misses a trick. The point is that nearly *all* classes, except the super wealthy elite that Standing identifies, suffer and are exploited by neoliberal capitalism; whether this manifests itself in being removed from participating in the market and job security or by being bonded to the market by negative equity mortgages. In Standing's class analysis, there is no consideration as to why anyone who is not the 1% (or perhaps more accurately the 0.01%) would support neoliberal capitalism. It also ignores the gross inequalities between those who just qualify for entry into the 'salariat' and those who surpass it, but do not qualify as super wealthy either. The result being that a junior GP and David Cameron sit in the same class. The analysis offered forward, therefore, can be one dimensional and ignores how the ruling class seek to dominate us in different ways. This is somewhat understandable omission though. Standing's focus is on the 'precariat', and it seems that he is less concerned with any other group and explaining their motivations or circumstances.

Standing is at his strongest when discussing 'why the precariat is growing' (Chapter 2), as he offers forward a detailed analysis of global transformations in the world economy since the 1970s that in no small part offers forward a convincing account as to why so much labour has become insecure, flexible and precarious. Alongside the emergence of this trend, we also witnessed an onslaught of neoliberal policies designed to cripple and destroy the trade union movement. A fuller discussion of the lengths the 'old working class' and their agencies went to in trying to stave off the attack that has led to the emergence of the precariat (in the West anyway) might have allowed Standing to extend this group more sympathy than he does. The 'old working class' therefore, is not simply a made up of fearful, right-wing prone, immigrant-hating people; indeed, the 'old working class' is made up of people who know only too well about the damage that can be done by divisive politics (as they are often victims of such politics), and who also (historically) engaged in struggle to attempt to prevent the trends which have developed. It is also the case that currently approximately seven million workers in the United Kingdom are in trade unions, which suggests that they are not a spent force, and in that sense, not an insignificant friend of the 'precariat'. The point about the damage being done to the precariat (if one believes that it is a distinct group at all) is that it affects all of us. It affects all of society. The welfare state was an expedient compromise in post-war Britain to manage capitalism and the fact that it also managed inequality was adjunct. The super elite that Standing refers to are not interested in 'managing inequality' even as an appendage and are only interested in managing capitalism in order that it benefits them. Standing is obviously interested primarily in the precariat (presumably because he thinks so few others are), but we cannot view the violence done to them in isolation; moreover, if they are to be successful in whatever quest Standing imagines them on, then they need allies who have access to organizing agencies and funds (presumably paid for via union subs). If Standing wishes to see a 'political paradise', those most exploited by capitalism need to recognize a common cause and use whatever vehicles are available to them (even if this is trade unions), rather than further divisions and references to overgeneralized notions of some kind of multitude precariat.

After the publication of *The Precariat*, Standing wrote a piece in *The Guardian* where he addressed 'what needs to be done', arguing for:

> a reinvention of the progressive trinity of equality, liberty and fraternity. A politics of paradise will be built on respect for principles of economic security and all forms of work and leisure, rather than the dour labourism of industrial society. The precariat understands that, and politicians on the left should listen. (Standing 2011b)

Many on the Left would agree with Standing regarding what is needed. The rub, however, is where Standing chooses to lay the blame, and this is often with those who have organized collectively or have been accustomed to working in reasonably secure full or part time labour – thus creating division, when none really need exist. It seems much better to target those that are inflicting such violence on all those exploited in a society, and thus the reason we need to theorize and understand these complex elite, and their myriad of supports. Various aspects of welfare society are being eroded, which are making life less secure for a good number or people, and even if they believe they will retire happily, and 'dodge the bullet' (so to speak) these groups still are able to extend sympathy and empathy to the *indignados* (in Spain), as indeed are many of them not also parents? Thus, any problem Standing sees as a problem for his precariat is a problem for all. Welfare capitalism was not built by just one group demanding it. Despite it being somewhat of an expedient compromise, welfare capitalism was constructed by people who inhabited all positions on the political spectrum (admittedly for different motivations). Trade unions have made great attempts in recent years to lobby on behalf of groups that Standing would recognize as being in the precariat, and indeed groups like Age Concern and the Fawcett Society (I could name many others) are also dedicated to campaigning on what Standing identifies 'precariat issues'.

Perhaps, the best way to sum up how I felt after reading *The Precariat* would be to recount a recent encounter I had with an individual who Standing would identify as being a precariat. Whilst writing this review, I found myself in Cardiff (Wales) for a conference. Whilst out and about I got chatting to a pub doorman called Howard. Howard was on a notional 6 hour per week contract, but often ended up working either more or fewer hours, had little/no job security, and by Standing's own definition should really qualify as a precariat. Howard asked me about the book I was carrying. I explained the concept of the 'precariat' as fully as I could, and how Standing claims this group differs from the working class and is indeed a new emergent class. After a while, giving it some thought, Howard replied, 'interesting idea, but I'm not buying it'. On the whole I have to say, that despite my sympathies with Standing's cause, I agree with Howard.

References

ONS (Office for National Statistics). 2013. *Labour Force Survey (LFS)*. London: Office for National Statistics.

Standing, G. 2011a. *The Precariat: The New Dangerous Class*. London: Bloomsbury.

Standing, G. 2011b. "Who Will Be a Voice for the Emerging Precariat?" *The Guardian*, June 1. Accessed September 8, 2013. http://www.theguardian.com/commentisfree/2011/jun/01/voice-for-emerging-precariat

Jo Grady
University of Leicester, Leicester, UK
j.grady@le.ac.uk

http://dx.doi.org/10.1080/23269995.2014.880258

Where's Howard?[1]

Guy Standing

Thanks are due to the three readers who took the trouble to read and comment on *The Precariat*. One of the features of that fascinating masque *Comus* is that Milton gave the devil the best lines. The best critiques are those that represent the author correctly, and I would like particularly to thank Jörg Wiegratz for trying to do that.

Jo Grady ends her critique by citing a pub doorman, Howard, but one really wonders if she described the precariat in a way that I, or the many people who have told me they belong to it, would have done, or if she described it in a neutral tone. And one wonders if he responded in the way stated. Anyhow, that is all clean fun.

One suspects that the definition of the precariat was not correctly conveyed to Howard, since Grady herself seems to think that the main characteristic is 'employment insecurity', which is not the case. In her critique, it is also regrettable that the positive, radical or transformative characteristics of the precariat do not receive a mention. Nor can I recall saying anywhere that the precariat is 'replacing' the proletariat; the two will continue to co-exist, although the one is growing, the other shrinking. Rightly or wrongly, the book states that the proletariat will not disappear.

However, it is a waste of scarce space to dissect textual inaccuracies. I want to use this response to summarise the key arguments as developed through a series of books, bearing in mind that *The Precariat* was, as Wiegratz recognises, an attempt to write a narrative accessible to a lay audience – most notably to those in or fearful of joining the precariat – as much as to academics, drawing on more than a decade of conceptual and empirical research, cited in the book's bibliography.

Defining the precariat as a class-in-the-making

For better or for worse (and clearly Grady and Catherine Lawlor think for the worse), the underlying objective of my work over the past 20 years has been to escape from the suffocating paradigms of what I call *labourism* and *neo-liberalism*, as well as from the sterile dualism that has characterised some quasi-Marxian labour process analysis.

While one is bound to be only partially successful at best, what one can say is that the concept and the book must have something going for them because I have received thousands of emails, letters, phone calls, invitations to speak and blogs from a wide range of people in numerous countries, many testifying to their personal identification with the precariat. As evidence, that may not be much better than Grady's friend Howard. But as I have put it in a number of public gatherings of those describing themselves as in the precariat, 'there is something in the water'.

Intellectually, one can define the precariat – and the other groups outlined in the class framework – as having a combination of distinctive relations of production, distinctive relations of distribution and distinctive relations to the state.

The first has received most attention from critics, many of whom stop at that point. The distinctive relations of production start with the absence of all seven forms of labour-based security listed on page 10 of the book and mapped in statistical detail in preceding academic books, journal articles and International Labour Organisation (ILO) reports. Wiegratz, having read my earlier defence against the type of charges made by Lawlor in her final acerbic comments, poses an important question in asking how a multidisciplinary team would investigate the matter.

In the 1980s and 1990s, within the ILO, I designed and implemented large-scale surveys, called Enterprise Labour Flexibility Surveys (ELFS) and People's Security Surveys (PSS), in trying to do precisely that. These were conducted in thousands of firms and, in the case of the PSS, covered many thousands of workers in 20 countries. I would be the first to admit to shortcomings, but they were the most detailed statistical attempts to capture the changing nature of labour relations of which I am aware. Identifying the growth of workers with insecure labour relations of many types fed into a detailed empirical book (Standing 1999) and a comprehensive ILO (2004) report that I coordinated and prepared.

I will not repeat findings from those years of trial-and-error. But surely critics should be fairer to colleagues than rely on talks with Howard for their opinions of somebody's work. We all have access to the web and can consult it to discover a work's antecedents. This is also one reason why these days it is less important to give a source for every stylised fact given in a text, because with a few taps on the computer one can identify a source for a stated fact or finding. Had Lawlor done that in connection with the book's statement on charity staff leaving for supermarket jobs to escape stress, she would have found that it came from a Unison report. Lawlor is an expert on Michel Foucault. Had the strict criteria she advocates been applied to his work, he would never have published anything.[2]

Anyhow, insecure labour in a contractual sense is not the fundamental point. Critics of the concept of the precariat have dismissed it on the grounds that there has always been precarious labour. Do they really think one does not know that? The point is that in the case of the precariat this feature is combined with other factors in a distinctive way, quite unlike precarious labour in the nineteenth century. That at least is the hypothesis, to be refuted or refined through subsequent research.[3]

Perhaps the characteristic that resonates most with members of the precariat is the absence of occupational identity, the inability to define and retain control over an occupational narrative or trajectory. That goes with growing statistical evidence of a low and declining level of social mobility. The analogy of a lottery society, of winner-takes-all, loser-loses-all markets, is increasingly apt.

At risk of castigation for overgeneralisation, one may suggest that in the early days of industrial capitalism, a docker or a miner may have had casual labour, but he was probably regularly a docker or miner. The precariat typically cannot own to a clear occupational identity, knowing that whatever is cited today is likely to change within months, weeks or even days.

The matter does not stop there. The precariat is also distinguished from the proletariat by having to do a great deal more work-for-labour relative to labour, and is typically exploited off formal workplaces and outside the bounds of formal, remunerated labour, as well as on workplaces and during remunerated labour. By contrast, the proletariat, in modal terms, was and is exploited at the workplace during designated working hours, clocking in and clocking out.

In that regard, it was pleasing to see Wiegratz's focus on *precariatisation*, because that contrasts with the well-established concept of proletarianisation, so brilliantly analysed by the great historians of the rise of industrial capitalism, most notably E.P. Thompson.

The rising amount of work-for-labour (and work-for-state) being forced on the precariat is why the book suggests a need to move away from the imagery of industrial time to one of *tertiary time*. Rightly or wrongly, this concept is presented as central to understanding the precariat, and it regrettable that some critics seem not to notice it at all, even though a whole chapter is devoted to it.

There is another aspect of the distinctive relations of production that does seem to be historically unique, and which, incidentally, seems open to good multidisciplinary Ph.D. research. The claim, or hypothesis, is that the precariat is the first mass class in history that is expected to have a level of qualifications (or that under-theorised notion of 'skill') greater than the level of labour it is expected to undertake. One would be prepared to bet that Howard would recognise himself if Grady had described the precariat in those terms. In Marxian terms, his labour power was being debilitated by his labour.

This feature has a series of implications for research and social and labour market policy. The book hypothesises that it creates deep alienation, *status frustration* and different forms of relative deprivation, in different ways for the several factions within the precariat. It also generates several types of *precarity trap*, a theme developed more in a new book, *A Precariat Charter: From Denizens to Citizens* (Standing 2014).

The second defining dimension of the precariat is that it has distinctive *relations of distribution*. As an economist, I have tended to emphasise this aspect. None of the three reviewers touches on it. The definition hinges on the concept of *social income*, explained in the book and developed in more detail in the preceding technical books. Perhaps it is because she has not come to terms with it that Grady claims that in my class analysis 'there is no consideration as to why anyone who is not the 1% (or perhaps more accurately the 0.01%) would support neoliberal capitalism'.

On the contrary, it is because the *structure* of social income (as well as its level) varies so much that one can make sense of the emerging class structure and the political orientations of its components. The plutocracy and elite, clearly earning all their income from capital and rental income, are financially advantaged by the neo-liberal model. But so too are large and growing parts of the salariat and the proficians, which is one reason for differentiating them from the old proletariat.

Today, in the United States, for instance, salaried employees in corporations on average receive about a third of their social income from capital, in the form of shares and profit-sharing bonuses. In Germany, the estimated equivalent is about 40%. If they perceive a direct trade-off between wages and profits and that a growing part of their income will come from profits, they will tend to support policies and institutional changes that will push down wages, if they are motivated by short-term material interest.

Proficians, even more so, depend on profits and the ability of corporations and bureaucracies to pay for consultancies and their fancy projects, as well as rates of return to private investments. As a result, being detached from the compensatory mechanisms of the welfare state, they will tend to support a neo-liberal agenda of lower direct taxation and a shrinking welfare state. There are contradictions in that way of thinking, but one can at least understand why they would support a neo-liberal agenda. I cannot think of a way of stating that more clearly than is done in the book.

The different political interests also become clearer when thinking of the changing character and structure of both state benefits and enterprise benefits. Under the neo-liberal state, the upper-income detached classes and parts of the proletariat benefit enormously from the panoply of *subsidies* built up as incentives and rewards for money-makers. None of these go to the precariat, which on the contrary suffers from the deliberate and very systematic erosion of rights-based universal benefits and services.

In short, the claim is this. The precariat is the first mass class that has to rely almost entirely on money wages for its social income. If Howard is part of the precariat, he would understand that. One wonders if Grady told him that this is a defining aspect of the precariat.

The third defining feature is that the precariat has distinctive *relations to the state*. This is hard to summarise adequately. Wiegratz recognises its significance in the book's framework, but it is not clear if he appreciates the centrality of what is happening. Perhaps I am being unfair in concluding that.

Here the concept of *denizens* should help. In the middle ages, a denizen was someone who came into a town and was granted by the burghers a range of rights that was more limited than granted to the town's citizens. Later, the term came to be used to describe a contractual relation imposed on certain migrants, as an 'in-between' civil status. That is still the case, in effect. But the precariat is the first class in history that has been subject to a state-led erosion of rights, turning more people into denizens.

In the new book, a more systematic attempt is made to show how the precariat has been losing civil, political, cultural, social and economic rights, *de jure* and *de facto*. That is quite unlike what has been happening to the salariat or proletariat. And in this respect as with the others, it can only lead to obfuscation if they are seen as all bundled together in one united working class.

In sum, the precariat can be defined in class terms – by relations of production, relations of distribution and relations to the state. This combination produces particular consciousness. At present, it is still a class-in-the-making, in that members of it know more about what they are against than have a united view of what they want instead. Will it become a class-for-itself? And if so, how? I have tried to answer those questions in *A Precariat Charter.*

Trades unions and the precariat

Part of the animosity by some critics with labourist values towards the analysis seems linked to the critical comments in the book on trades unions.[4] As someone who has been a trade union member for longer than he cares to admit, and as someone who has been working for and with a union for the past 15 years, I can claim some experience and evidence of sympathy. But the industrial trades unions of the twentieth century are in deep existential danger.

Historically, they were a great powerful progressive force from the nineteenth century into the late twentieth century. But they were trapped by their intrinsic labourism, which is the essence of the critique in the previous longer book, *Work after Globalization: Building Occupational Citizenship* (Standing 2009). For me symbolically, this was exposed when the international body of trades unions refused for years to allow affiliation by the Self-Employed Women's Association (SEWA), the association representing women outworkers in India. The pretext was that it was not a union because it did not represent and bargain on behalf of *employees* with capital.

Grady misses a key point in her characterisation of poor Howard in saying he had no 'job security', when what she almost certainly meant was no employment security. That is crucial to understanding the difficulty facing unions. Through the twentieth century, after the defeat or subordination of craft unionism (symbolised by the amalgamation of the AFL-CIO), unions gave priority to employment security and labourist social security rather than to occupational security or 'the right to practise'.

They opted for a social compact in which they gained so-called 'labour rights' (labour-based security) in return for ceding the right to manage to capital, in the process allowing management to alter the technical division of labour without much restraint, even if some unions sometimes manned the barricades in extremis.

They thus opposed occupational guilds and their tradition of 'self-regulation' and stood by as complex neo-liberal state regulation of occupations through licensing, usually via financial institutions, was steadily strengthened. Again symbolically, just as the international unions blocked organisations like SEWA from being recognised in the ILO, so they have always opposed the presence and legitimation of occupational associations inside its umbrella. It is not some critic who is 'dividing the working class'; it has been deeply divided for more than a century, and unions have played a role in that.

Even today, if unions are confronted by a trade-off between jobs for their members and improved benefits for the precariat, their governance structures will push them in one direction, whatever rhetoric they might adopt to suggest otherwise. If there is a trade-off between jobs and the environment or pollution, they seem invariably to choose the former.

Regrettably, there are plenty of examples that could be cited. One should not be surprised by this or indeed be very critical. Unions have been constructed to represent their members as employees bargaining with employers.

We need unions. But we should not be apologists and claim they represent a united working class. It is not united, and they have never actually stood for it. If they had, a regime of work rights (including equal rights for women's work (sic) and the right to practise) would have been constructed rather than a so-called labour rights regime.

Grady claims that 'trades unions and other mobilising institutions' were 'quickly dismissed by Standing'. It is hard to understand how anybody could say that and claim to be fair. The whole thrust of the argument in *The Precariat* and, at length, in the last two chapters of the book on which it is based is that the emerging global labour market and economic system require a combination of new policies of income security and new forms of representation security based on collective Voice institutions.

Grady further claims that the book 'ignores the fact that in recent years it has been trades unions that have been campaigning on the very issues that Standing claims are central to the precariat'. She then lists things not mentioned in *The Precariat* and omits what is mentioned. One wonders if this is a fair way of conducting a critique.

Grady's claim provides an excuse to relate an anecdote. In 2012, I was invited to present the themes to a trade union leaders' summer school in the north of England. There were long-standing friends in the audience; some resentment from older men there, a lot more empathy among younger participants. Towards the end, I asked rhetorically, 'Why is it that trades unions over the years, and even now, have been among the most vehemently hostile to a basic income?' After all, this is a pivotal proposal in *The Precariat*.

In the discussion group afterwards, a young Italian trades unionist said he had been thinking about it. 'I think I know the reason', he said, 'It is because we would lose control and people would not join trades unions'. I looked at him and said, 'If you think about it, that is a pretty bad statement about trades unions. They should be appealing to people to join for better reasons than that'. I could have added that people with basic security are actually more likely to join collective bodies than those without it.

Grady was unfair. The good news is that there are signs of change, even if unions are having to be dragged out of their labourist bunker. But let us not pretend that they have been doing what the precariat needs or what the book advocates.

In brief, what is required is a reinvention of collective association. The way this is presented in the books is as a synthesis of the time-honoured occupational guilds, which had their faults as well as good qualities, and trades unionism, with all their good qualities without the bad.

Collective bodies are the very antithesis of neo-liberalism. That is why they are needed now as much as ever before. They must be revived in new forms suitable to the globalising labour and productive process, reviving and strengthening values of social solidarity and social empathy. To do that, they may have to start by accepting that wage bargaining is not the most important part of the challenge ahead.

Why is the precariat the new dangerous class?

A key issue in debates around the precariat relates to its political orientations. Most fundamentally, its material foundations give it a sense of alienation from other class interests and lead it to reject the old mainstream political traditions, including social democracy as developed in the twentieth century and neo-liberalism.

The idea of a dangerous class has historical connections. Essentially, in the way used in the book, it means the emerging mass class that rejects the existing social and political order, largely because it does not recognise its aspirations and needs as being addressed within that order.[5] It does not mean it is prone to violence, crime and drugs, which is how some reviewers have presumed.[6]

This differs from Marx's definition, in that he saw what he called the lumpen-proletariat as entirely negative, being used as strike-breakers and so on. By contrast, today we need terms for differentiating between those on the margins of society, socially and economically damaged and essentially anomic, and those who are central to the emerging system of production and labour and work.

The *lumpen-precariat* is roughly equivalent to Marx's notion, in that it conveys being a group at most helping to prop up an existing order. But a group that drifts into crime and social illness is not actually dangerous in the political sense. Lock them up or send them for therapy that can be the moralistic reaction. It does not challenge the legitimacy of the existing order.

The precariat is a dangerous class-in-the-making because its combination of characteristics leads it to reject the old social democratic political strategy and the neo-liberalism that predominates within the modern state.

Some would describe the precariat as apolitical, since almost everywhere voting in parliamentary and local authority elections has been falling, mainly among the young. Thinning democracy is dangerous. But it favours the neo-liberal model, since the groups that favour it have a greater tendency to remain politically engaged in the conventional sense.

However, if one wishes to be optimistic, one can say that the consequential loss of support for labourist and social democratic variants of a leftish politics must sooner or later induce a reorientation towards values and aspirations of the precariat. It is this thought that underpins the new book, which hinges on the question: How would a Charter of demands by the precariat of 2014 differ from a Charter of demands that might have been made by the proletariat in 1914? (Standing 2014).

Notes

1. With apologies to Martin Handford, the creator of Where's Wally? In the United States and Canada, Wally is called Waldo.
2. It should not be necessary to point out that there is a big difference between citing anecdotal evidence to illustrate an analytical point and implementing policy based on anecdotal evidence.
3. One attempt to develop a sevenfold class framework was the BBC's Great British Class Survey in 2013. Elsewhere, I have expressed reservations about that particular way of conceptualising and measuring, for focusing overly on relative incomes.
4. Jo Grady even goes so far as to assert that I 'lay the blame … with those who have organised collectively or have been accustomed to working in reasonably secure full or part time labour – thus creating division, when none really need exist'. Although trades unions made historically strategic errors when they had the power to effect social change, this assertion is unfounded and unfair.
5. Among those who have used the term in ways that underlie the idea in *The Precariat* was Henry Mayhew, the great observer and student of London's proto-proletariat in the late nineteenth century. For an interesting modern interpretation, albeit of a different class than the precariat, see Jankiewicz (2012).
6. This may have been connected with the timing of the book's publication, which was just before the riots and arson that started in Tottenham in August 2011. Pictures from those riots were used to illustrate several subsequent newspaper interviews with the author.

References

ILO (International Labour Organisation). 2004. *Economic Security for a Better World*. Geneva: International Labour Organisation.

Jankiewicz, S. 2012. "A Dangerous Class: The Street Sellers of Nineteenth-Century London." *Journal of Social History* 46 (2): 391–415.

Standing, G. 1999. *Global Labour Flexibility: Seeking Distributive Justice*. Harmondsworth: Macmillan.

Standing, G. 2009. *Work After Globalization: Building Occupational Citizenship*. Cheltenham: Elgar.

Standing, G. 2014. *A Precariat Charter: From Denizens to Citizens*. London: Bloomsbury.

Guy Standing
School of Oriental and African Studies (SOAS), University of London
G.Standing@soas.ac.uk

http://dx.doi.org/10.1080/23269995.2014.888278

CONCLUSION

The precariat, intergenerational justice and universal basic income

Juliana Bidadanure

School of Politics, Economics and Philosophy, University of York, York, UK

This inspiring special issue provides an overview of the multidimensional nature of precariousness in the neoliberal world. It takes issue with the numerous forms of insecurity that a multitude of people experience in their daily lives. The authors alternately employ the concepts of *precariat, precariatization* and *precariousness* as tools to address the ways in which people stand in relation to the labour market, to their workplace, as well as to their homes and families. The shrinking of the welfare state, the disappearance of the public sphere, as well as the outsourcing and the robotization of jobs all participate in the making of an insecure social reality that turns a growing class of employed, self-employed, unemployed, carers and migrants into actual or potential members of the precariat.

In this conclusion, I aim to emphasize two major aspects of the debate that I believe deserve to be discussed further: on the one hand, questions of intergenerational justice and, on the other, the radical policy proposal of a universal basic income. Through this discussion, I hope to point to further avenues for research. Although intergenerational justice has not been explicitly discussed in this special issue, I will show that it relates quite extensively with the discussions around the precariat. In fact, I will argue that the precariat, as an analytical tool, shares many features with the intergenerational approach, which critically examines period, age and cohorts effects in societies. The second topic – basic income – is explored by Guy Standing in his book on the Precariat and elsewhere (Standing 2013a, 2006). Basic income is also the explicit focus of Bill Jordan's (2013) contribution to this issue and is mentioned by most of this issue's contributors, without however being their explicit central focus. I will demonstrate that the poignancy of the precariat analysis cannot fully be grasped in isolation from the correlated radical basic income response that Standing puts forward.

Intergenerational justice

Standing's analysis of the precariat shares many features with intergenerational analyses, which look at how current economic and social trends affect different age groups and birth cohorts. Intergenerational analysts and people interested in intergenerational justice, more generally, often worry that the interests of the generation of young people today are not taken seriously (Griffith 2011; Howker and Malik 2010; Tremmel 2010; Willetts 2010; Chauvel 2010; Coatman and Shrubsole 2012). The 'jilted generation', 'precarious generation', 'jobless generation' or 'internship generation', as it is now often referred to, indeed suffers staggering levels of unemployment, poverty and exclusion. And yet, there is a tendency in the media and amongst politicians alike to emphasize personal desert and render young people responsible for their own situation. Discourses on youth tend to revolve around their alleged laziness, bad attitude and strong sense of entitlement (Jones 2011). Young people are asked to 'stop whingeing, stop complaining, and just get on with it' (Howker and Malik 2010, 2). The Intergenerational Foundation recently published a report on the perception of young people in European countries (Leach 2011): 'British people in their 20s achieved the lowest scores of any country in relation to being viewed with respect. (…) In terms of contempt, British people in their 20s came first. (…) When asked to rate overall how positively or negatively people felt towards those in their 20s, respondents from the UK gave its younger people the lowest score of any country, coming 29th out of 29 countries' (Leach 2011, 3). In the UK, over a million youth are NEETS – not in education, employment or training. At the same time, benefits for the young are still very limited. The vast majority of internships are unpaid and unemployed young people may well be soon threatened with loss of their benefits if they do not accept to work for free as part of the new workfare proposals of the British Government (Malik 2011, 2012; Tapsfield 2012).

The first point in common between the precariat as an analytical tool and the field of intergenerational justice is thus that an important focus is placed on young people. The precariat brings together a variety of individuals from all generations, but the young make up for a very substantial part of the precariat, as illustrated by Armano and Murgia's (2013) claim that: 'Young people are far more likely than other age groups to be employed in precarious jobs, independently of their education and skills' (Armano and Murgia 2013, 486). In times of economic crisis and job scarcity, new entrants' integration in the labour market is jeopardized. The young's transition to 'adult life' takes a slow turn. Young people from disadvantaged backgrounds are of course the first exposed, but young people whose parents hold relatively stable jobs are also affected. As Armano and Murgia (2013) demonstrate, even highly educated or highly skilled young people are now likely to lead a precarious existence. The multiplication of zero-hour contracts and the development of freelancing and internships are concrete examples of the normalization of insecurity essential to the making of a precariat.

Even if young people do not make up a homogeneous category and even if different youths are equipped and supported differently, the precariatization of most sectors of the economy has become part of their social reality, as an age group. Worse, what is so problematic about precarity at a young age is that it risks clustering into further disadvantage over people's lifespan: 'If early precious years are spent groping around in precarious jobs, the capacity to develop will be permanently impaired' (Standing 2011, 78). Therefore, nothing suggests that youth precarity is just a phase that will be overcome over time. On the contrary, everything seems to suggest that if young people as an age group are doing quite badly, they are also likely to do badly over their complete lives. As the generational sociologist Louis Chauvel (2010) argues, cohorts that are socialized in a context of job scarcity remain 'scarred' throughout their lives and enjoy comparatively lower wages, opportunities and employment rates than other cohorts: 'when the difficulties disappear, the cohorts who faced these problems continue to suffer from long-term consequences of past handicaps' (Chauvel 2010, 16). The problem with the young precariat is thus that the young as a birth cohort – the jilted generation – will not get the same job or income opportunities as their parents as they age.

In intergenerational terms, we may then conclude that the young are being failed in at least three ways: they are being subjected to high risks of unemployment, poverty and exclusion, which is highly imprudent because these may cluster into further disadvantages over their lifespan; as a result, as a generation, they may be scarred by these young experiences of insecurity and lead more insecure lives than the generation before them; last, their substantive exclusion from the productive sphere and from politics (young people vote much less and have few political representatives) is worrying in terms of their ability to stand as political equals in our society. The trends that the analytical lens of the precariat illuminates are therefore closely related to questions of intergenerational justice.

This leads us to the second way in which the precariat analysis and the intergenerational approach converge. As is now evident, they are both fundamentally dynamic analytical tools. The young from across traditional social classes, generational analysts argue, are affected by the flexibilization of the labour market, job scarcity and the lack of investment in their future. In the same way, the precariat is not a homogeneous group, but it grows with the very diverse categories of people who find themselves falling into it over time. Standing's approach emphasizes processes and changes, as does intergenerational analysis. In other words, new precarious modes of living are being normalized as new cohorts of young people evolve in the labour market. New forms of occupational insecurity are spreading through a growing proportion of younger cohorts. The dynamic, temporally sensitive nature of the analysis is thus a central aspect of Standing's class analysis. Those who miss this basic feature are likely to misunderstand the relevance and the salience of his framework.

For this reason, it seems to me that some of the criticisms that have been raised against Standing's analysis are in fact analytically on par with some of the criticisms that have been raised against the generational approach. Both criticisms point to legitimate worries, but miss what really makes the analysis relevant. When Standing defines the precariat as a 'class-in-the-making' (552) made of people living lives of insecurity, perhaps the important bit really is not 'class' but 'in the making'. The point is not to identify rigid categories in which people fall or do not fall. It is not to define and delineate clear boundaries, nor is it to describe clear patterns of distribution. The point is to show that something like a precariat is growing and that the traditional working class is shrinking: 'the two will continue to co-exist, although the one is growing, the other shrinking' (Standing 2013b). It aims to show that the precariatization of the labour market has become more and more normalized. What is more, it aims to show that, it is a process and many people are heading towards these precarious lives. When Jo Grady (2013, 544) argues that 'Standing never really convincingly differentiates the precariat from the working class' and yet, that he creates false divisions between the two classes, perhaps she underestimates the importance of this point. Standing is concerned with highlighting a dangerous direction, not with specifically trying to delineate the working class from the precariat.

This criticism seems to me to be analytically on par with the left-wing critique of intergenerational justice. The intergenerational lens, just like the precariat, magnifies the transformations in our societies that give rise to precarious lives. The aim of these analyses (or at least some of these analyses) is not to create false lines of conflicts between old and young people or between the working class and the precariat. Nor is it to create false amalgamations between the rich young and the poor young or between the poor retired and the migrant denizens; it is to show where we are heading. Endorsing a generational lens simply helps in emphasizing that:

> an unequal social order is being constructed along generational lines by paying off baby-boomers and exposing young people to the hard realities of a reorganized economy. This is not a wealth transfer from young to old, or a neglect of the interests of the young simply because they don't vote: it is part of a strategic restructuring of how our economy and society work in favour of capital, focusing its efforts on the weakest points of resistance. (Little 2014a, 10)

In other words, a new settlement manifests 'in an emerging generational politics produced by the material effects of neoliberalism on the lives of young people' (Little 2014a, 7).

Left-wing critics of both the precariat and the intergenerational lens may not be voiced by the same individuals, but they share the same worries: are we not emphasizing the wrong antagonisms? Pitting the elderly against the young? The working class against the precariat? The baby boomers versus their children? Or, as Shiv Malik expresses it: 'why fight the vested interests of your parents when you should be fighting those of the upper classes? Or, to put it another way, how does fighting the baby boomers stop the fat cats from making off with society's plunder?' (Shiv Malik 2012, 7). Surely, there is something prima facie worrying about the intergenerational lens. Intergenerational discourses have often been used to justify austerity politics: in the name of the young, the discourse goes, we should cut public deficit and stop spending so much of the public money on welfare. For this reason: 'Many on the left are suspicious of generational politics, on the grounds that it is stopping people talking about class' (Little 2014b). Any discourse, framework or concept may be appropriated in one direction or another, but there is much more to the intergenerational analysis than the debt-ridden pro-austerity turn it took in some discourses.

Very interestingly, at one point in her review, Jo Grady criticizes Standing along explicitly generational lines: the traditional, older members of the working class, who held comparatively more stable careers should not be opposed to the young precarious, she argues: 'even if they believe they will retire happily, and "dodge the bullet" (so to speak) these groups still are able to extend sympathy and empathy to the indignados (in Spain), as indeed are many of them not also parents?' (Grady 2013, 546). This seems to provide even more ground for thinking that the rejection of the precariat as a tool of analysis shares many characteristics with the suspicion against intergenerational analysis. But the point of Standing's analysis, surely, and of some of the intergenerational approaches, is not to create arbitrary divisions, but to say that the current difficulties and insecurities experienced by the young are in fact the sign of the new order establishing itself. Moreover, both approaches have the potential to even strengthen the class analysis to which critiques subscribe. As Ben Little (2014a) argues, the strategic restructuring of the economy creates new spaces of insecurity that 'work in favour of capital, which focuses its efforts on the weakest points of resistance – which include the economy's newest and most vulnerable entrants. Class is just as important as it ever was' (Little 2014a, 13). Mere love of parents for their children is not a strong objection to the generational analysis. Affection and care only mean that those who are more privileged have access to stronger safety nets, which in turn dangerously increases social inequalities. Through the precarization of the youth, as an age group, the notion of families as the only collective from which individuals should seek support is normalized (Little 2014a). Because families are so unequally advantaged, here again, the intergenerational and precariat lenses intersect and reinforce traditional class analysis.

I thus hope to have suggested that the two analytical tools of the precariat and intergenerational comparisons should be understood and approached as dynamic lenses that help to identify the trends, processes and changes that are relevant for social justice. Further directions for research must include more explicit linking of the two lenses: analysis of the phenomenon of precarization and how it affects different age groups and cohorts; research on how the young cope and react to the prospects of lives of uncertainty; analysis of how existing social inequalities between families are being exacerbated by the challenges the youth currently face with research on intergenerational mechanisms of solidarity which are arising as a result; analysis of discourses of intergenerational justice and the purpose they serve, as well as normative and conceptual attempts to provide more intersectional tools of generational analysis, without losing the sociological relevance of existing tools.

Basic income

This leads me to the second important idea to emphasize when we address the precariat: the solution to the problems highlighted – namely the implementation of a basic income. Basic income is a radical policy proposal that would consist in an unconditional monthly cash allowance above subsistence level delivered to all without means testing, extending from the beginning of adulthood to death. I think that one cannot really grasp the strength of Standing's concept of the precariat in isolation from the solution that he puts forward. The previous concerns I highlighted about the precariat analysis and the intergenerational lens were that they create erroneous antagonisms. The opposite worry also exists, however. At the same time as they create wrong divisions, the two approaches are criticized for lumping very different kinds of individuals together in the same bag: the young highly educated and the NEETS (young people not in education, employment or training). Seriously? The retired and the migrant? Honestly? This scepticism is fairly understandable. However, I think that the radical policy proposal, which Standing advances, rises up to the challenge. Focusing on the basic-income solution, one can see that the idea of the precariat in fact consciously and willingly unites more than it divides, thus creating the space for a common political consciousness.

In another paper on basic income, Bill Jordan (2011) addresses the unifying potential of basic income. He calls upon the history of the campaign for a basic income in the 1970s in a small industrial town in Southwest England. He describes the mixture of groups who fought for the radical policy: workers who had been made redundant, Trotskyist trade unionists, the long-term unemployed, single parents and disabled persons. The challenge for basic-income proponents is precisely to succeed in linking basic income to the multitude of insecurities from which people suffer. Building ties between the highly educated but economically insecure and the lumpen proletariat under the categorical group of the precariat can seem arbitrary, but it becomes less so when one realizes that a substantial basic income would provide both with a lifetime of basic economic security. The strength of both the identification of an emerging precarious class (the problem) and basic income (the solution) is that they both have the potential to appeal to a broad mass of people. When examining the precariat as an analytical tool, one should not underestimate the political potential it creates. The Occupy or indignados movements, for instance, in this respect, were not from a specific traditional social class, but shared a common anger for the many insecurities the current system produces.

Grady (2013) and Standing (2013b) had an interesting discussion in this special issue about trade unions. It seems that Standing' s analysis of the precariat and rejection of labourism may be in tension with trade unionism. Interestingly, trade unions are slow in accepting basic income as a potentially transformative and progressive tool for reducing the effects of the neo-liberalization of the economy. This seems to suggest, once again, that the concepts of precariat and basic income are as interconnected as I am trying to suggest. One way to explain the reluctance of unions to side with basic income, or Grady's doubts on the precariat as a useful analytical tool, is that it seems to give up on jobs and on the traditional working class as the adequate space for the struggle to be led. Why not a guarantee of employment instead of a basic income? Why not strengthen the working class as a group instead of claiming that more and more people are becoming precariatized? Many replies exist in the already vast literature in defence of basic income: including Standing's argument that a basic income is a requirement of a meaningful right to work; the view that basic income gives people the freedom to say no to oppressive, exploitative forms of work and that it would thus signal the beginning of non-alienated work (Jordan 2011; Widerquist 2013; Pettit 2007). Basic income would also empower the working class and unions in their struggle against exploitation. But its extension beyond the traditional working class is both a normative and a strategic requirement.

Defending basic income is very straightforwardly relevant, or should be, for those who emphasize trends of growing structural oppression and insecurity. Not only would it offer the time for people to build lives around things they find valuable, instead of alienating and exploitative forms of living, but it would also allow people to lead a more multidimensional existence, around care, volunteer work, leisure, political engagement and so on (Standing 2006). The best way to get people not to be political is to make them precarious. If young people were not so focused on making ends meet, they would probably become a more disruptive force. Basic income is not an end, it is a beginning. It has the potential to change the rules of the game, empower the most vulnerable and act as a shield between individuals and those who have a fundamental interest in their existence to be insecure. In this sense, unions should support it, because it would surely amplify the voices and struggles of the working class.

Further research on the precariat must not miss the fundamental link between the problem and its solution, because, as I have tried to show, one justifies the other, and this works both ways. In the same way, quibbling about the categorical boundaries does not help. Debate on the precariat should be as dynamic as the analytical framework itself. It should acknowledge its fundamental predictive nature and the scope for political awareness and change that arises from it.

References

Armano, E., and A. Murgia. 2013. "The Precariousnesses of Young Knowledge Workers: A Subject-Oriented Approach." *Global Discourse* 3 (3–4): 486–501.

Chauvel, L. 2010. "The Long-Term Destabilization of Youth, Scarring Effects, and the Future of the Welfare Regime in Post-Trente Glorieuses France." *French Politics, Culture & Society* 28 (3): 74–96.

Coatman, C., and G., Shrubsole. eds. 2012. *Regeneration, Radical Futures*. London: Lawrence & Wishart.

Grady, J. 2013. "*The Precariat: The New Dangerous Class*, by Guy Standing. Review." *Global Discourse* 3 (3–4): 543–546.

Griffith, M. 2011. *Hoarding of Housing: The Intergenerational Crisis in the Housing Market*. London: Intergenerational Foundation.

Howker, E., and S. Malik. 2010. *Jilted Generation: How Britain Has Bankrupted Its Youth*. London: Icon Books.

Jones, O. 2011. *Chavs: The Demonization of the Working Class*. London: Verso.

Jordan, B. 2011. "Prospects for Basic Income: A British Perpective." In *Arguing about Justice. Essays for Philippe Van Parijs,* edited by A. Gosseries and Y. Vanderborght, 253–260. Louvain la Neuve: Presses Universitaires de Louvain.

Jordan, B. 2013. "Authoritarianism and the Precariat." *Global Discourse* 3 (3–4): 388–403.

Leach, J. 2011. *The Poor Perception of Youger People in the UK*. London: Intergenerational Foundation.

Little, B. 2014a. "Class and Generation Under Neoliberalism." In *After Neoliberalism: The Kilburn Manifesto*, edited by S. Hall, D. Massey, and M. Rustin, 1–16. http://www.lwbooks.co.uk/journals/soundings/manifesto.html

Little, B. 2014b. "The British Left Needs a New Politics – One that Addresses Class and Generation." *The Guardian*. http://www.theguardian.com/commentisfree/2014/feb/13/british-left-new-policies-class-generation

Malik, S. 2011. "Young Jobseekers Told to Work without Pay or Lose Unemployment Benefits." *Guardian,* November 16.

Malik, S. 2012. "Borish Johnson Launches Unpaid Work Scheme for Young Londoners." *Guardian,* August 28.

Pettit, P. 2007. "A Republican Right to Basic Income?" *Basic Income Studies* 2 (2). https://www.princeton.edu/~ppettit/papers/2008/A%20Republican%20Right%20to%20Basic%20Income.pdf

Standing, G. 2011. *The Precariat: The New Dangerous Class*. London: Bloomsbury.

Standing, G. 2013a. "Why a Basic Income Is Necessary for a Right to Work." *Basic Income Studies* 7 (2): 19–40.

Standing, G. 2013b. "*The Precariat: The New Dangerous Class*, by Guy Standing. Where's Howard?" *Global Discourse* 3 (3–4): 546–553.

Standing, G., and E. O. Wright. 2006. "CIG, COAG, and COG: A comment on a debate". In *Redesigning Distribution*, edited by E. O. Wright, 175–198. London: Verso.

Tapsfield, J. 2012. "Hundreds of Thousands of Young People Could Be Stripped of Housing Benefit and Forced to Live with Parents." *The Independent,* June 24.

Tremmel, J. 2010. *A Young Generation under Pressure? The Financial Situation and the 'Rush Hour' of the Cohorts 1970–1985 in a Generational Comparison*. London: Springer.

Widerquist, K. 2013. *Independence, Propertylessness, and Basic Income: A Theory of Freedom as the Power to Say No*. New York: Palgrave Macmillan.

Willetts, D. 2010. *The Pinch, How the Baby Boomers Took Their Children's Future – and Why They Should Give It Back*. London: Atlantic Books.

Index

Note: Page numbers followed by 'n' refer to notes